Craig R. Evans

MARKETING CHANNELS

INFOMERCIALS
AND THE FUTURE OF TELEVISED MARKETING

PRENTICE HALL
Englewood Cliffs, New Jersey 07632

.4/94

28722358

Prentice-Hall International (UK) Limited, *London*
Prentice-Hall of Australia Pty. Limited, *Sydney*
Prentice-Hall Canada, Inc., *Toronto*
Prentice-Hall Hispanoamericana, S.A., *Mexico*
Prentice-Hall of India Private Limited, *New Delhi*
Prentice-Hall of Japan, Inc., *Tokyo*
Simon & Schuster Asia Pte. Ltd., *Singapore*
Editora Prentice-Hall do Brasil, Ltda., *Rio de Janeiro*

10 9 8 7 6 5 4 3 2 1

Library of Congress Cataloging-in-Publication Data

Evans, Craig Robert.
    Marketing channels : infomercials and the future of televised
marketing / Craig Robert Evans.
        p. cm.
    Includes bibliographical references and index.
    ISBN 0-13-075151-0
    1. Television advertising. 2. Advertising—Television programs.
    3. Marketing channels.   I. Title.
HF6146.T42E974   1994

659.14'3—dc20   93-23345
                                                                CIP

ISBN 0-13-075151-0

PRENTICE HALL
Career & Personal Development
Englewood Cliffs, NJ 07632
Simon & Schuster, A Paramount Communications Company

Printed in the United States of America

DEDICATION

To generations of loved ones, past, present, and future.

ABOUT THE AUTHOR

Craig Evans's first look inside a television station came when he was 10 years old, auditioning for the *Ted Mack Amateur Hour*. While it quickly became clear that a career in front of the cameras was unlikely at best, the boy fell in love with what was going on behind the cameras. Fascinated by the hustle and bustle, the lights and the sets, the cables and banks of monitors, young Evans knew then and there that television was for him.

During college at Drake University, he followed his inclination and joined the staff of two television stations in Des Moines where he was given the opportunity to learn the ropes shooting, producing, writing, and directing. Having grounded himself in the basics, in 1985 he decided to take his skills and go where the big money is: advertising. While holding down a full-time job as an account executive at Colle & McVoy in Minneapolis, he earned his MBA in marketing in the evening at the University of Minnesota.

In 1988 he moved to CMF&Z Advertising, a Young & Rubicam subsidiary located in Cedar Rapids, Iowa. There he spearheaded a series of highly successful video brochure mailings to a targeted audience of VCR owners—this at a time when VCR penetration was only 30 percent. Called "Earmail," it involved sending 50,000 tapes promoting Dow Chemical's Lorsban™ corn insecticide to midwestern corn growers. The following year he headed up the development of PowerPac™, an interactive computer disk catalog for John Deere Power Systems.

Always the futurist, Evans was among the first people in the industry to see the potential in the long-form, 30-minute infomercial, not just as a hawker of diet plans and kitchen gadgets, but as a powerful new marketing tool for big-ticket, high-involvement products from blue-chip marketers. In 1991, on the strength of an article published in *Cablevision*, he was offered, and accepted, a position with Home Shopping Network in Tampa. There he created a new marketing arm called Showcase Video Network whose mission was to create self-liquidating, long-form commercials for national brand advertisers. Bothered by the catch-as-catch-can nature of current infomercial exposure, he started to refine an earlier idea of marketing channels as a permanent, schedulable location for airing these category-specific, high-profile messages.

Mr. Evans's interests—past, present, and future—involve the practical application of innovative communications technologies as visual marketing mediums.

ACKNOWLEDGMENTS

It's incredible . . . the number of people who contributed to the synthesis of this treatise on marketing via television in the 1994–1997, five-hundred-channel universe. I started compiling names early on in hopes of including everyone, but I'm sure that someone will, undoubtedly and unfortunately, be overlooked. And for that I ask, ahead of time, for forgiveness.

Here's a listing of those I'm remembering to acknowledge: Ron Howes for his organization of thought, construction of sentence, colorful anecdotes, and most important, attitude. I had the good fortune of tapping Ron for both his vocation and avocation in the creation of this manuscript.

Publishers Larry Selby, Judy Weiss, and Joe Tessitore at Prentice Hall for their professionalism, encouragement, and expedience.

Prentice Hall editor Karen Hansen who, like myself, became truly engrossed in the subject matter.

Researcher Phil Hjemboe for tireless hours at the University of Iowa library finding the most obscure of facts.

Kathryn White whose meticulous attention to detail in the preparation of the manuscript saved us all countless hours trying to redo what we probably would have not done properly in the first place.

Dr. Richard Cardozo, Professor of Marketing at the University of Minnesota Carlson School of Management who, in 1985, pointed out that in marketing, being different is usually better [sic]. A once-in-a-lifetime moment of inspiration.

Eric Barnouw, whom I have never met (in person), but had the good fortune of stumbling across while researching the roots of television. Eric's books on the history of radio and television are among the most thorough works on a subject I've ever had the pleasure of reading. To a first-time author (such as me), Eric is definitely an example of what I aspire to . . . or what I would like to be when I grow up.

I want to thank specifically several key contributors of the facts and statistics found in this text:

Mr. John Quarderer and Mr. Steve Ridge of Frank Magid Associates, (319) 377-7345

Mr. Brad Fay of the Roper Organization, (212) 599-0700

Ms. Kathy St. Louis of *Response TV* magazine, (714) 493-2434

Ms. Maria Almeida of TRADE/Retail and Distribution Services Group, Deloitte & Touche, (212) 492-2600

Mr. Steve Crane, (312) 464-0880, and Mr. Rinker Buck, (212) 536-5336 of *AdWeek* magazine

Mr. Scott Tillett of CompuServe, (614) 457-8600

Mr. Paul Nicholson of Television Business International, 011-4471-352-3211

Mr. Gerald O'Connell of ModemMedia for his concise overview of the current and future players of the interactive television industry, (203) 853-2600

Mr. Allen Weiner of the *San Francisco Chronicle*, (415) 777-6036

Dr. Otto Westphal of Clinic La Prairie, Lake Geneva, Switzerland, for reminding me of the importance of the scientific method in the construction of this book. As such, I've attempted to adhere to this time-honored dictum by building a logical, cumulative case for the marketing channels. I'm also leaving the door open for improvement of the concept. Throughout this text I've tried to give credit where credit is due. My goal is not to take ownership of anyone's original "great thought" as much as to juxtaposition it with other great thinking. I hope you will agree, after reading the book, that the result is indeed, Gestalt.

And, most important, my wife, Nancy, and children, Seth and Maria, for their patience while Dad pursued his off-hours writing.

Now that the work is completed, I stand by and wait for any industry change this thought may have put into motion. I truly believe in the marketing channels concept and how, if implemented as described in this book, a "win-win-win" scenario for manufacturers, advertising agencies, and consumers can come about. In a small way, through this concept, I hope to help make the world a better place. What more can anyone ask?

An ancient Chinese proverb-curse reads: "May you live in interesting times." May we all be so fortunately "cursed" as to be inspired with interesting thoughts and concepts, to live in times of plentiful answers, and through these answers, create opportunities to contribute to the world we help form.

Craig Robert Evans
Cedar Rapids, Iowa
August 1993

PREFACE

For television advertisers—from *Fortune* 500 giants to Mabel's Main Street Notions Shoppe—things have been going from bad to worse. The three decades following 1950 had been sweet, indeed. There were only three commercial networks from which to choose. Audiences were large and easy to track. In terms of numbers and demographics, advertisers got exactly what they paid for. As if that weren't sweet enough, Americans were hypnotically fascinated by both the medium *and* the message, easily amused by programs and commercials alike. Indeed, during the sixties many commercials became so irreverent and outrageous they generated more Monday morning coffee break conversation than most regular programming.

Then, along about 1980, the tidy little world that had been the television advertiser's suddenly got messy: cable had arrived. While network executives nervously pooh-poohed the danger, subscribers began to sign up by the millions. It soon became clear that network ratings were deteriorating, but where were these viewers going? Cable channels had little or no accountability. As an advertiser, you *knew*, deep down in your heart that the championship game on ESPN was a potentially good buy, but you couldn't *prove* it.

Along with basic cable channels came pay cable channels. Sure, they were commercial-free, but they were clearly attracting viewers from commercial channels. How many viewers? Who knew?

With the arrival of the remote control unit and the VCR, commercials became completely optional. Unless your commercial was immediately relevant, your audience would zap merrily away, up and down the dial. Or, devotees could tape their favorite daytime soaps for after-work viewing and fast forward through the commercial breaks. Plus, the proliferation of video rental outlets, from dedicated chains to supermarkets, further diminished the advertiser's audience.

The mid-eighties saw the situation get even messier. Home shopping channels allowed viewers to shop from their living rooms, providing a sort of electronic mall which circumvented advertisers altogether. And with Reagan-era deregulation in full swing, commercial time limits were erased, leading to a barrage of long-form, 30-minute infomercials, most of them hawking unbranded, unadvertised products like kitchen gadgets, cosmetics, and real estate schemes. What were these aberrations doing to commercial viewership? Who knew?

As destructive as these changes have been to the advertiser, the worst is yet to come. Looming on the horizon is the most fearsome spectacle of all: the 500 channel universe. Just as broadcasting is attempting the painful transformation to narrowcasting, it now faces the specter of splintercasting. In an age of technologically advanced channel surfers and voluntary commercials, how will television advertising adjust?

It can be done. What's required is a totally new way of looking at the function of television as it relates not just to advertising, but to retailing as well. I've called this new approach a paradigm shift. It involves a perceptual shift from looking at television not as strictly an entertainment medium, but also as a marketing medium. Joining entertainment channels in the 500 channel universe will be what I've called marketing channels . . . channels that put the lie to the old adage that nobody tunes in to watch commercials. Marketing channels won't account for all the new programming required by 440 additional channels, but the excess capacity could easily accommodate the 20-30 proposed herein. This book is organized and written to show you where the broadcast industry has been, where it is now, and to suggest a path ahead that can be advantageous to advertisers, broadcasters and marketers alike.

❖ Chapter Surfing: A Quick Look Through This Book

Chapter 1

Would it surprise you to know that today's basic broadcasting format—entertainment programming carrying commercial messages—was not the first, or even the second or third scheme devised for the new medium? Indeed, radio was around for more than two decades before the first commercial was even broadcast in 1922. And did you know that prior to the quiz show scandals of the mid-fifties, most television programming was conceived and produced not by independent studios, but by advertising agencies? It's all here, from the mendacity of Dr. Brinkley, the goat gland transplant king, to the genius of Desi Arnaz, to revolution wrought by an obscure game show contestant named Herbert Stempel.

Chapter 2

The first radio commercial, broadcast in 1922, was a rambling, ten minute harangue against city living, for which a suburban Long Island housing developer paid $50. It was a terrible commercial by any standards. Radio sets were scarce, hardly anyone heard it. It sold $127,000-worth of homes in just three weeks. Since the advent of television, commercial breaks have lengthened, while commercials have shortened. If you're over fifty, you may remember seeing 2-minute commercials in prime time. Today, we're down to 15-second spots, headed for 5-second billboards. For three decades, advertisers were secretly confident that even bad commercials worked, given enough exposure. But all that began to change in 1980. Cable technology was catching on fast providing the networks with unexpected competition, remote control devices and VCRs made commercial watching optional, and a former radio sportscaster from the midwest, with a bent for deregulation, moved into the White House. From then on it was "anything goes."

Chapter 3

Did you know there are better and cheaper ways to bring multiple channels to your living room other than the existing cable system? There are. And did you know there was an interactive cable operation—where subscribers not only watched and listened, but could communicate back to a central computer? There was, in the early eighties. And how are things with pay cable and Pay-Per-View? The eighties saw more chaotic change than any other period in broadcasting history. Companies were established, franchises were granted, subscriptions poured in by the millions. Great, huh? Well . . .

Chapter 4

The explosive growth that characterized cable in the eighties left the market saturated. Subscriptions were rapidly reaching a plateau. New programming ideas came and went. And then came a bombshell—digital compression technology was about to make it possible to supply subscribers with at least 500 channels. This at a time when most Americans agree that there really isn't enough worthwhile programming to fill 36 channels, let alone 500. Keep in mind that 500 channels operating 24 hours a day will consume 12,000 hours of programming a day, 84,000 hours a week, and 4,368,000 hours a year. Even if we find we can keep these channels busy, what about next year? Can we create more than four million hours of worthwhile new programming annually? Clearly a new way of looking at the medium is in order: a paradigm shift. Instead of looking at programming as being stricly entertainment-based, we need to begin to look at it from a marketing standpoint. How? Well, it's been done before . . . a long time ago.

Chapter 5

While everyone else was trying to figure out how to attract big prime time audiences and high-rolling advertisers with boffo entertainment, a few pioneering individuals were making big sales from small audiences in off hours. Sometimes, off-off hours. Yes, the Popeil brothers and their imitators were spinning 2-minute strands of cheap time into gold. Sure we laughed. And we made fun of them with comedy skits from *I Love Lucy* (VitaMeataVegaMin) to *Saturday Night Live* (the Super Bass-O-Matic). But we bought their kitchen gadgets and apparently indestructible knives and pocket fishermen by the millions. In the eighties, the rules changed and the 30-minute infomercial made its appearance. The classic format featuring the glib, fast-handed, stand-up presenter remained, to be joined by others fashioned to look like game shows and talk shows, often featuring celebrities from the entertainment or sports world. The kinds of products advertised were expanded to include real estate schemes, self-help programs, cosmetics, jewelry, diet and exercise programs. Why does this kind of advertising work? How can such phenomenal sales result from such off-hour exposure? The fact is, the rules of sales resistance on television have established that infomercials work worst on Wednesdays and best on Saturdays and Sundays.

But there are other kinds of infomercials we see every day, not on television but rather in our capacity as buyers of products from automobiles to business supplies. We see them in retail outlets, perhaps demonstrating the newest model sports car. They come through the mail, offering complete lines of merchandise. We see them at the office as annual reports or in presentations. They demonstrate features, detail advantages and clarify benefits. Are these video brochures and video catalogs suitable for television? Yes. Are we likely to see them there? Yes. But first, we need to examine today's changing retail scene.

Chapter 6

The flight to the suburbs following World War II doomed the downtown retail establishment and opened the door to the malls. Since the arrival of the discount store, the malls have begun to empty. Dozens of other retail formats are being tried today, including factory outlet stores, specialty shops, and in Bloomington, Minnesota, a super mall. While the price-conscious public shops at the discount

stores, busy, time-conscious, two-career families are seeking alternatives. They want value, which they define as quality at a reasonable
(not necessarily low) price. And they don't have time to shop-and-
compare. They rely on brands. And more and more, they are shopping by catalog, without leaving home. It is possible these people
could be induced to buy big-ticket merchandise from blue-chip
marketers simply by watching their television sets? Hmmm.

Chapter 7

Infomercials appeal to a downscale market, right? They prey on the
gullibility of the bored, the poor and the uneducated, right? "People
like us" don't watch, let alone buy merchandise from them, right?
Well, if you agree, you're wrong on all three counts. While less than
ten percent of Americans buy from long-form commercials, many of
these are upscale catalog buyers and baby boomers. But what about
those 24-hour shopping channels? Surely "people like us" don't buy
from them? Preposterous. And yet, if that's true, why did programming genius Barry Diller, upon leaving the Fox Network, cast his lot
with the shopping channel, QVC? Does he know something we
don't? Bet on it.

Chapter 8

Clearly the paradigm shift has begun. The visionaries among us have
already begun to look at television as more than simply an entertainment medium. The marketing possibilities inherent in the long-form
commercial, the shopping channels, on-line computer services and
emerging interactive technologies will change not just our viewing
habits, but our buying habits as well. The restless, fluid state of
television technologies extends to the television audience as well.
We're watching more television than ever, and we're worried about
it. We decry the incidence of violence, yet can't seem to get enough.
We angrily zap programs and commercials we don't like. We surf
maniacally up and down the dial, hoping for something better on
the next channel we come to. Younger boomers watch two or even
three programs at once, surfing back and forth between channels.
And the kids . . . well, they're "zoning out" completely by surfing

without regard to content. They're watching *television*, not programs. Where is all this leading? The answer is clear. It is leading *away* from exclusively entertainment-based programming, and *toward* something entirely different.

Chapter 9

If we begin to look at television as marketers, rather than as entertainers, the need is clear for what I have called marketing channels, made possible by the same digital compression technology that is fast bringing us 500 channel availability. Imagine, if you will, a block of category-specific marketing channels designed to attract buyers of expensive, considered-purchase products from blue chip marketers. Programming largely originates with advertisers themselves and may be product specific or brand/image oriented. It provides useful information to shoppers currently in the market to buy. The idea plays right into the lifestyles of today's busy 2-income families. By making selections of, say, automobiles from *The Car Buyer's Channel*, prospects can narrow their choices from the comfort of their living rooms and remove most of the hassle inherent in the current retail system. As marketing manager of Channel 397—*The Car Buyer's Channel*—what kinds of programming would *you* select to attract maximum advertising revenues? See if your picks agree with mine.

Chapter 10

Given the nature of the automotive industry's current retail structure, which has remained basically unchanged since 1910, it seems an obvious choice for a marketing channel. Despite the fact that brands have proliferated alarmingly, that automobiles have become far too complicated for the average Joe to understand, and that most automobiles today are purchased by women, the industry stubbornly refuses to change its ways. Buyers must still run all over town, listen to conflicting claims from competitive salespeople and then haggle over prices. And as a final gesture of arrogance, most dealerships are closed on Sundays, the only convenient shopping day for most of the new car buying public. Clearly, an automotive marketing channel represents a vast improvement over this archaic retail structure. Long-form commercials produced by the manufacturer, with a reputation to maintain, will provide welcome relief from the suspicion so often generated by the glib salesperson who may have been working for the competitor two weeks earlier. Unbiased head-to-head comparison programs can help narrow choices. Independent pricing programming will help alleviate the feeling that you've just been had. By the time you're ready to enter the marketplace you're armed with information and ready to make a better buy.

While not all industries are such ideal candidates for a marketing channel as automotive, there are others with apparent potential. Most are marketers of complex, high-involvement, considered purchase products; the kinds of products people worry about buying to the point where they feel the need for studied comparisons. Others are included simply because, at any given time, 100% of Americans are actively in the market for products in these categories. That and the fact that these industries spend upwards of $8½ billion per year in advertising. I've identified a total of sixteen industry categories. Is yours included? (More in the Appendix.)

Chapter 11

Okay, so marketing channels look like a great idea. Now, how do they come about? I've put together a list of minimum requirements needed. Will the first company on the block with a marketing channel(s) come from the cable industry? Or the broadcast networks? Perhaps the motion picture industry will be first. Or the business community. Or the entertainment industry. Or maybe, just maybe, one of the many gifted individuals who dominate the world of communications today will break out on his own and amaze the world. (To make it easier, I've developed a three-channel phase-in . . . sort of a marketing channel starter kit.)

Chapter 12

If I'm right, marketing channels will provide a link between passive, entertainment-based television as we know it today and the exciting interactive television world of tomorrow. The link up of television and telephone technology, made possible by computer technology, will revolutionize not just television, but our entire retail system. When we can go to school, conduct business and do our shopping from home, what will happen to such institutions as the packaging industry? Or the U.S. Post Office, for that matter? The electronic superhighway of the next century will change the way we live forever.

❖ A WIN/WIN/WIN SITUATION

It doesn't happen often, but marketing channels represent a rare three-way win situation. Marketers of products and services win because they now have a cost-efficient way to deliver entire sales messages, product introductions, or feature demonstrations to interested, ready-to-buy audiences. Advertising agencies win because they now have a specific location in the 500 channel universe to place advertising that viewers seek out. And most important of all, the viewer/consumer wins since Marketing Channels provide an easier, more sensible shopping alternative for evaluating and buying products. The *Yellow Pages* and *Consumer Reports* of television—all wrapped up in a single channel.

Such is the promise of marketing channels.

FOREWORD

"Revolutions are not made; they come. A revolution is as natural as the growth of an oak. It comes out of the past. Its foundations are laid far back."

WENDELL PHILLIPS, 1852

Ed and Mabel Vinger of suburban Minneapolis plopped down on their comfortable sofa. It was 7:00 P.M. and the kids were in their room playing the Sega Channel. Ed was uneasy. His plumbing business was in trouble. With the advent of the *How-To* Channel and Pay-Per-View videotaped programming, more and more folks were doing plumbing work themselves. He was still hoping for that middle-class tax cut. Unfortunately, the outdoor news billboard on the drive home said that the chances were slim.

Ed picked up and clicked the universal remote control. The high-definition, wall-mounted Zenith immediately glowed brightly. Before choosing regular TV or N-Vision from the first menu, Ed checked his monthly billing and viewing status report.

"Mabel," he said, "how many more hours of Terminator III do we have?" "We rented it at 6:00 P.M. yesterday. Right before dinner, remember?" she replied. "Oh. That's right." Ed was still having trouble getting used to having a first-run movie for 24 hours without ever physically touching a video cassette.

Ed quickly chose the regular TV window and selected the Comedy category from the list. After scanning the twenty or so choices, he clicked on the new Tim Allen Special and pushed the *View it* button. He had heard about it a couple of weeks ago from two guys in the coffee shop. The show had just begun with the telephone range. Ed pushed *Freeze,* hit the telephone key on the remote control and shouted at the television screen, "Who is it?"

"MCI calling, Mr. Vinger. We wanted to talk to you about our new . . . (click)." Ed hated salespeople almost as much as he hated dripless faucets. "Damn it, Mabel! I thought we turned off the commercials!" "Only on the television. Not on the telephone. That costs an extra $5.00 a month, Dear," she replied. "We've got to cut some corners."

No longer interested in Tim Allen, Ed scrolled to *The Car Buyer's Channel.* He clicked on to the Saturn icon and in an instant a gleaming red Saturn SVII appeared on his television screen. Ed selected the rear camera angle and asked for an engineering report.

"Whew," he whispered to himself. "That is one fine-looking car. I wonder if it's the 1997 model?"

* * *

The story I've just told is not a futurist's fantasy. This future is upon us. Within literally a few years our sofas will feel more like flying carpets and our living rooms will become more akin to an entertainment bubble than we can imagine. For marketers, advertisers and broadcasters, we must begin to look at television as we now know it in a whole new way. Used correctly, we all can thrive.

Marketing Channels chronicles how the foundations and seeds of tomorrow's communications wonderland were planted long ago. *Marketing Channels* also outlines strategies to consider implementing now that will help our industry prepare for the near future.

Craig Evans has done a great job peering down the Electronic Highway and revealing a clear vision of what he calls marketing channels. *Marketing Channels* outlines how the incredible advances in communication technology will affect advertising, advertisers and consumers alike. Messages, media and audiences are about to become precisely arranged and comfortably coexisting.

There are, perhaps, four or five media plans as we know them remaining for most advertised brands in this country. We leave the Era of Television and move toward the Age of Teleactive. Bravo, Craig. Hurrah for the revolution.

DAVID VERKLIN
Senior Vice President
Corporate Media Director
Hal Riney & Partners

**1992 *MediaWeek* Magazine
Media Director of the Year**

**1993 *Advertising Age* Magazine
Advertising Agency of the Year**

CONTENTS

1

BROADCASTING AS IT WAS

"Fifty-seven channels, and nothin' on."

BRUCE SPRINGSTEEN

Once again we are about to be overtaken by technology, like it or not. Digital compression is making it possible for cable technology to bring up to five hundred channels—maybe more—to our living rooms. Are we ready for this?

The answer, of course, is no.

The next question is, "Since we really don't have enough quality programming to fill the 57 channels Springsteen was singing about, what in heaven's name are we going to put on the other 443?" The mind boggles.

We've come to regard television as basically an entertainment medium. Yes, it brings us news and educational documentaries, but the documentaries are entertaining and the news is . . . well . . . happy news. Only during aberrant moments of history, such as Operation Desert Storm or the shooting of the Viet Cong hostage by Vietnamese General Nguyen Ngoc Loan, does television deviate from the entertainment mode. Presumably the entertainment mill is operating at top speed now, bringing us our usual fare consisting of sitcoms, game shows, documentaries, soap operas, made-for-TV movies, kiddy cartoons, sports events, exposé programs, talk shows and real-life mystery, crime, and rescue shows. And above all, the channels are strewn with reruns, from classic movies to TV sitcoms like *I Love Lucy* and *Cheers*; one can even catch reruns of game shows like *The $25,000 Pyramid* and *Hollywood Squares* (True or false, George Gobel: President Reagan was once a Democrat.). If it weren't for new movie releases, shopping channels, and infomercials, there wouldn't be much on television that hasn't been seen before.

So far, what's been proposed to fill the new channels is more of the same and variations on a theme. Premium services may grab up blocks of channels to "multiplex" movie offerings, giving subscribers numerous options, probably on a Pay-Per-View basis. Spin-offs from existing channels have also been proposed: from *MTV* may come country-western or rhythm and blues channels, or from *ESPN* may come a channel devoted exclusively to auto racing. There may be entire channels devoted exclusively to fare such as game shows, soap operas, talk shows, military shows, videoshopping malls, cooking shows, or crime shows.

The one thing all these proposals have in common is the fact that they are all entertainment based. These are the kinds of suggestions one expects from people who look at programming from the viewpoint of seventy years of broadcasting entertainment. That's fine, of course. But it would seem that the advent of five hundred channels could, and should go further. Rather than simply regarding this windfall as an entertainment-based challenge, what would happen if we regarded it instead as a marketing-based opportunity? Entertainment-based programming is fraught with peril. If it succeeds, everybody wins: the producers who develop it, the sponsors who buy it, and the broadcasters who air it. But if it fails, it is costly to all.

This book will suggest a new way of looking at programming at least some of the newly available channels. It calls for a genuine paradigm shift, a way of looking at programming that is totally different from the way we've looked at programming in the past. That is to say, *let's look at programming not as entertainers, but as marketers.* Said another way, instead of programming seeking a specific audience, why not locate audiences seeking specific programs. Let's look at true marketing channels, places where viewers can find useful information that is genuinely relevant to today's life-styles. Let's look at television not just as an escape from the world, but as a way to cope better with the world. Let's look at programming not just as a tenuous carrier of commercials, but as an adjunct to the American retail system. Unlike entertainment-based programming, marketing-based programming is not fraught with risk. Because advertisers, not entertainers, provide the programming . . . because the programming is of genuine use to a constantly renewing audience of consumers . . . and because the broadcaster is freed from whim and changing tastes, everyone wins.

We tend to think that broadcasting has always been an entertainment medium, that its use as a carrier of commercials has always been as obvious as it is now. Not at all. Some seventy years ago, in fact, nobody really knew quite what to make of it.

❖ RADIO DAYS: WHAT HATH GOD WROUGHT?

Since the beginning of the Industrial Revolution, each new technology has spawned its own breed of dedicated enthusiasts. It has been said that these were individuals of an entrepreneurial spirit, seeking ways to turn this technology into money. And while in the early days monetary wealth often resulted from their tinkering, one doubts that wealth was the driving force behind them. Sure, fortunes were made by clever people finding new ways to put James Watt's steam engine technology to work, or to expand on Otto Lilienthal's studies in glider technology. Still, it seems the real driver behind these people was not cash, but curiosity.

As proof, let's examine the wireless communications technology introduced by Guglielmo Marconi at the turn of the century.

Immediately, broadcasting techies went to work. Some, who worked for large corporations, were able to convince often skeptical board members that fortunes were to be made and extensive budgets were necessary. Others, with no corporate connections—teachers and factory mechanics, farmers and craftsmen—worked in garages and basements with minimal equipment purchased at hardware stores or forged at blacksmith shops. All of them, from the head of broadcast development at AT&T to the letter carrier assembling a cat's whisker receiver set on the kitchen table, had one thing in common: an irrepressible curiosity. For years people worked on Marconi's ideas, distilling them, refining them, taking them further and further.

By 1912 there were so many of these experimenters cluttering up the airwaves that the government, at the urging of the military, was forced to pass a licensing law. During World War I, the amateurs were ordered off the air altogether. Meanwhile, Westinghouse, General Electric, and Western Electric (a subsidiary of American Telephone & Telegraph Company), liberally fed by government contracts, proceeded to redefine the state of the art. At the war's end, radio found itself in the position of the corpse at an atheist's funeral: all dressed up and no place to go. The sophisticated technology which had been developed was to be relegated, it seemed, to serving the Merchant Marine as a ship-to-ship or ship-to-shore communications device.

Someone at Westinghouse, no one knows who, thought that radio seemed just too grand a thing to end up as a device for keeping track of tramp steamers. This unknown genius suggested that the receivers used by the Signal Corps might, if they broadcast something interesting to listen to, attract buyers.

Westinghouse was intrigued enough with the idea to test it out. In November 1920, the company went on the air over station KDKA, Pittsburgh, and the magic of radio began to capture the imagination of the American people. Demand was immediate as buyers rushed to the new "Radio" counters at their local department stores.

By 1922 more than four hundred radio stations were on the air, along with thousands of hams. The fact that receivers were still few and far between, despite the miniboom in sales, failed to dispel the optimism of these cheerful pioneers. And while the amateurs found their reward in simply scratching their curiosity itch, the corporate moneymen were thinking in terms of profits. Early plans for turning profits were largely a product of existing corporate cultures. AT&T, for instance, first thought of using its new radio station as a sort of phone booth. (AT&T even referred to radio stations as "toll stations.") The idea was that anyone with the desire and the cash could drop by the studio, broadcast a personal message to the world, and then simply pay for the time. After a full month with no takers, it became clear that the future for this idea (shades of today's public access TV channels) was perhaps limited.

AT&T next turned to programming as a possible scheme for making money with radio. Songs and recitations by company employees were soon replaced by professional talent, and on August 28, 1922, AT&T's first "toll station," WEAF in New York broadcast its first commercial, a spot read by the advertiser himself, entreating city dwellers to move to a new housing development on Long Island.

> ... get away from the solid masses of brick, where the meager opening admitting a slant of sunlight is mockingly called a light shaft and where children grow up starved for a run over a patch of grass and the sight of a tree. Apartments in the congested parts of the city have proven failures. The word neighbor is an expression of peculiar irony—a daily joke.

The spot went on for another 10 minutes. And proving for the first time the adage that even bad advertising works, it sold homes in the suburbs . . . $127,000 worth of homes in just three weeks. The sponsor bought three more afternoon spots for $50 each and an evening spot for $100. Despite the demonstrable success of the experiment, revenues for the first two months of operation netted WEAF a mere $550. Just prior to the Christmas season, an advertising executive named William Rankin of the Rankin Agency bought a $100 evening period to discuss radio advertising with potential sponsors. Sifting through the many replies, Rankin was intrigued by a small company that manufactured a beauty product called Mineralava. His agency put together a radio promotion built around the film actress Marion Davies, who discussed her beauty secrets and offered an autographed photo to anyone who wrote in. The response was overwhelming, the lesson was clear, and other sponsors soon got the message. The Rankin Agency tied the commercial to a series for one of its clients, and within six months WEAF had signed up sixteen new sponsored series.

To keep agencies like Rankin interested in radio, AT&T offered to pay all agency-submitted material a 15 percent commission, following the lead of the print media. Not surprisingly, the technique created much interest on the part of agencies, and did much to speed up the commercial success the industry was to enjoy.

But if AT&T considered radio as a sort of telephone, the other players in the burgeoning new industry—RCA, GE, and Westinghouse—saw the new medium, not surprisingly, as a way to sell the home radio sets being manufactured by their separate divisions. Sponsors offered musical groups such as The Rheingold Quartet, The Cliquot Club Eskimos, The Ipana Troubadours, and Schrafft's Tea Room Orchestra to the stations where they were broadcast free of charge. Although these sponsors didn't broadcast commercials, they enjoyed the product name identification. This sort of programming soon had people lining up to buy radio sets. Not everyone, however, was pleased with this trend toward commercialism of the public airwaves. Secretary of Commerce Herbert Hoover, for example, worried about the commercialization of radio, seeing its role as one of public service. But already the future of radio was taking shape.

It was becoming clear that Americans didn't want a variation on the telephone. Nor did Americans want a pulpit from which to preach. What Americans wanted from broadcasting was—purely and simply—entertainment. The pattern for broadcast programming was set. Profits gleaned from broadcasting would rise or fall on the basis of entertainment.

Radio caught on quickly. All America, it seemed, was in love with the magic idea of bringing everything from sporting events to theatrical productions to musical performances into their living rooms. Sales of radio receiver sets boomed, and what had first been considered an expensive luxury had become, by 1925, a household necessity. Sponsors were soon lining up with money. The problem these broadcasters faced in the mid-1920s was not so much profits as programming. Stations signed up local attractions from foot games to organ recitals and in 1923 listeners tuned in to *H. Kaltenborn and the News*. That same year, AT&T linked its New Yor station, WEAF, to its new Washington, D.C., station, WCAP, and formed the beginnings of a network. Aggressively, AT&T next turned to "licensing" other stations to join its fledgling network. In addition to its licensing fee, AT&T required these stations to buy transmitters from its subsidiary, Western Electric, at a cost of $10,000 each. Despite this near blackmail, the lure of advertising profits and increasingly sophisticated network programming brought in a number of takers.

The network, with its ability to carry a single message to a broad audience, appealed to large regional and national advertisers. Soon, single-sponsor programs were being developed by advertising agencies for network use, including *The Ampico Hour, The Maxwell House Hour, The Palmolive Hour, The Cities Service Orchestra,* and *The General Motors Family Party*. In the years ahead, advertising agencies like Young & Rubicam, William Esty, and J. Walter Thompson would expand their programming to include drama programs—many of them original—detective shows, and eventually the great comedy programs of the 1930s and 1940s.

In September 1926, AT&T's three major competitors, RCA, GE, and Westinghouse, announced the formation of the National Broadcasting Company, Inc., and the network concept was on its way. Advertisers flocked to the new network until, by 1927, NBC had two networks in operation: the Red Network with programming fed by WEAF (acquired from AT&T) and the Blue Network with programming fed from station WJZ, also in New York.

During this period, programming was produced largely by advertising agencies, which tied the sponsor's radio show into print, outdoor, and promotional campaigns. The networks, being almost entirely dependent on sponsors for programming, were inclined to give the sponsor free rein. No advertising claim was too exaggerated, no technique too outrageous. This lack of control, among other complications ranging from wave length to competitive scheduling, led to the Radio Act of 1927. Within short order the Federal Radio Commission (FRC), forerunner of today's Federal Communications

nmission (FCC), went to work on the industry's many problems.
ne Radio Act made it clear that the airwaves were not owned by
ither the networks or the sponsors, but rather by the people of the
United States. From now on, Big Brother would be watching.

But not for long. The stock market crash of 1929, coupled with
competition caused by the appearance of the new CBS network,
created a climate where the sponsor was king. Network executives
and government regulators looked the other way; discretion, along
with taste, went out the window. "Dr." John Romulus Brinkley,
owner of a Kansas station, was allowed to continue advertising
various nostrums as well as goat-gland transplants long after the
American Medical Association had branded him a quack. The American Tobacco Company, whose research indicated potential cigar
buyers were turned off by rumors of cigar makers licking cigars for
extra adhesion, came up with perhaps the most tasteless advertising
slogan in history for Cremo cigars. As the Cremo Military Band
finished each rousing rendition, the announcer would shout, "There
is no spit in Cremo!"

Often, too, popular stars became closely associated with sponsors, who enjoyed the rub-off as well as free product mentions such
as Jack Benny's cheerful show opener, "Jell-O again." Other such
associations were Bob Hope's with Pepsodent and Edgar Bergen and
Charlie McCarthy's program, which was originally *The Chase and
Sanborn Show.*

Variations on the theme of one-sponsor shows were to last well
into the television era with programming such as *The Colgate Comedy
Hour, The Texaco Star Theater,* and, of course, the granddaddy of them
all, *The Hallmark Hall of Fame.*

In the years ahead, the network concept found complete acceptance. In addition to the formation of CBS, NBC's Blue Network
became ABC. The entertainment value of the programming continued to improve, largely because of the evolution of what Erik
Barnouw has called the "two worlds" of radio broadcasting.[1] During
the 1930s, while prime-time periods were sold out, other less attractive time periods went begging. These were soon put to use carrying
public service programming that not only kept the stations operating, but tended to keep the federal regulators from being too hard

on the sponsored shows. Despite insufficient funding, as the decade wore on the public service/educational world began to attract narrow but highly interested audiences of its own. The dedicated people who labored in this underfunded world managed to offer a sort of counterprogramming to the sponsored world. Much like publicly funded broadcasting today, they occasionally took on corporate inequities or exposed social injustices. And while they couldn't afford the likes of Benny, Bergen, and Hope, they presented entertainment's lesser lights such as Huddie Ledbetter ("Leadbelly"), Woody Guthrie, and opera's Paul Robeson. During the period 1935–1940, the self-supported world of radio combined with the expensively sponsored one offered the American public a rich mix of quality programming choices.

The impact of radio following World War I was every bit as great as the impact of television following World War II. For better or worse, families gathered around the radio set most every evening, for a walk down *Allen's Alley* or a visit with *Fibber McGee and Molly* at 79 Wistful Vista. Radio announcers became as well known and popular as movie stars, and radio actors became movie stars themselves. Demographic segmentation, though the term itself was still half a century away, occurred naturally. With the exception of the war years, most women stayed home, listening to *Ma Perkins* and *One Man's Family.* Women's products, notably soap, found listeners . . . and buyers. Kids ran home from school in a hurry, tuning in *The Green Hornet, Superman, Sergeant Preston of the Yukon,* and *Jack Armstrong, All-American Boy.* And on Saturday mornings there was the wonderful Nila Mack waiting to take children into the fun and fantasy of *Let's Pretend,* sponsored by Cream of Wheat. Cereal and candy companies stood in line, waiting to pick up the tab. These shows, like most shows of the time, were produced by advertising agencies for individual clients, which meant the principal actors and announcers usually delivered the commercials.

And, of course, there were game shows, which, despite very small prize money, drew very large audiences. Typical of these early game shows was *The Bob Hawk Show* heard over CBS in 1945. Hawk, the quiz master, combined gags and questions. Studio contestants were asked five questions, each worth $10. Contestants had the option of dropping out at any time, but if all five questions were answered correctly, the contestant was declared a "Lemac" (the sponsor's name—Camel—spelled backward). Ecstatic winners were awarded $50 and serenaded by the show's peppy quartet.

You're a Lemac now,
Yes, a Lemac now,
You're up among the scholars,
You've won your fifty dollars,
You're a Lemac now.©

Radio game shows were almost exclusively nighttime fare, as were early television game shows. Nowadays, of course, game shows are strictly daytime. There is a reason for that, having much to do with the way television programming is conducted today. It makes for an interesting story.

❖ TELEVISION: THE TORTOISE THAT BEAT THE HARE

So, here was radio. Not since the automobile had technology made a greater impact on American society. And yet there were some people who, as early as the 1920s, blew right on past radio—all the way to television. One of these visionaries was David Sarnoff, head of RCA, who in 1927 predicted that within five years television sets would be as common as radio sets in American homes. His prediction, of course, was off by some fifteen years. He could not have foreseen distractions like the stock market crash, the Great Depression, aggressive competitors, government interference, or World War II.

While Sarnoff pushed his company into television development, his competitors did the same. By 1927, GE was experimenting in Schenectady, producing pictures on postcard-size screens. On September 11, 1928, GE broadcast the first television drama, a melodrama called "The Queen's Messenger." Out in the hinterlands, dedicated amateurs, mostly radio hams, were picking up these early television experiments on homemade picture tubes, delighting in the snowy black-and-gray silhouettes they managed to receive.

The Great Depression served to postpone, but not cancel, television development. Work moved ahead on both transmission systems and receivers. By 1939, Sarnoff felt the time was finally right, and the RCA exhibit at the World's Fair not only demonstrated the new medium but also featured a display of 5-inch and 9-inch home viewing sets ranging in price from $200 to $600. Enthusiastic visitors were regaled with programming from Radio City and, on May 17, the Columbia-Princeton baseball game courtesy of RCA's mobile unit.

Before Sarnoff could convince the public that the new medium was more than just a living room novelty, international events were to turn the attention of the government to radio, considered essential to the war effort, and to a new technology called radar. Licensing was suspended for the duration and television was put on hold. But while television marketing efforts were suspended, technological development continued impressively. The new image-orthicon tube provided clarity without the hot, intense lighting and bizarre green-face/purple-lip makeup required earlier. Also during this period, experiments in color technology began.

By 1945, economists were making dire predictions. The wartime economy, they said, would collapse like a house of cards, plunging the country once more into economic depression. And so it might have been had not the Marshall Plan, through the simple expedient of rebuilding the war-torn world, kept American factories bustling, American workers working, and the taxes rollin' in. Obligingly, Rosie the Riveter returned to hearth, home, and savings account, sick and tired of shortages and rationing. Johnny came marching home with a pocketful of cash and a strong aversion to further deprivation of any kind. America was in the mood to treat itself to some fun. One of these former servicemen, General David Sarnoff, realized that his prophecy was about to be realized.

Many of the returning servicemen were experienced in electronics: they had served as Navy radar operators and communications people, Signal Corps personnel, Air Force radiomen, and traffic control operators. These men, plus women who had worked in the wartime electronics industry, formed a valuable core of expertise for the fast-growing television industry. By 1947 the fruits of their labor were entertaining the customers in every tavern within range of a signal. Sports programming drew patrons as never before, and the obscure world of professional wrestling came into its own, bizarre, preposterous, and above all, popular. The tavern owners' euphoria, however, was short-lived as loyal patrons bought home sets and, instead of stopping off for a quick one with the boys, ran home to catch the *Camel News Caravan* with John Cameron Swayze.

Meanwhile, a funny thing was happening at the corporate level. Until now, profits from the "radio side" had been used to make up for losses on the "television side." But that picture was changing. Seeing the potential of television, more and more profits were diverted, radio budgets were cut, and listeners—along with expensive, quality programming like the NBC Symphony Orchestra conducted by Arturo Toscanini—fell by the wayside. As the cost cutting continued, a long-standing policy of live, unrecorded programming was dropped, and in 1947 the first disk jockey saddled up and rode out onto the airwaves. Television was killing radio, stealing its listeners, draining its resources.

Radio and taverns weren't the only American institutions changing profoundly because of television. As stations proliferated in city after city, movie theaters began to close, restaurant patronage dropped dramatically, bookstores and libraries lost business, and attendance at sporting events fell off. What was causing this retreat to the living room? Largely, zaniness.

❖ HATS AND HORNS: EARLY NETWORK PROGRAMMING

In 1948, *The Texaco Star Theater* went on the air and within weeks its star, Milton Berle, became the most recognized man in America. Berle was outrageous, preening, primping, camping it up in drag (see Figure 1-1). He had the greatest double take in the business—a toothy, self-centered smile of braggadocio which, two beats after the putdown, turned to a scowl of outrage. America loved him, calling him "Uncle Miltie," "Mr. Tuesday Night," and even "Mr. Television." The network offered him a $200,000-a-year contract guaranteed for the next thirty years, unheard of at the time. His ratings went through

Figure 1-1

Television's Mr. Tuesday Night

"Uncle Miltie" swings out in full regalia. Milton Berle, already a star on radio, became America's first television superstar and perhaps the most recognized man in America. Zaniness was, indeed entertainment capable of drawing large television audiences. (Courtesy Shooting Star International.)

the roof, attracting the best guest stars available. And while Berle dominated Tuesday night, a new show took over Saturday night.

Introduced in 1949, *Your Show of Shows* boasted an ensemble cast and a writing team that has perhaps never been equaled. The stars, Sid Caesar and Imogene Coca, were two people with one brain. Their on-screen by-play was telepathic, their timing together flawless. Two of the writers on the show, Carl Reiner and Howard Morris, doubled as actors. Even writers who declined to act, like Neil Simon, Mel Brooks, Woody Allen, and Larry Gelbart, for example, went on to change the face of American entertainment—television, movies, theater. Both shows had good runs—*Your Show of Shows* went off the air in 1954 after five years, followed by Uncle Miltie in 1956 after seven years.

While the zany, hats 'n' horns comedy of the principals was the mainstay of both shows, variety acts—singers, comedians, ventrilo-quists, acrobats—played a significant role. *Your Show of Shows* was live, and a full 90 minutes long.

Top guest stars were seen each week, one of whom was the nominal "host" of each show. Ballet and opera sequences added to the sophistication of the show—all of which may help account for the success of another show introduced in 1949. It was called *The Toast of the Town,* and its host was arguably the host least likely to succeed—a gaunt, homely, awkward man almost completely lacking in either poise or charisma. His name was Ed Sullivan. A columnist for the New York *Daily News,* he had no prior performing experience, a fact that became immediately obvious. On stage he moved like a sort of manic puppet speaking in a hopelessly nasal voice, stumbling over his words. There was one thing about him that wasn't obvious at first. He was a genius.

Perhaps the doubters should have suspected they were wrong. The guest list for his very first show included America's most suc-cessful musical team, Rodgers and Hammerstein, as well as a prom-ising new comedy team called Martin and Lewis. Something old, something new. This formula, pairing off unlikely talents, was to keep Sullivan's show on the air continuously for twenty-two years, solid proof that entertainment, as opposed to education and even information, was what American broadcasting was all about.

Like radio network programming, television programming during this period was still being produced in New York by advertising agencies on behalf of their national clients. The networks were paid by the sponsors with the agencies receiving their customary 15 percent commission from the networks. It was, in essence, the established method of radio remuneration.

There were two notable exceptions to the radio concept. In 1950 Desi Arnaz and his wife Lucille Ball formed a production company called Desilu, not in New York, but in Los Angeles. Desilu was originally formed to produce just one show . . . but what a show it was. It was called *I Love Lucy*, and it was to make television history. Today, after years of reruns, probably no other television show has been seen by more people, worldwide, than *I Love Lucy*. Ironically, despite its West Coast origins, it was the ultimate "New York" show, with almost every episode taking place in Ricky and Lucy's tiny Manhattan apartment which they rented, of course, from Fred and Ethel Mertz. *I Love Lucy* was sold to CBS, which offered it to a number of sponsors rather than just one. The following year another West Coast entry called *Dragnet*, a holdover from radio, was picked up by NBC and sold the same way. *Dragnet*, based on case histories from the files of the Los Angeles Police Department, featured an enormous number of exterior shots, making the Los Angeles area, and weather, mandatory.

The "magazine concept" of several sponsors per episode had its proponents, but a complete switch from the radio concept of a single sponsor seemed a daunting challenge. The idea clearly needed a champion, and in Sylvester L. "Pat" Weaver it found one. In 1952, Weaver was named president of NBC and immediately went to work on a programming idea that was simple enough for the network itself to produce and that could be sold to sponsors on the magazine concept. The *Today* show went on the air in 1952, in a competitive vacuum at 7:00 A.M. It was shot at very little expense in studios at NBC. There were no expensive location shots, no tricky camerawork, nothing fancy . . . just the host, mellow Dave Garroway and his comical sidekick, a chimp known as J. Fred Muggs. Yes, a chimp. You had to be there. The closest *Today* ever came to exteriors were shots of crowds of fascinated onlookers standing on the sidewalk outside, gaping through huge glass windows at the cameras inside. In 1954 Weaver repeated the success of the *Today* show with the *Tonight* show, a similar showcase for the versatile Steve Allen. Here again, production values were kept to a minimum. Allen expanded slightly on *Today's* version of the exterior shot by going out to meet the people on the street, almost always with hilarious results. Allen's on-the-street interview with a drunken sailor is a comedy classic.

❖ 1953–1955: THE GOLDEN AGE

Perhaps television never reached higher, dramatically, than in the live dramas of this brief, glowing two-year period. An incredibly talented group of writers arrived on the scene almost simultaneously—people like Reginald Rose, Rod Serling, and Paddy Chayefsky. They fueled a number of top-quality, live drama shows including the *Philco Television Playhouse*, the *Goodyear TV Playhouse*, *Kraft TV Theater*, *Studio One*, and the *U.S. Steel Hour*. Obviously, these were single-sponsor shows, sold on the radio concept of remuneration. All were shot in New York in immense studios capable of holding a number of carefully placed sets. Because of this, certain restrictions were placed on writers. There could be no wide-angle exterior shots; in fact, exterior shots were best avoided altogether as they tended to look phony with their fake trees and painted skies. This tended to minimize action and put a premium on dialogue.

These restrictions actually helped television discover something it did best. The close-up. Plays like Rose's *Thunder on Sycamore Street* and Chayefsky's *Marty* used close-ups to involve viewers intimately. Also, since dialogue was so important to these dramas, writers took great pains to write exactly as people talked. Real people, not actors. And plots followed suit, dealing with real problems—love, security, boredom, prejudice. Sadly, except for a few grainy kinescopes, many of these masterpieces were never seen again.

The public responded to these intensely atmospheric dramas in vast numbers, a tribute to the talent of the writers, directors, and actors. Future film superstars like Paul Newman, Rod Steiger, and William Holden learned their craft in early live drama. Only the sponsors worried. Their products were intended to solve real-life problems from halitosis to headaches instantly. The real-life problems in shows like *Thunder on Sycamore Street,* a story of the effects of prejudice on a neighborhood when "undesirables" moved in, were not so easily solved. These dramas were the subject of kaffeeklatsches and workplace conversations for days after viewing. Programming was, again, evolving nicely . . . independent of sponsors.

So what went wrong? Why was the Golden Age of Television so brief? A number of things, actually. With the advent of videotape, outdoor action was possible. The live dramas were certainly involving, but not necessarily entertaining in the plebeian sense of the word. The sponsors became more and more reluctant. And most of all, the talent, both in front of and behind the cameras, was literally driven away by the communist witch hunt that was going on. If you were on the blacklist, you couldn't get hired. Even if you weren't, most of the people on the blacklist were the cream of the crop. It became more and more difficult to work in New York under the watchful eye of the government and the sponsors. The talented men and women who had spawned and nurtured the Golden Age went elsewhere for employment. But a new summit of quality television programming had been reached.

❖ 1955: COPS AND COWBOYS

Looked at in terms of genres, the police/private eye categories surely provide us with the greatest longevity. Cop shows were popular on radio almost from the beginning. Colorful characters such as *Mr. Kean, Tracer of Lost Persons,* and *Yours Truly, Johnny Dollar,* kept radio listeners interested for years. And action-packed classics like *Gangbusters* and *Mr. District Attorney* dominated their radio time slots. As television began to catch on, some of these radio cops successfully made the transition to television: *Martin Kane, Private Eye, Man Against Crime,* and others. It was a natural transition. Most of the action was interior. There were few sets: the detective's office, the bar where he slugged 'em down between cases and conferred with his buddy the bartender, maybe a darkened warehouse or a nondescript apartment constituting the scene of the crime. While poisoning and stabbing might be employed by the murderer, still the gun was the preferred method of dispatch. There was something ultimately satisfying about the loud report of the gun, the sparks flying from the short barrel, and the smoke hanging in the air that made for better television . . . more viewers, anyway.

Regardless of the genre of choice at any given moment on television from 1948 until today, cop shows have always been with us.

By 1955, the Hollywood movie studios finally began to give up the losing fight with television. Up to this time, studio magnates had haughtily dismissed the idea of producing television programming. Indeed, their art form was best experienced on the silver screen, not over a blurry, flickering tube. The first man to understand "if you can't beat 'em, join 'em" was Jack Warner of Warner Bros. The studio put together a package of three programs which were picked up by ABC. Two of the programs were considered "sure things" by both the studio and the network. The third, a cheaply produced Western called *Cheyenne* with a nobody named Clint Walker in the title role of frontier scout Cheyenne Bodie, was generally considered "filler." Both sure things were off the air the following season. *Cheyenne* had an eight-year run. Not only that, but it spawned a whole host of adult Westerns, called "oaters," including *Maverick, Sugarfoot, Colt 45,* and *Lawman* from Warner Bros. and, from other studios, *Wyatt Earp, Gunsmoke, Death Valley Days, Broken Arrow, Adventures of Jim Bowie,* and many more.

Early in the game, agencies and sponsors expressed an interest in "consulting with" the studios on plot lines and story elements. Jack Warner brusquely torpedoed the idea, a policy that stands to this day. Sponsors may express their support or nonsupport only by buying time or holding back. They may not have creative input.

The public took to these telefilms, as they were called, enthusiastically. Film freed the home viewer from the constraints of the studio . . . interior locations, the by now overused close-up, the total reliance on dialogue to advance the plot. More significantly, the influx of Westerns in the late 1950s contributed to the demise of the old radio method of remuneration (sponsor produced) in favor of the magazine concept (network produced, many sponsors). An easier, more sensible system of sponsorship was emerging. It would eventually allow agencies to get out of the production business and back into the advertising business. It gave the sponsor more flexibility for less risk. It allowed a sponsor to buy in on new programming without investing its own production money up front; if the show bombed, the sponsor simply pulled out and went elsewhere. It saved the big Hollywood studios from oblivion and spawned the science of demographics which was to revolutionize broadcast advertising in the years ahead.

But there was one more event of 1955 that was to do more than anything else to destroy the old single-sponsor radio concept, although it wasn't immediately obvious. The seeds of that destruction took root in the season's most successful new show, *The $64,000 Question*.

❖ SCANDAL! THE END OF SPONSOR CONTROL

In 1955, the battle of the cosmetic companies was in full swing. Hazel Bishop stubbornly held the largest share of the market, with Charles Revson's Revlon seemingly locked in second place. Upset, Revlon was known to be unhappy with its advertising agency and was looking for a new one. Enter Norman, Craig & Kummel, one of Madison Avenue's finest, with a new quiz show idea. No more gags and games, no more $50 jackpots; NC&K proposed a show where winners could win the astonishing sum of $64,000. (This at a time when $5,000 per annum was considered a good living wage.) Revlon was quick to see the marketability of such a concept, transferred the account to NC&K, and went for it.

Within weeks the show commanded an incredible 85 percent share of viewers. Demand for the first product advertised, Living Lipstick, quickly outstripped supply. Host Hal March opened each show with an earnest appeal to the women of America to be patient, the company was working as hard as it could to bring Living Lipstick back to the cosmetic shelves of their nearest store. Soon, Revlon moved into the lead, leaving Hazel Bishop behind.

Obviously, such a success story spawned imitators, notably *High Finance, Twenty One,* and *The $64,000 Challenge.* These shows and others scored big with the public, but soon began to draw suspicions from the government. A former contestant on *Twenty One* named Herbert Stempel claimed the show was fixed. Because he wasn't particularly popular with viewers, Stempel claimed, the sponsors ordered the producers to make sure he was defeated. Furthermore, he charged that the man who eventually beat him, Charles Van Doren, a popular Ivy League professor from a prominent family, had been given the answers in advance. At first, Van Doren denied any wrongdoing, but in 1959, before the House of Representatives special subcommittee on legislative oversight, he confessed that Stempel's accusations were true. Soon other witnesses came forward to admit that they, too, had been coached.

What the subcommittee learned was that popular contestants—those whom viewers wanted to win—were helped, while less popular contestants were deliberately set up to fail. While not the method, certainly the motivation for these actions came from the sponsors. It was a natural hangover from early radio shows where sponsors felt they owned the airwaves, forgetting they were public property. As the government began to take its oversight duties seriously, and as the networks concentrated on damage control (such as the establishment of network "Standards and Practices" units), the big-money game shows, fresh out of credibility, vanished from the nighttime schedule.

❖ THE 1960s: ROLLER-COASTER YEARS

Through the 1950s, ABC was the perennial weak sister in the ratings game. While CBS and NBC jockeyed for the top slots, ABC had to be content to bring up the rear. Yet throughout the decade, the network had learned a lesson or two, the most important of which was that Americans had an apparently insatiable appetite for violence. Being the network with the least to lose, ABC was becoming the risk taker, and in 1960, with the introduction of *The Untouchables,* all that risk taking paid off. *The Untouchables* provided its loyal viewers with more violence per minute than any other show on television. The FBI unit headed by Robert Stack as the intrepid Elliot Ness disposed of Chicago gangsters at an alarming rate. Adding to the violence was another plot requirement in the show: before Ness & Co. dispatched the gangsters, the gangsters had to dispatch other gangsters in their territorial wars. Gangsters were gunned down, run over, drowned in vats of illegal booze, tossed from buildings, and burned alive.

So outrageous was the violence on *The Untouchables* that even its imitators never matched it. Shows like *The Roaring Twenties*, *Surfside 6*, and *77 Sunset Strip* never achieved the heights of violence reached by *The Untouchables*.

All this violence, coupled with ubiquitous Westerns and banal sitcoms, was bound to cause a reaction from someone, somewhere. It was not long in coming, directly from the new Kennedy administration.

❖ THE VAST WASTELAND

The Untouchables, of course, was not the biggest news in 1960. The big story was the election of John F. Kennedy to the presidency. Kennedy, elected largely on the strength of a television debate, understood the power of broadcasting, particularly television, better than any president before. He empowered the FCC, which had remained relatively silent through the Eisenhower years, and replaced its chairman with a strong advocate of program reform named Newton Minow. Minow stepped boldly into the age of violence and vapidity with a no-nonsense speech delivered at the 1961 meeting of the National Association of Broadcasters. Minow began by praising broadcasters for all the good things television was bringing into the living rooms of America—documentary shows like *See It Now*, *Victory at Sea*, and *CBS Reports*; outstanding dramatic shows such as *Playhouse 90* and *Studio One*; live public service programming such as the Army-McCarthy hearings and the presidential debates. When television was good, Minow said, it was very, very good. But when it was bad . . .

> I invite you to sit down in front of your television set when your station goes on the air and stay there without a book, magazine,

newspaper, profit and loss sheet or rating book to distract you—and keep your eyes glued to that set until the station signs off. I can assure you that you will observe a vast wasteland. You will see a procession of game shows, violence, participation shows, formula comedies about totally unbelievable families, blood and thunder, mayhem, violence, sadism, murder, western badmen, western good men, private eyes, gangsters, more violence, and cartoons. And endlessly, commercials—many screaming, cajoling, and offending . . .

Minow's finish was ominous indeed.

I understand that many people feel that in the past licenses were often renewed *pro forma*. I say to you now: renewal will not be *pro forma* in the future. There is nothing permanent or sacred about a broadcast license.

"Newton's law" was not wasted on the broadcasters. Worried about the handwriting on the wall, they sought out and found nonviolent programming capable of ousting the violent programs. A comparison of top ten shows illustrates how seriously broadcasters were taking Minow's message. The list of top ten shows for 1960–61 the season, before Minow's warning shot, was one of violence:

1960–61 Season

1. *Gunsmoke*
2. *Wagon Train*
3. *Have Gun, Will Travel*
4. *The Andy Griffith Show*
5. *The Real McCoys*
6. *Rawhide*
7. *Candid Camera*
8. *The Untouchables*
9. *The Jack Benny Show*
10. *Dennis the Menace*

The year after the warning, network programming had taken on a totally different look:

1962–63 Season

1. *The Beverly Hillbillies*
2. *Candid Camera*
3. *The Red Skelton Show*
4. *Bonanza*
5. *The Lucy Show*
6. *The Andy Griffith Show*
7. *Ben Casey*
8. *The Danny Thomas Show*
9. *The Dick Van Dyke Show*
10. *Gunsmoke*

The two surviving Westerns—*Bonanza* and *Gunsmoke*—were among the least violent of their kind, dealing instead, often humorously, with relationships and family interaction.

Prompted by the success of the James Bond films which dominated the movie theaters of the 1960s, and growing media interest in international intrigue inspired by the cold war, spy adventures naturally began to appear on television as well. The years 1964 through 1966 saw the introduction of such genre shows as *The Man from U.N.C.L.E.*, *The Girl from U.N.C.L.E.*, *I Spy*, and *Get Smart*, to name a few. These secret agents were, in a way, the exact opposite of cowboys. Where *Gunsmoke's* intrepid Marshall Dillon was steadfastly honest, four square in the right, standing on the streets of Dodge City face to face with the evil gunmen, Napoleon Solo, the man from U.N.C.L.E., practiced trickery and deceit, as devious and cunning as the enemy spies that were his nemesis.

Also during this time, just as the Vietnam situation was beginning to deepen, World War II shows enjoyed a brief period of popularity. Shows like *Combat, Rat Patrol, McHale's Navy, Twelve O'Clock High, Hogan's Heroes,* and *The Wackiest Ship in the Army* took over time slots vacated by the Westerns.

Despite the shock of the Kennedy assassination in 1963, violence was back in vogue. America's appetite for mayhem had not yet been sated. Like alcoholics, we kept coming back for just one more. Then, in one year, things changed.

❖ 1968: HITTING BOTTOM

By New Year's Eve 1967, most Americans were convinced that things simply couldn't get much worse. Vietnam was beginning to look like a hopeless trap, a swamp of body counts and body bags. Hawks were becoming doves, and in March 1968 the Great Hawk himself, Lyndon Johnson, announced he would not be a candidate for president. It seemed that communists were in control around the world. In August the Czechs rebelled against their communist masters and the free world thrilled . . . until Soviet tanks entered the streets of Prague and brutally, quickly, all too easily it seemed, reestablished control.

But there were horrors enough at home. In April, Martin Luther King, Jr., was assassinated on the balcony of a Memphis motel, and on June 5, Robert Kennedy, Democratic presidential candidate and brother of the slain president, was gunned down in the service hall of a Los Angeles hotel. By default, the Democratic nomination fell to Johnson's vice president, the last standard bearer of the old Democratic liberal-populist wing. At the Democratic convention in Chicago that summer, student protesters succeeded in provoking what was termed a "police riot." America watched it all on television. The images were unforgettable—the cops and the clubs, the bleeding kids being shoved into paddy wagons, the angry face of Mayor Daley. Finally, America hit bottom. Real life had, at last, become more violent than the fictionalized violence on television.

The shock of 1968 changed America forever. People began to realize that the age, sex, and racial differences that had played such a divisive role in the culture of the 1960s must somehow be addressed if we were to survive the 1970s. The change was reflected on television as exemplified by the success of *Rowan and Martin's Laugh-In*. Introduced in the 1967–68 season, *Laugh-In* was characterized by irreverence. Hosts Dick Martin and Dan Rowan presided over an ensemble cast of attractive young men and women, many of them black. Each week a celebrity guest star joined the madness. *Laugh-In* finished the season a respectable twenty-first in the ratings. In the 1968–69 season, the show went to first place, a position it was to reoccupy in the 1969–70 season.

Much of the material was risqué for television at the time, including its trademark shot, a pretty girl, scantily clad, twisting suggestively and chanting "Sock it to me, sock it to me" until she was hit in the face by a bucket of water. This scene, unthinkable a few years earlier, became so acceptable that President Nixon was persuaded to utter the phrase, *sans* the face full of water.

Another running gag on *Laugh-In* illustrates the way television was changing with regard to race relations. The first show where a black man was heavily featured, *I Spy*, had been introduced in 1965. Two secret agents, Bill Cosby and Robert Culp, maintained a scrupulously egalitarian relationship throughout the run of the show. Generally, Cosby played his role exactly as a white man would have; only occasionally did one or the other partners resort to a quick line or two of black dialect, always done with great good humor, never denigrating.

Laugh-In ignored such niceties altogether. Minstrel skits featured white players in blackface and black players in whiteface. One running gag, usually featuring Sammy Davis, Jr., was based on an old Pigmeat Markham vaudeville skit and was called "Heah come de Judge." Davis, in full British courtroom regalia including white powdered wig, would mount the bench to the chant "Heah come de judge, heah come de judge." He would then proceed to listen to case after case, dispensing immediate justice by clouting litigants with a grossly oversized rubber gavel. Occasionally "de judge" was played by Arte Johnson, a white player, in blackface.

Suddenly, it seemed, blacks were everywhere on television. Within three years blacks had starring roles in major top twenty-five shows like *The Bill Cosby Show*, *The Flip Wilson Show*, and *Julia*, starring Diahann Carroll. Blacks were also seen in strong supporting roles in new shows like *Mission: Impossible* and *The Mod Squad*. Asians, too, began receiving serious parts on shows like *Hawaii Five-O*, a far cry from the role of Hop Sing, the stereotypical Chinese cook on *Bonanza*.

At the same time, minorities began to show up on commercials. National marketers were discovering that it was good business to at least give a nod to their black customers. The success of shows like *Julia,* along with other more somber television images on the news—lines of heroic freedom marchers being attacked with fire hoses and police dogs in the South, thousands of young black men who, while second-class citizens at home, turned out to be first-class fighting men in Vietnam—was winning the admiration of sympathetic whites. Perhaps these whites weren't marching through Dixie with the handful of white clergymen, college kids, and liberal old ladies from Back Bay, but they applauded those who did. The sight of a black face in a commercial, therefore, was a signal not only to blacks, but to an ever-growing number of openly sympathetic whites: the manufacturers of Gloop Candy are with you, on the side of truth, justice, and the American way. Folks who felt a little guilty about not facing fire hoses and police dogs could assuage their consciences just a little bit by spending a quarter on a Gloop Chocolate-Nut Roll.

If minorities were being better served by television, so were young people. During the 1960s, with the Old Establishment still in control (if not in the White House), young people had been considered out of control. They were called Flower Children (read: "airheads") and Hippies (read: "militant troublemakers"). But as the first of the baby boomers began to come of age, numerically and politically, in the early 1970s, television programming reflected the change.

The science of demographics, too, came of age. It was discovered that audience size was, in many cases, less important than audience makeup. Long-running shows like *The Red Skelton Show, Jack Benny, Gunsmoke, Bonanza,* and even the longest-running show of them all, *The Ed Sullivan Show,* fell to the god of demographics. Their still-large audiences consisted primarily of older people, well beyond the years of acquisition. One by one they fell to youth-oriented shows like *Happy Days, LaVerne and Shirley, The Six Million Dollar Man,* and *Starsky and Hutch.* Two of these new shows, Norman Lear's *All in the Family,* introduced in 1971, and Larry Gelbart's *M.A.S.H.* in 1972, began to deal in serious social issues despite their comedy format. They produced episodes dealing with bigotry, homosexuality, menopause, and other subjects that had been considered taboo up till then. The Old Establishment, however, was not yet dead. There were rumblings in Rhode Island.

Folks in Rhode Island had begun asking Senator John Pastore of that state to please do something about all this sexual frankness on television. Since these folks were registered voters, and since Senator Pastore was no fool, he pressured FCC chairman Richard Wiley to please do something about all this sexual frankness on television. Since Pastore was chairman of the appropriations subcommittee that controlled the FCC's budget, and since Wiley was no fool, he appealed to the broadcasting industry to please do something about all this sexual frankness on television and exercise "self-regulation." Since the FCC controlled licensing, and since the broadcasters were no fools, they established the National Association of Broadcasters Code Authority, which immediately designated 7:00 to 9:00 P.M. as "family time" during which shows would be carefully monitored and regulated for objectionable programming.

Family time, however, was a short-lived concept. Norman Lear and Larry Gelbart brought suit, and the court found family time in violation of the First Amendment.

❖ THE 1980s: HERE COMES CABLE

For years, broadcasters had resented the fact that Big Brother, in the form of the FCC, always seemed to be looking over their collective shoulders. The election of Ronald Reagan in 1980 seemed to bode well. Reagan was a passionate believer in deregulation—the less government interference the better, he believed. Within a year the administration deregulated industries from the airlines to the savings and loan institutions. Entire government entities were dismantled or severely weakened from the Environmental Protection Agency to Housing and Urban Development to, finally, the FCC. The broadcasters' dream had come true. And as we'll see in Chapter 3, their worst nightmare began. But, first, having examined the evolution of television programming, let's take a look at what has been going on in television advertising.

❖ ENDNOTE

1. Eric Barnouw, *Tube of Plenty: The Evolution of American Television* (New York: Oxford University Press, 1990).

2

TELEVISION ADVERTISING:
FROM CLOUT TO CLUTTER

It's been said, nobody ever tunes in a television show to watch the commercials. True enough. But this is not to say people *don't watch* commercials. They do. And they act on them; the very first commercial, the one in 1922 for the housing development on Long Island, sold $127,000 worth of homes, remember. Seven decades of experience, along with a great deal of testing, have proved that commercials can build positive images, affect attitudes, and make sales.

The key to the success of any commercial is relevance. If the message is made clear, and if it relates to a real consumer need, it will work. It doesn't have to be expensively produced, it doesn't have to be clever, but it does have to be relevant. Because if it is, if it relates to an immediate consumer need, people will watch and respond. While nobody tuned in just to watch it, it interested them, it involved them, and it worked.

As we'll see later in this book, the combination of a new form of commercial advertising, linked with the concept of marketing channels, greatly enhances the relevance of commercials and puts the lie to the old adage that nobody tunes in to watch the commercials. First, however, it is important to understand the changing relationship between advertising and television. And to understand that, we are currently at a point of significant and critical change in that relationship.

❖ THE GOOD, THE BAD, AND VANCE PACKARD

For more than forty years, television programming, like a cork afloat on a sea of circumstance, bobbed along without apparent purpose, direction, or destination. Buffeted here and there by the winds of popular whim, alternately shackled and ignored by the gale force opinions of government bureaucrats, programming was powerless to chart its own course. The frequently raised charge that television programming was responsible for leading the nation (especially the nation's youth) into violence and hedonism was never quite true. Television didn't originate evil, it merely disseminated it. The people who programmed television were not leaders, but followers. Businessmen in a capitalistic system don't make waves, at least not purposely.

Unlike programming, television advertising has always enjoyed relative immunity from either public whim or government interference. A 60-minute show dealing with murder and mayhem could, it was felt, have an undesirable effect on susceptible youngsters, but the most a 60-second commercial could hope to do was get noticed if it were properly done and motivate a viewer to seek out and buy a product at a favorite retail store. Separating the weak-willed (meaning everyone else but me) from their moral teachings was considered much more serious than simply separating them from their money.

In 1957, Vance Packard published *The Hidden Persuaders*, a book that spawned other books, articles, speeches, and sermons critical of advertising.[1] The industry, it was claimed, shamelessly manipulated its audience, turning ordinary consumers into mindless zombies, shuffling off to the marketplace to do the advertisers' bidding. Among the techniques advertisers used, Packard and his latter-day disciples have charged, was "subliminal advertising." The most famous example of this technique was an oft-illustrated whiskey glass shown in extreme close-up, with the sponsor's product being poured over a jumble of ice cubes. Using the patterns in the photo, an imaginative artist was able to outline suggestive words and parts of women's bodies. According to the theory, these subliminal words and pictures were registered in the subconscious where they remained until the poor puppet of a reader stood in front of the shelf at the liquor store where they were called up and acted upon. The fact that readers were almost universally unable to see this subliminal smut without help seemed to say more about the critics' overly active imaginations than the advertisers' cunning. Said one art director, "If making sales with advertising were as simple as Vance Packard says it is, I'd be a whole lot richer than I am."

Subliminal advertising, it was claimed, was also used in television commercials. Suggestive words and phrases were inserted on individual frames of film that, while not consciously seen, were nonetheless picked up and recorded in the subconscious, ready to be recalled at the supermarket or automobile showroom.

If television programming was a cork on a storm-tossed sea, television advertising was a shark, gliding through the shallows. The trends in advertising on television remained clear and largely consistent from the 1950s to the mid-1980s.

> Commercial breaks have gotten longer and longer.

> Commercial length has gotten shorter and shorter.

> Commercial costs (both production costs and time costs) have gone from relatively cheap to wildly expensive.

> Commercial placement has gone from hunch buying to high science.

> Commercial content has gone from "hard sell" to "image."

❖ THE LENGTHENING OF THE BREAK

By the 1960s the National Association of Broadcasters (NAB), reacting to public complaints that there were just too many commercials on television, issued a guideline: affiliates should limit commercial prime time to 10 minutes an hour and all other day parts to 16 minutes. Following a lawsuit in the 1970s, the NAB commercial code was struck down, and since then, broadcasters have given in to the temptation to squeeze in just one more commercial. Little by little, year by year, the trend continued. And still continues today.

Obviously, week-to-week changes and monitoring difficulties make exact figures difficult, but the trend is clear. Studies funded by cable interests vary somewhat from those funded by network interests. Arguments break out as to what, exactly, constitutes commercial time. Is a station promo a commercial? Or a public service announcement (PSA)? The cable industry claims that the results of the Arbitron research (see Figure 2-1) is flawed in that the figures for the networks do not include either PSAs or station promos. Add these in, say the cable people, and the network figures closely approximate the cable numbers.

Not surprisingly, advertisers are becoming concerned with the amount of clutter. Sharp media buyers are using it as an argument to obtain lower rates. On the other hand, consumer unhappiness with the situation, since the advent of remote control, has abated— the zapper makes commercial viewing optional.

❖ COMMERCIAL LENGTH: HOW MUCH IS ENOUGH?

That first radio commercial, broadcast in 1922, was 10 minutes long. It was broadcast into a vacuum, with no competition and few listeners. The listeners it had, however, were so thrilled with the miracle that was taking place in their own homes that they would listen with rapt attention to anything that came over the wireless. Did it sell homes on Long Island? Reportedly, the sponsor was pleased, although he never established a regular radio advertising schedule.

By the late 1940s, the most common length for commercials on radio was 60 seconds. There were, of course, exceptions. Afternoon children's shows, for example, might run longer, explaining various offers—a free prize packaged in with Wheaties or Cracker Jack or a "send-in-the-boxtops" offer for a decoder ring or an official glow-in-the-dark arrowhead magnifying glass.

Figure 2-1

Clutter Facts

Commercial Comparison
(Cable and Broadcast):
Prime Time Commercial Minutes Per Hour (1991)

A&E	9:35		
CNBC	13:09		
CNN	13:22	**Averages**	
Discovery	10:37		
ESPN	9:54	Cable	11:12
Family	11:38	Networks*	9:12
Lifetime	11:42	Fox	11:04
Nashville	12:54	Ind. Stations	11:21
Nick-At-Nite	10:53	Synd. Prog.	13:21
TNT	10:05		
USA	10:29		
WTBS	10:22		

The Arbitron Company - 1991

*ABC, CBS, NBC

What's on the Broadcast Networks When the Show's Not (1989)

	Network Prime time	Network Daytime
ABC	10:42	16:39
CBS	11:40	16:45
NBC	10:58	16:37
FOX	13:23	--

Commercial Minutes Per Hour

Changes in Total Non-program Time Per Hour 1984-1989

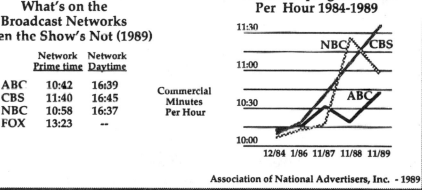

Association of National Advertisers, Inc. - 1989

Per-hour commercial time ranges from a low of 10:42 minutes (ABC) to a high of 13:22 minutes (CNN). While there is some dispute about the accuracy of these figures, the trend is clearly up, and sensitive to change. Notice in the chart at the right how NBC, finding itself leading the networks with nearly 12 minutes of commercial time per hour in 1988, dropped to just 11 minutes the next year. CBS, on the other hand, shot past 11:30 minutes, boldly going where no network had gone before. Courtesy Association of National Advertisers Inc., and the Arbitron Company.

And because it was common for radio hosts to deliver the commercials live and in person, commercial length could vary widely. The dean of these hosts, Arthur Godfrey, surely the most trusted man in America when it came to product promotion, had a penchant for pretentious, rarely used words. Clever advertising copywriters began putting at least one such word in their copy. Godfrey, who never read scripts in advance, would come upon the key word unawares, would repeat it, along with sponsor's name, insert it later, perhaps applying it to a product attribute, or use it along with a sponsor reference while interviewing guests. "Well, Daphne," he might say to an author 10 minutes after delivering the commercial, "let's hope your new book becomes as *ubiquitous* as the *Better Homes and Gardens Cook Book.*" It wasn't unusual for a sponsor like BH&G to garner 2 or 3 minutes of playful commercial time for the cost of a 60-second spot.

Early television at first generally copied this 60-second commercial format. Around this time, advertisers introduced the segmentation of commercial length: those selling low-involvement products such as toothpaste and laundry products and those promoting high-involvement products like refrigerators and automobiles. While the 60-second spot remained the norm, advertisers of low-involvement products soon found that once you'd said "gets clothes whiter," or "gets teeth whiter," there wasn't really a whole lot more to say. The 30-second spot, it was felt, could do everything the 60-second spot could do, for less money. Sponsors of big-ticket items such as appliances found it difficult to explain all their new features, advantages, and benefits in 60 seconds and opted for longer spots.

Other tricks were being used in these early days to keep costs low. Animation became popular. While animated commercials were more expensive to produce than live action, they eliminated talent residuals. Live actors and actresses had to be paid, and repaid, every thirteen weeks. Animated stars such as Ipana's Bucky Beaver and Gillette's parrot did not. Perhaps the most imaginative way to avoid high residual payments was developed by Old Gold cigarettes. Live dancers with cigarette packs covering everything but their legs gave the impression of a live commercial, but with minimal residuals.

While advertisers of low-involvement products were finding happiness on the low side of 60 seconds, advertisers of high-involvement products were discovering the advantage of 90-second and 120-second spots. Because television was a visual medium, it lent itself to the art of demonstration. There was a lot that needed showing and telling about, say, the new electric dishwashers that were just coming on the market. The long-form commercial proved itself ideal. Soon, attractive, personable (and above all, sincere) men and women were explaining charts and product cutaways, demonstrating results, and testing appliances and automobiles live and on camera.

The fact that many of these early spots were live (read: "unpredictable") gave added impact to the product message. The presenter would hold his Zippo lighter in close-up and prove it would light on the first try. It always did. Timex watches were subjected to incredible tortures live and on camera to prove that the product could "take a licking and keep on ticking." It always did. Well, almost always. Only once did a problem occur. The watch was fastened to the propeller blade of an outboard motor. The propeller blade was brought up from the transparent plastic tank used in the demonstration and the watch was gone. A search of the tank and the immediate stage area failed to turn up the watch. The audience, not to mention the normally suave commercial announcer, broke into gales of laughter. Thinking quickly, the announcer assured the audience that when the watch was eventually found, it most assuredly would still be ticking.

Another such on-camera save was pulled off by game show host Garry Moore for Winston cigarettes. Moore, an experienced, heavy smoker, delivered the commercial while actually smoking a Winston. His habit of dragging deeply and then, without exhaling, resuming the commercial worried the sponsor. Moore assured him there was no problem. Then one evening he lit up, leaned back and began extolling the mildness of Winston. "Winston gives you the smoothness and easy draw that other cigarettes lack," said Moore, taking a heavy drag . . . and bursting into a coughing spell. Amidst the laughter of the audience and the panel, Moore saved the day with perhaps the cleverest ad-lib in television advertising history. "See," he said, "Even the *thought* of another cigarette makes me cough."

Of course, the classic mishap occurred in 1954 during a commercial for Westinghouse refrigerators. Contrary to advertising legend, long-time Westinghouse spokeswoman Betty Furness (see Figure 2-2) was *not* on-camera talent that night; it was one of the few occasions when June Graham acted as her substitute. The hapless Miss Graham stepped up to the refrigerator and touched the magic button with her elbow to demonstrate how easily the door could be opened even with both hands full. The door remained shut. "Someone's been playing tricks," she ad-libbed, trying again. Again, nothing. She then had the presence of mind to suggest perhaps someone had forgotten to plug in the unit. The director went to close-up as June continued to describe the wonders to be found . . . just inside the door. Finally the camera pulled back to reveal the refrigerator, which June tried again, with some trepidation, and presto! Greatly relieved, but with great professionalism, she confidently delivered the rest of the commercial, all the way to the tagline, "You can be *sure* if it's Westinghouse." Her big smile on "sure" brought a well-deserved round of applause from the studio audience.

(Note: The version just quoted, the "June Graham" scenario, is the one provided to interested authors by Westinghouse. There are others, however—most everyone but the Westinghouse PR staff—who swear that Betty Furness was on duty as usual that night and cite the existence of a kinescope that proves it. While unable to locate the kinescope, in the face of all this certainty the author is tempted to believe that a "cover-up" may have taken place. By Westinghouse? By Miss Furness? Or even (gasp!), by a future employer in a very high place?)

In those early days television was a novelty, and so were television commercials. People watched the animated characters and celebrity presenters with rapt attention. As a result, sponsors began to understand that a schedule of commercials, no matter how amateurish by today's standards, was a ticket to sales. This remarkable clout extended from national to local sponsors. If you wanted to be the biggest Chrysler-Plymouth dealer in Walla Walla, you'd have to get on the tube. If you wanted to sell more television sets than anyone else in Teaneck, television was the answer. Retailers enthusiastically jumped on the bandwagon.

Figure 2-2

Betty Furness for Westinghouse

Betty Furness, for many years the spokeswoman for Westinghouse, was not on duty the "night the door wouldn't open." Still, most people—even people who saw the spot—insist it was she and not substitute June Graham. So closely did the Westinghouse commercials associate her with the industry, ten years later she was appointed to head up Consumer Affairs during the Johnson administration. Courtesy Westinghouse Electric Corporation.

As a result of this fascination, commercial time became more expensive. These increased costs gradually began to reduce the frequency of the long-form, 2-minute prime-time commercials, a trend that has continued until today when the majority of prime-time spots last 30 seconds. The most recent time period for commercials is 15 seconds, and most evidence indicates that 5-second "video billboards" are just around the corner. The result of all this is a confusing jumble of messages and products, too often ignored. The loss of clout is disheartening to sponsors.

Nor is television alone responsible for the current glut of advertising to which we are exposed. Recent evidence indicates that the average American is exposed to more than 1,000 advertising messages a day. On an ordinary shopping trip, we are bombarded from all sides. Besides the commercials we hear on the car radio and the extensive gallery of billboards and buses we drive past, messages come at us from the supermarket cart, over the PA system, from point-of-sale displays, on the grocery bag, and even on the receipt. We arrive home only to discover a mailbox full of advertising. We no sooner get inside than the phone rings, and we reach it just in time to hear the beginning of a telemarketer's spiel. After dinner, Dad relaxes in front of the television (more commercials), Mom browses through her favorite magazine (ads, ads, ads), while Junior searches the CompuServe system (more advertisements) looking for the latest electronic game and Sis is entertained by a rock singer extolling her favorite soft drink at the beginning of her rented video.

Interestingly, each medium is clearly distinguishable from the others in effect. According to a study by *Marketing and Media Decisions* magazine, specialty magazines provide the best ad environment and reader involvement; radio is the most cost efficient; direct mail is best in terms of targeting and measuring results; general interest magazines attract the highest-quality ads; cable offers the greatest potential for creativity; and network television, despite the beating it has taken from cable, still provides its advertisers the biggest reach and the greatest influence over consumer motivations.

Still, pity the poor television advertiser. Not only is he forced to compete with scores of new advertisers created as commercial length shortens, he also must compete with an array of new media. And if all that isn't bad enough . . .

❖ ENTER THE ZAPPER

Like any number of post-1950 devices—automatic car door locks, electric toothbrushes, and the like—it seemed silly at first. "The day I get too lazy to change channels is the day you can take me out and shoot me." Prior to deregulation, back in the days when the vast majority of American viewers were limited to three commercial channels and one public channel, the remote-control channel changer *did* seem . . . well . . . unnecessary. But the advent of cable, with its wide range of channels, suddenly gave the device credence. Nobody wants to stand there, uncomfortably bent over, flicking through thirty-eight channels. Ownership of zappers has grown from 16 percent in 1981 to over 90 percent in 1992. Today's advertiser not only has to compete with the bathroom, the refrigerator, or the crossword puzzle, but with the zapper as well. Almost overnight, commercial watching became voluntary. Today's viewer has no patience with boring formula commercials. No longer can commercials ride the coattails of entertaining programming; commercials today have to be as entertaining as the programming itself. At this writing, director Rob Reiner is producing a commercial for Coca-Cola Classic, shot in the style of his hit movie, *When Harry Met Sally.* Other major brand-name advertisers like Nike are commissioning Hollywood mogul Michael Ovitz for TV work. The time-honored rules of television advertising have begun to go out the window.

Prior to the ascension of the zapper, research had uncovered strict rules for television commercial writing. Perhaps the guru of this school was Rosser Reeves, champion of the USP (unique selling proposition). This theory held that the key to sales was discovering one product characteristic that was different from any of its competitors and driving it relentlessly home. In practice, these USPs usually took the form of some obscure chemical property not found in other products. Thus words like *simethecone, Flouristan,* and *GL-70* came briefly into popular usage.

The commercials spawned by this school of advertising were, except for the USP, remarkably similar. Generally they took place in the kitchen, bathroom, or laundry room. The sponsor's name and the USP were always mentioned as quickly as possible. The format was always problem/solution. They were usually 60 seconds in length. Gimmicks were encouraged. For example,

OPEN ON MOM ABOUT TO PUT JUNIOR'S FILTHY SWEAT
  SOCKS IN WASHER.

MOM (TO CAMERA): I was so embarrassed. Coach Smith said he
  was going to change the name of Junior's team from White
  Sox to Gray Sox.

ANIMATED EFFECT: PARROT WEARING BASEBALL CAP
  SWOOPS IN AND LANDS ON BACK OF WASHER.

MOM: Wha . . . who are you?

PARROT: Squawk! I'm Polly, the Soft-Rain parrot.

AS MOM GAINS HER COMPOSURE, THE PARROT PRODUCES
  A BOX OF SOFT-RAIN DETERGENT FROM UNDER HER
  WING.

MOM: Soft-Rain?

PARROT: *New* Soft-Rain, with activated *Polyacterine*, the detergent
  that's specially formulated to chase gray away. Let's give it a
  try.

MOM PUTS SOCKS IN MACHINE, PARROT ADDS DETER-
  GENT. ANIMATED SEQUENCE SHOWING TINY RAIN-
  DROPS PENETRATING SWIRLING LOAD OF GRAY
  WASH, SWEEPING AWAY DIRT PARTICLES, AND LEAV-
  ING THE WASH WHITE.

V.O. ANNCR: *Polyacterine*, the active cleaning ingredient in new
  Rain-Soft detergent, penetrates deeply into dirt, blood, or
  grass-stained wash leaving it not just clean, but *Polyacterine*
  clean.

FADE TO SLIDE: NEXT DAY

CUT TO EXTERIOR, 2-SHOT MOM AND COACH WATCHING
  PLAYERS WARM UP.

MOM: Well, Coach, what do you think of your Gray Sox now?

CUT TO CU SOCKS ON JUNIOR. THEY LOOK DAZZLING.

COACH (ABASHED): Looks like we're the White Sox again. How did you get Junior's uniform so clean?

BACK TO 2-SHOT. COACH HEFTS BAT TO HIS SHOULDER.

MOM (SMUGLY): Oh . . . a little bird told me.

ANIMATED PARROT LANDS ON COACH'S BAT.

PARROT: *Squawk! Polyacterine!*

MOM AND COACH LAUGH AS PARROT SQUAWKS.

CUT TO GLAMOR-SHOT OF RAIN-SOFT BOX WITH ANIMATED PARROT.

V.O. ANNCR: Try New Rain-Soft laundry detergent . . . with deep-cleaning *Polyacterine.*

Commercials like these, backed by tremendous media expenditures and introduced with enormous reach and frequency, continued to launch many low-involvement products well into the 1970s. Advertising creative people, frustrated by these formula commercials, began to rebel in the early 1960s, encouraged by the Volkswagen campaign launched in 1959 by Doyle, Dane, Bernbach. This historic campaign is remembered largely as a print campaign, although its effect was visible in all media. The opening ad featured a stark, simple photo of the little Volkswagen bug with a headline exhorting readers to "Think Small." It taunted the fin-tailed American dinosaurs of the highway, promoting Volkswagen's smallness as being an advantage in city driving, city parking, and gas mileage. Other ads in the campaign were equally revolutionary. One, based on research that indicated Americans thought the car was funny looking, carried the headline "It's ugly, but it gets you there." Perhaps the most famous ad in the series carried the one-word headline "Lemon" and went on to explain that a quality control inspector had rejected the car because the dashboard clock didn't work. As the funny-looking little car scored sales, racked up market share, and led the way for the upcoming invasion of foreign cars still with us today, advertisers began to realize that simplicity and relevance were more effective than hype.

The campaign did much to encourage advertising creative people to throw off the bonds of formula commercials. The 1960s saw a brief golden age of advertising in all media. DDB quickly became a major agency, acquiring an impressive client list of well-heeled, blue-chip accounts. For one brief shining moment, creativity was "in," and the opinion of copywriters and art directors took precedence over that of account supervisors and research directors. Creative boutiques and "hot shops"—DDB wannabes—sprang up. But while imitation may be the sincerest form of flattery, it is also hard to achieve. Some of these "creative campaigns" were successful because of their relevance to the marketplace needs. More, however, were creative only; charming, funny, but ultimately irrelevant to the viewer. By the mid-1970s innate fear of flying without research combined with a softening economy frightened sponsors back to the "let's play it safe" mode, and once again commercials were dictated largely by research.

While low-involvement products were fighting the formulas, big-budget, high-involvement products were facing the battle of the budgets. Even the prosperous automobile industry occasionally choked on the price of commercial airtime. The old 2-minute spots demonstrating and describing the features, advantages, and benefits of the new models simply couldn't be justified on a cost basis. To maintain effective frequency levels, advertising objectives were changed. Commercials were no longer expected to educate viewers on new models, but to bring viewers to their local dealerships where salespeople would do the educating. The result was a strong shift to "image" advertising on the part of many of these big-ticket items. While perhaps you couldn't explain the workings of the new Dyna-Flyte transmission in 2-minute detail, you could compare the new model to a Mustang or a Jaguar or a Barracuda in 30 seconds of quick-cut action, gut-wrenching music, and a few well-chosen lines of *basso profundo* copy. And you could position your buyers as virile young successes as opposed to the unexciting wimps who bought competitors' models.

Image advertising had a tendency to work for a while but fade in the long run. Advertising research companies sprang up like weeds, out to prove that formula spots were not only safer, but more effective over time. Small, highly creative advertising agencies flashed briefly, added millions of dollars in billing overnight, and then, just as briefly, they disappeared as clients reverted to the safety of conservative, old-line agencies. Accounts fragmented or were pirated off by various talented agency principals.

The battle between safe, research-oriented commercials and creative, image-oriented advertising became irrelevant with the arrival of the remote-control device. A new set of rules was called for. The old rule that the sponsor's name should be mentioned in the first 5 seconds didn't seem relevant anymore. The sponsor's name immediately signaled the beginning of a commercial and a subsequent grab for the zapper. "I'm not really interested in this product, so I guess I'll see what else is on."

European advertisers had been up against this problem for years. In many countries, commercials are barred from interrupting the program and are placed instead in a lengthy segment at the end, competing not with the entertainment segment of the show but with each other. By the mid-1980s, European commercials began to resemble minimysteries, opening with a sequence aimed at piquing audience curiosity to the point where they were "hooked" and then leading them through the story until the product was revealed at the very end. Unable to count on entertainment programming to carry them, these commercials became as entertaining as the shows.

A classic of this genre is a commercial developed by Young & Rubicam/Stockholm. It follows a little old lady home from the grocery store. Although the viewer can see a piano being hoisted into a third-floor window directly ahead of her, she seems oblivious to the danger. Quick intercuts between the old lady, slowly trudging, and the piano, inching upward. Suddenly, the rope breaks and piano falls . . . landing directly behind the old lady, who blithely continues her walk. At this point, the first and only mention of the sponsor is made . . . Trygg-Hansa Insurance.

While such commercials broke traditional rules of advertising, they had the advantage of staying the channel surfer's thumb. Today, many American commercials use this minimystery format.

Another genre first developed in Europe is the pure image, make-the-customer-figure-out-who-the-advertiser-is format. Seemingly unrelated images are shown, forcing the viewer to guess who the sponsor is . . . never revealing the answer until the last few frames. Levis, shot with a denim-blue tinge, are a classic example of this genre, as are Nike sports shoes and Chanel perfumes. Again, the objective is to keep the zapper from doing his thing.

Other techniques for staying the zapper's itchy trigger finger include new wave video techniques; storytelling (usually humorous) with a beginning, middle, and end; and the use of celebrities. Bookend spots, placed at the beginning and end of a commercial cluster, are another.

One of the biggest problems facing advertisers today is placement within the line-up of commercials during the break. If the first commercial in line loses the audience, nobody will be around to see your beautifully crafted and expensively produced spot. Complaints from advertisers are being heard by network officials who are looking for ways to "clean up" commercial breaks by rescheduling network promos and station identifiers. Just as magazines charge a premium for favored pages such as inside front cover or back cover, one expects networks may eventually charge more for the "first in line" spot in a break.

❖ THOSE WERE THE DAYS

During the three decades prior to 1980, television had created for itself a comfortable corner in America's living room. Evolving from successful radio networks, its *metier* was pure entertainment. Even its informational and educational programming was delivered as entertainment, from so-called "happy news" shows to *Sesame Street* and Disney's nature series, where the laid-back voice of Rex Allen lazily anthropomorphized the actions of wild animals.

Following the early demise of the Dumont Network, CBS, NBC, and ABC settled in for a long run. For those interested in human nature, or perhaps "American nature," ABC provides an interesting lesson. In 1950, ABC was Tail-end Charlie, far behind its two formidable competitors. Then in 1955, purely by accident, ABC released *Cheyenne* and discovered a rich vein of violence. It was clear that the American appetite for violence was hearty indeed. In quick order,

ABC released a string of violent Westerns and then, in 1959, turned to urban violence. Always ready to toss a little more raw meat into the nightly schedule, ABC led the ratings by 1980. Is there a lesson here? Michael Medved, in his book *Hollywood vs. America*, thinks so.[2] But that discussion is for another time.

Another curiosity present during the first thirty years was the variety show. Such shows had been a hallmark of radio. *The Ed Sullivan Show*, introduced in 1949, survived with no change in format until 1971, when it fell victim to demographics. During the run of the Sullivan show and beyond, other variety shows enjoyed enormous popularity. These included early shows like the *Texaco Star Theater* and *The Colgate Comedy Hour*, on through *The Jackie Gleason Show, The Dean Martin Show, The Red Skelton Hour,* and *The Carol Burnett Show.*

The years before 1980 were the years of true *broad*casting. If you were watching television, you were watching one of the three commercial networks or, in some markets, the public television channel. Decision making was easy. Usually the family could agree on which program to watch. The rule-of-thumb was one television set per household. Nothing else was needed.

But the times . . . well . . . the times they were a-changin'. Those days, those comfortable, fun-to-remember days were about to end. All hell was about to break loose. And the agent of change was a man who had already made his mark on broadcasting . . . more than forty years earlier.

❖ ENDNOTES

1. Vance Packard, *The Hidden Persuaders* (New York: D. McKay, 1957).
2. Michael Medved, *Hollywood vs. America: Popular Culture and the War on Traditional Values* (New York: HarperCollins, 1992).

3

CABLE, COMPETITION, AND CHAOS

On a warm spring day in 1934, a tall, good-looking young man entered the lobby of radio station WHO in Des Moines, Iowa. The receptionist was impressed.

"May I help you?" she smiled.

The young man removed his hat and smiled back. "I'm the new sportscaster," he said. "My name's Reagan. Ronald Reagan. But you can call me Dutch."

"Dutch?" she asked. "Why Dutch?"

"Why not? That's what everybody calls me."

Within a month his pleasant voice and easygoing personality won him a large following of fans. If he sometimes got his facts and statistics a little twisted . . . well, so what? How could anybody hold a little thing like that against a nice guy like Dutch Reagan (see Figure 3-1)?

His employers loved him. Not only was he popular with listeners, but he showed a great deal of ingenuity as well. In those days sportscasters generally called baseball games, play by play, directly from the studio, picking up their information as it came in on a Western Union line. Once, during a Cubs/Cardinals pennant game, with Dizzy Dean on the mound for St. Louis' famous Gashouse Gang, the telegraph line went down. Calmly and without a trace of panic, Reagan proceeded to call seven straight minutes of foul balls until contact with Western Union was reestablished. For weeks, fans asked Reagan whether that wasn't some sort of record for foul balls. With all the professionalism of a magician who refuses to reveal the secret behind his tricks, Reagan never let on.

Then in 1937, while he was covering the Cubs at their Catalina Island training camp, a Warner Bros. talent scout, impressed with his good looks and easygoing manner, offered him a screen test, which he passed with flying colors. As an actor, he proved himself competent, if not inspired. It was as if acting was secondary to a new and more exciting passion which was developing in his character: politics. In 1947 he was elected president of the Screen Actors Guild. Like his actress wife, Jane Wyman, Reagan was a liberal Democrat. Anticipating the coming rise of television, and concerned with the treatment of actors as the new media expanded, Reagan put together an agenda calling for a favorable system of residual payments. By the time he left that office in 1952, the Guild had won its residual payment system, which is still in use today, as well as a strong pension and welfare program for Guild members.

In the late 1940s, the television networks, quite naturally, took a great deal of interest in things like residual payments. But neither the networks nor the Screen Actors Guild paid much attention to a new but not very impressive technology operating on the fringe of the industry. It was developed in response to a problem. John Walston, a television set dealer in Mahoney City, Pennsylvania, was having sales difficulties due to poor reception in his area. Mahoney City was just outside the nearest local coverage. Walston built a tower antenna on his store to demonstrate how clear television could be, and when his customers insisted on equivalent reception, he offered to let them hook up to his tower for the mere cost of the antenna installment lines.

Figure 3-1

Ronald Reagan During His Radio Days at WHO/Des Moines

While his acting career in movies and television was perhaps less than distin-guished, Ronald Reagan's political career was, of course, spectacular. And his influence on broadcasting over a period of fifty years was enormous. Courtesy WHO Radio.

The folks in Mahoney City weren't the only people plagued with poor reception. People who lived in mountainous regions, or in downtown areas of major cities surrounded by tall buildings, found their reception varied from poor to nonexistent. Many small-market cities had access to only one local network station, a situation that could be frustrating at times.

And people who lived in Austin, Texas, had a special problem all their own. Although clearly a large market and the capital of one of our most populous states, Austin's television fare was limited to station KTBC, owned by the Texas Broadcasting Company. Despite repeated appeals by other broadcasters anxious to establish stations in the lucrative market, action was blocked year after year by the Federal Communications Commission (FCC). With no competition, KTBC, the only game in town, was able to charge what some advertisers considered exorbitant prices, becoming in the process the most profitable station in America. It has been suggested that politics played a part in this situation. Senator Lyndon B. Johnson of Texas had many close friends on the FCC, and while no paper trail exists between them, still there was talk. Despite these accusations, the lucrative situation endured for years, much to the delight of the owner of the Texas Broadcasting Company, Claudia Taylor Johnson, better known as Lady Bird.

While the problem of limited television reception in Austin was unique, there was hope for the small-town viewer in isolated or mountainous areas. It was called coaxial cable. Signals could be picked up by large antennas, usually built on the highest ground available, and sent to homes via a coaxial cable system. The cable had two advantages over broadcasting technology. The reception on all channels was noticeably clear, unusual during a time when most broadcast viewers spent a great deal of time fine-tuning between each station change. And although early cable companies simply rebroadcast existing network fare, it was possible for cable to supply several additional channels of programming. Its only clear disadvantage—the fact that subscribers had to pay a fee for the service, though inordinately comforting to network executives—didn't seem to be much of a deterrent to service-starved viewers.

The attitude of many network executives toward cable was remarkably naive. It was felt that as networks placed affiliates in more and more cities, cable would eventually find itself with no market. After all, who would pay for something they could get for nothing? Meanwhile, they simply added cable viewers to their viewership figures to drive up advertising cost per minute.

By 1964, almost unnoticed by the networks, there were more than a thousand local cable companies operating in the United States. Furthermore, these small entrepreneurs had learned a lesson. While it was true that people weren't likely to pay for something they could get free, it was also true they'd gladly pay for something extra—like free movies, uncut and without commercials, which the cable operators began to supply on their unused, open channels.

A curious phenomenon of this period was a brief fascination with locally produced programming designed purely to fill up the dial. With plenty of unused channels, cable companies would offer a public channel, free, to anyone who had something thought to be worthy of presentation (not unlike AT&T's first radio "toll booths"). Public channels brought out every high school magician and church choir soprano for miles around. During dead time, cable stations would often simply turn a camera on a basketful of newborn puppies or a fish tank. While the fish tank was generally ignored, the puppies, when awake, were capable of drawing an audience.

In 1967, hoping to boost the UHF (ultrahigh frequency) system in large cities, the FCC put a de facto ban on urban cable systems, stopping further development in the top one hundred markets. Restricted to small towns, cable stations owners began to regroup and consolidate. Community access programming was upgraded from fish tanks to clocks, ticker tapes, rolling weather reports, municipal meeting coverage, and public service programming.

Meanwhile, the FCC went to work trying to figure out just what to do about this new development. In 1970 it decided that broadcasting networks should not be allowed to own cable networks, and CBS was ordered to sell its cable assets. And in 1972 the ban on the top one hundred markets was removed. Having spent five years on a leash, the cable industry came out of the gate both healthy and hungry. And almost immediately ran into a brick wall. The national economy began to worsen. New systems failed to grow enough to produce cash flow. And because cable systems needed local approval to operate in most cities, opposition appeared at once. Network stations, sensing a chance to stymie cable competition, enlisted the help of church groups to halt franchise acceptance with talk about "X-rated movies coming to your living room."

Still, progress was made. In November 1972, Time, Inc., introduced a new concept called pay-cable TV. Something in excess of three hundred New York City patrons to Time's new *Home Box Office* service enjoyed a hockey game broadcast in New York. The new service also offered a schedule of relatively new movies. For the first time, cable subscribers were paying a fee in excess of the basic cable fee. Within two years, Home Box Office had grown to 57,000 subscribers, which was still not enough to turn a profit. Facing failure, Time, Inc., gambled big. It committed $7.5 million over a five-year period to put Home Box Office on RCA's new Satcom 1 satellite. While this made the service theoretically available to all 4,000 U.S. cable systems, few if any of these systems had satellite-receiver dishes. But the quality of the movies on *HBO*, coupled with a second pay-cable channel, *Showtime,* in 1976, were clear money-makers, and satellite dishes sprang up like mushrooms after rain.

The year 1977 saw another innovation. Ted Turner, owner of *WTBS*, Atlanta, one of the nation's big independent stations, signed on Satcom 1 and became the first superstation. Cable stations could, for a small "per subscriber" fee add it to their basic cable offering, while Turner began selling time on *WTBS* at national rates with no expensive changes in programming.

Cable was, finally, coming of age. After the unfortunate false start of 1972, a strong period of growth began. More and more satellite services like *ESPN* (sports), *C-SPAN* (public affairs), *CNN* (24-hour news), *MTV* (pop-rock music), plus children's programming like *Disney* and *Nickelodeon,* and even adult programming like *Playboy,* attracted more and more subscribers. This "narrowcasting," with its ability to cater to a variety of tastes, gave cable companies an opportunity to grow into solid, solvent business entities.

❖ THE 1980s: CHAOS

We left Ronald Reagan, liberal champion of the Screen Actors Guild, a successful union politician but, alas, still struggling with his film career. In 1951 he appeared in *Bedtime for Bonzo* opposite a chimpanzee. Which probably helps explain why, in 1954, he accepted a position as host of television's General Electric Theater. His earlier-mentioned good looks and easygoing manner soon restored his popularity. Divorced from Jane Wyman, he married Nancy Davis, a minor actress with her own bent for politics. Conservative, Republican politics. Charming and gregarious, Reagan soon found himself in the company of giants of industry, movers and shakers, people who could really influence political action. He was impressed, and so were they. Thus began his move into the highest ranks of Republican politics. The union leader had become the champion of laissez-faire. The mediocre actor had become the master politician. The transformation was complete.

In 1966 he was elected governor of California, and by 1982 he was the Republican candidate for president. His opponent, incumbent Jimmy Carter, had campaigned on a platform of putting government back in the hands of the people. That had not happened. Reagan campaigned on a platform best described as eliminating government altogether, with the exception of national defense. It was exactly what Americans wanted to hear. Oh, sure, maybe he got his figures wrong once in awhile and maybe his statistics didn't always add up; still, how could you hold a few little oversights like that against a nice guy like Dutch Reagan? Strapped by a weak economy, and disgusted by Carter's concern for human rights overseas and his support of welfare programs at home, the country gave Ronald Reagan the White House along with a strong mandate.

Most network executives were behind Reagan, at least those who for years had hobnobbed with the General Electric types. True to his word, he gutted the welfare agencies. Members of the air traffic controllers union, underestimating his resolve, went out on strike. Within a few months the air traffic controllers were out of work. Ronald Reagan wasn't.

Next he turned to deregulation. One by one, American industries were left on their own, free to compete without government interference or restriction; the airlines, the savings and loan industry, the automobile industry. The network executives began to worry. For years the FCC had, with occasional exceptions, provided the industry with profitable stability. Not only had Big Brother watched the networks, but it had also kept an eye on potential competitors such as cable. Would Reagan deregulate the Federal Trade Commission, and thus the FCC? The answer was . . . of course he would.

Reagan's new head of the FCC, Robert V. Fowler, was an advocate of the conservative line. Regulation, he felt, was not only unnecessary, but undesirable. Government support of public programming, often used to promote the liberal agenda, was undemocratic, and the many regulations and restrictions that had put all power in the hands of a bureaucratic elite must be abolished. By leaving communications to market forces, the American people would finally be in a position to determine what they wanted to see and hear in their own living rooms. And wasn't that, after all, the true spirit of the First Amendment?

Of course deregulation worked two ways. If the FCC's regulatory function was severely weakened, so was its protectionist function. The networks, which years of tradition had transformed into national institutions, found themselves in a competitive market with no competitive edge. The cable industry, on the other hand, was in the midst of creative expansion. Dozens of new pay-cable channels were put on the market, each finding its niche. This growth, of course, was all made at the expense of network ratings. An unprecedented erosion of audience share began.

❖ THE ONSLAUGHT OF CABLE

The network executives had reason to worry. Cable was an idea whose time had finally come. Americans were fascinated at the diversity and willing to pay to get it. Best of all, they didn't even have to give up their favorite network shows. It was all there, coming out of that little box of entertainment in the living room.

Then, like an old knight unhorsed by a young champion, the network establishment gazed in horror as a platoon of new competitors entered the lists.

The first was QUBE, a stunning new technology from Warner Amex that could do everything cable could do with one remarkable difference: QUBE subscribers could communicate back. Much talked about, interactive television had finally arrived. One cable line carried television to the home, while an upstream line allowed viewers to interact with a central computer. Early tests in Columbus, Ohio, indicated great public acceptance. Within the next few years, the interactive functions were expanded from simple polling to the ability to order merchandise and take scholastic courses at home. Later advancements even afforded the viewer theft and fire protection. In the early 1980s, markets were opened up in a number of top one hundred cities.

Despite its early promise, QUBE was short-lived. It was expensive, for one thing. And subscribers often came to feel that the information they were providing could somehow be tapped and used against them—by the IRS, perhaps? Interactive television may simply have been ahead of its time. In 1984, QUBE folded. The possibilities of interactive television are still being explored today, mainly by phone companies. Their ability to reach virtually every phone subscriber anywhere in the world portends such things as banking by phone and shopping by phone. The new fiber optic technology should solve potential overload problems. The trouble seems to be one of perceived need. After all, in most instances an 800 number and a touch-tone phone are, in fact, an interactive system.

In 1983, Australian-born newspaper magnate Rupert Murdoch, among others, announced financial backing for direct broadcasting satellite (DBS) services. This technology, while still in the development stage, was based on the idea of satellite programming being acquired by individual satellite dishes in the customer's home, thus bypassing the television station and the cable system altogether. The technology was already in use by farmers and ranchers whose isolation made cable hookup unprofitable. While DBS worldwide remains a worry to broadcasting and cable interests alike, so far the status remains quo. For all the investment in DBS it remains today the only cost-effective way to reach that last small remnant of the population that lives beyond the signals, out where the cable lines end.

Next came microwave technology, followed by cellular technology. Both these systems are capable of transmitting audio and video signals just as effectively, but without the expense of conventional cable systems. A compact, inexpensive dish, either indoors or out, replaces all the miles of lines required with cable. These systems remain in various stages of experimentation today.

Probably one of the areas of greatest speculation is that of telephone companies entering the cable business. Telcos are big and massive, with lots of money—plus their fiber optic technology is clearly going to be important in the two-way interactive future predicted for television. Still it will take hundreds of billions of dollars and many years for them to be considered even an also-ran in the race against existing cable systems.

Despite the comings and goings of these rival technologies, the established cable system remains firmly in place. At the time of this writing, 65 percent of American homes subscribe to a local cable service. This, despite the fact that DBS, for instance, promises more for less. And despite the fact that public attitudes toward cable are changing. For the worse.

❖ THE 1990s: MIXED SIGNALS

Cable penetration is at an all-time high, but growth is slowing, as the market approaches saturation (see Figure 3-2).

Most people report they are satisfied with the programming they receive on cable. But the majority of Americans are unhappy with both service and rising subscription costs. In 1982, basic cable cost an average of $8.46. As of 1992 that rate now tops $18.85.

While basic cable subscriptions continue to grow, pay-channel sales are falling off.

Pay-Per-View (PPV)—events and Video-On-Demand (VOD)— seemed like such a good idea at the time. Highly touted ventures such as NBC's 1992 triple-cast of the Olympics were widely ignored, and subscriptions seem to have peaked at a very low level of pene-

Figure 3-2

National Growth in Cable Subscribers and Household Penetration, 1980–1992

	Household Penetration (%)	Cable Subscribers (000)	Pay Subscribers (000)
1992	65.1	60,123	26,273
1991	63.9	59,329	26,556
1990	61.0	56,336	26,758
1989	58.5	53,094	27,862
1988	55.5	49,408	27,384
1987	50.5	44,272	25,531
1986	48.1	41,479	22,669
1985	48.7	41,490	24,776
1980	28.3	21,834	8,701

A. C. Nielsen - 1992

In 1980, fewer than three out of every ten Americans had cable. Ten years later that figure had grown to more than six out of ten. And half of these also subscribed to pay channels in addition to basic cable channels. Courtesy A. C. Nielsen.

tration (20 percent in 1992). Unless prices come down, Pay-Per-View and Video-On-Demand seem unlikely to prosper.

Cable viewership skews toward the wealthy, "upscale" end. But even while advertising revenues increase, advertisers have begun to develop an attitude. It's often difficult for them to verify cable viewership using the traditional cost-per-thousand (CPM) model. While cable as a whole commands some 40 percent of the total viewing audience, single channels can claim only a fraction of that number. Advertisers continue to pressure cable for improvements in demographic and psychographic research. Too, VCR continues to confuse the issue: if 80 percent of cable subscribers currently own VCRs and that figure is expected to reach 90 percent by 1995, what are folks really watching tonight?

Finally, while most viewers report satisfaction with their pay-channel selections, these channels continue to lose subscriptions even as basic cable installations rise.

In the late 1970s the promise of cable was great indeed. It could do everything broadcast television could do, and more. It could entertain. And because of lower advertising costs, made possible by the plethora of channels, it could afford to inform and educate. To advertisers, it promised a clear, low-cost, enormously efficient way to reach potential customers, not just as mass audiences but almost as individuals.

Now, less than twenty years later, its promise seemed unfilled. In the public eye, the difference between network and cable has become indistinct and irrelevant. Today's average teenager neither knows nor cares. It's all TV. It all comes out of that box in the corner.

Making matters even worse for the networks was the fact that cable was attracting an audience that was, well, attractive (see Figures 3-3 and 3-4). Sure, it was smaller than the mass audience of the networks, but it was also better off. Upscale Americans, curious and intelligent, were delighted to give up mindless sitcoms like *Three's Company* for historical or nature documentaries, theater, music, even classic films. As we'll see in the next chapter, the cable industry has yet to explain this benefit to advertisers.

❖ THE GOOD NEWS AND THE BAD NEWS

As the cable industry enters the 1990s, things look generally good. Having attracted a large, affluent segment of the public, it is prosperous and comfortable. It seems to be the product of choice for American television viewers. Even its potential competitors—DBS, telcos, and so on—seem to have been relegated to the status of alternate delivery systems. After all, the important thing is not how programming is delivered, but rather the quality of the programming itself. It's a lot like ordering a pizza for delivery: carefully you select your toppings, make the crucial crust decisions, and consult coupons for special deals and bargain prices. After much deliberation, the order is placed and the pizza is on its way. Does anyone care how it arrives? Plane, train, or automobile . . . nobody gives a hoot. Entertainment is the pizza; cable is and will likely remain the preferred delivery system for years to come. It does the job and it's in place. And that's all that really matters to the viewer. That's the good news.

Figure 3-3

Cable Viewer: Facts and Demographics, 1992

Nationwide Cross Section　　　　Total U.S. Cable Households　**65%**

	U.S. Total	Non-Cable	Cable
Household Income			
$75,000 +	100	90	126
$40,000 - $75,000	100	99	116
$20,000 - $40,000	100	102	100
Under $20,000	100	102	76
Education			
College Graduate	100	97	113
Attended College	100	98	105
HS Graduate	100	101	104
Not HS Graduate	100	101	78
Occupation			
Exec. Mgmt. Adm.	100	95	123
Professional	100	95	107
Other Employed	100	98	106
Not Employed	100	105	86
HH Size			
3 + Persons	100	99	105
2	100	103	101
1	100	100	75
Age			
18 - 34	100	98	103
35 - 54	100	99	105
55+	100	105	92

Mediamark Research Inc., Spring 1991 as published in
1992 Cable TV Facts - Cabletelevision Advertising Bureau

A. C. Nielsen - 1992

As compared to the general population, cable viewers lead in important demographic categories such as income, education, occupation, household size, and age. These are the people advertisers are most interested in reaching. Courtesy A. C. Nielsen and Cabletelevision Advertising Bureau.

Figure 3-4

Cable Facts, 1982–1991

Top 10 Cable Network Advertisers*

	Expenditures ($ millions)
Proctor & Gamble	$ 112.0
General Motors	41.9
Anheuser-Busch	37.6
Phillip Morris	34.8
General Mills	33.4
Hasbro	29.6
American Home Products	25.4
AT&T	24.9
Mars Inc	21.9
Eastman Kodak	21.4

The Arbitron Company - 1992

*Measured Networks: ESPN, TBS, USA Network, MTV, CNN, Family Channel, Lifetime, TNT, Nickelodeon

Audience Share Trends: Cable vs. Broadcast

Total Day Viewing Shares
Total U.S. Households

82/83 83/84 84/85 85/86 86/87 87/88 88/89 89/90 90/91 91/92

NTI montly CSR, B/C years 1982/83 - 1990/91

Top 10 Multiple System Operators

	Basic Subscribers	
Tele-Communications Inc.	9,686,000	(2/93)
Time Warner Cable	6,807,330	(1/93)
Continental Cablevision	2,855,000	(10/92)
Comcast	2,852,000	(2/93)
Cablevision Systems	2,008,986	(2/93)
Cox Cable Communications	1,722,007	(1/93)
Jones Intercable/Spacelink	1,586,233	(3/93)
Newhouse Broadcasting	1,321,806	(12/92)
Adelphia Communications	1,189,000	(12/92)
Cablevision Industries	1,175,422	(10/92)

Cablevision magazine - Capital Cities/ABC Inc., Diverisfied Publishing Group
Cabletelevision Advertising Bureau - 1992, 1993

The decade of the 1980s saw broadcast's share of audience and advertising budgets (or at least parts of budgets) once pledged to networks shift to cable. This prosperity was responsible for the establishment and subsequent success of solid multiple-system operators (MSOs). (Courtesy Cabletelevision Advertising Bureau and The Arbitron Company).

The bad news is, the market seems to have reached its saturation point. Most of the people who want cable have it. Projections indicate a decline in pay channels such as the movie channels. Pay-Per-View television, introduced with such great expectations, just hasn't caught on (Figure 3-5).

According to a study conducted by the Electronic Industries Association, when respondents were asked to name the most enjoyable way to watch a movie, only 2 percent mentioned PPV. Even movies that are purchased rank higher, at 5 percent, while movies in the theater tie with TV movies (including commercials) at 16 percent. Interestingly, commercial-free pay-cable channels are named by 22 percent of respondents, while video store rentals top the list with 36 percent preference. Then there's the cost factor. If a single PPV movie costs between $2 and $4, why not spend $10 for *HBO* and get 30 days of a variety of movies 'round-the-clock? This "accidental rivalry" between pay-cable channels and video store rentals may, as The Conference Board figures indicate (Figure 3-6), be even more heavily skewed than suspected. Notice how high video rentals rank and how low pay-cable channels rank.

"Cable has made the vast wasteland vaster, and no less a wasteland."

JOHN CARMAN, Television Critic, *San Francisco Chronicle*

It seems cable is offering nothing more than the same old thing. The mixed signals cable is receiving in the 1990s indicate that the battle between the networks and the cable companies has ended in stalemate. The networks lost their autonomy in the late 1980s when the Reagan administration set them adrift on a sea of deregulation. No longer independent, now each of the three of the major networks is simply an arm of one of the giant, multinational corporations. Cable, while faring better, had begun the decade of the 1980s confidently aggressive. Cable programming, having patterned itself after network entertainment programming, never really broke new ground. It has, however, reached the same level of stagnation. Today its growth curve indicates it entered the 1990s not with a bang, as expected, but a whimper. What went wrong? Is there any way to break the present gridlock? Is there any way cable can live up to its bright promise of the 1970s?

It all depends . . . on how you look at it.

Figure 3-5

Notable Pay-Per-View Events, 1989–1992

1992	Estimated Number of Homes Buying	Price
Evander Holyfield-Riddick Bowe fight	929,000	$36.95
Olympics Triplecast 15-day package*	165,000	125.00
Olympics Triplecast 1-day package*	35,000	19.95
Holyfield-Larry Holmes fight	666,000	35.95
Guns 'n' Roses rock concert	140,000	24.95
1991		
Metropolitan Opera	34,000	34.95
Holyfield-George Foreman fight	1,400,000	35.95
1990		
New Kids on the Block rock concert II	154,000	19.95
Wrestlemania VI wrestling	675,000	29.95
Holyfield-James (Buster) Douglas fight	1,059,000	36.50
1989		
Rolling Stones rock concert	170,000	22.50
Sugar Ray Leonard-Robert Duran fight	695,000	35.00

Paul Kagan Associates, Inc. - 1992

* As cited in *The New York Times*

While an estimated 20 to 21 million homes have access to Pay-Per-View, it seems to be largely a fight fan's medium, at least as far as special events are concerned. Rock concerts are a long way back, and interestingly, the much-publicized Olympic triple-cast barely beat out the Metropolitan Opera. Courtesy Paul Kagan Associates, Inc..

Figure 3-6

Consumers Rate Products and Services (Select Listing from Fifty Items)

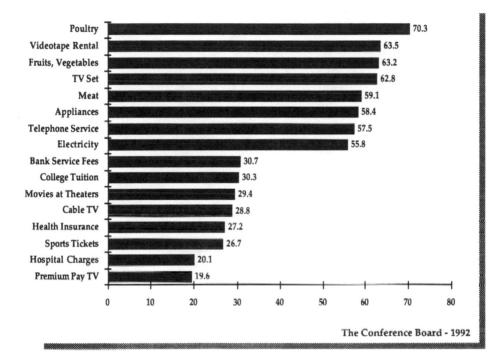

The Conference Board - 1992

When consumers were asked to rate items on a three-level value scale—good, average, and poor—videotape rental ranked second, while premium pay TV came in dead last. Courtesy The Conference Board.

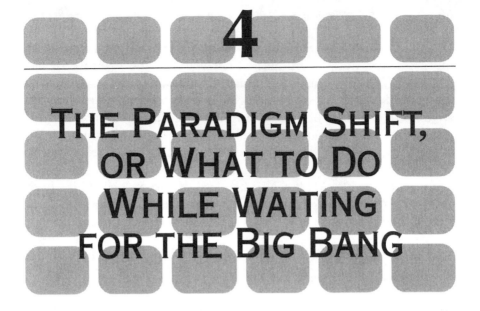

4

THE PARADIGM SHIFT, OR WHAT TO DO WHILE WAITING FOR THE BIG BANG

Overheard in an advertising agency:

"*Arts & Entertainment*? Yeah, they fit our psychographics nights and weekends. Daytime, though, I'm not so sure. They'll go to an old movie or a rerun of *Rockford Files*."

"Look, I know *ESPN* is the only station in the market carrying the Notre Dame game, but I can't propose it to my client without some indication of CPM."

"I know it's a good buy, but what about share?"

"What's the difference in demographics between the women watching *Lifetime* and the ones watching the network soaps?"

Psychographics? CPM? Share? Demographics? Does that sound familiar to you? Of course. It's the language of broadcast media advertising. And as long as cable continues to play on broadcasting's home court, the stalemate will continue.

Much of cable's early promise has been fulfilled. Reception is universally excellent. The subscribing viewer has more channels, hence more choices. Satisfaction with programming is generally high. But the unique promise of early cable, the promise of *narrowcasting,* has been arrested in midcareer. The idea behind narrowcasting—the idea that had so much original appeal to advertisers—was the creation of channels limited to single-interest subjects, so that audiences would be numerically small *but demographically pure.* Unlike broadcasting, where the audience selects a channel, narrowcasting creates a situation where the channel selects the audience. A few cable channels like *MTV, CNN,* and *ESPN* come close. Most, however, though not as broad as network broadcasting, are far too broad to be called narrowcasting. It has to do with programming.

❖ ART IMITATES . . . OLDER ART

As Batra and Glazer point out in their book, *Cable TV Advertising: A Strategic Overview,* the technology of any new entertainment medium goes into place long before anyone has figured out what to do with it.[1] So what happens? The new hardware is programmed with the old software. Film used the software of theater. Radio used the software of vaudeville, Chautauqua, and the musical concert hall. Television used the software of film and radio. And cable television used, and still uses, the software of broadcast television.

In the case of cable's predecessors, each grew into an entity distinct from its original programming. Talented people working in early film discovered that the camera could create dimensions that theater couldn't match; close-ups could bring viewers into the conversation . . . or the kiss. And outdoor filming could heighten the scope and the action as theater never could.

Radio writers eventually became skillful at blending the verbal dimension of theater with music and sound effects to create what has been called "the theater of the mind." By leaving the art direction up to the individual listener, theater of the mind remains, in many ways, the most arresting dramatic form of all.

Television's main contribution to entertainment has been, perhaps, its enormous variety. Early television took radio's music and variety programming and blended it with many of the lost trappings of vaudeville, from the sight gag to the double take to funny faces, silly walks, pratfalls, and outrageous costumes. And it added an exciting "you are there" visual dimension to sports, participation shows, interview shows, and especially news.

Cable, so far, has added nothing new to television programming. Old movies have been a staple of broadcast television since the late 1940s. If you like old movies, you'll love the *American Movie Classics*.

Sports have always been a mainstay of both radio and television. If you like sports, you'll love *ESPN*.

News has been popular with listeners since H. V. Kaltenborn in the 1920s. If you're in the mood for news, check out CNN, any time, day or night.

Popular music? Shades of *American Bandstand*? Tune in *MTV*.

The NBC *Movie of the Week*? Get a recent movie every two hours on *Showtime* or *Cinemax*.

Documentaries? *The Discovery Channel*.

Something for the kids? *Disney*.

Something for the ladies? *Lifetime*.

Something for the lads? *Playboy*.

Cable technology is new and exciting. But when it comes to cable programming . . . well . . . there seems to be nothing new under the sun. Cable has failed to compete by failing to fulfill the promise of narrowcasting. It's still playing broadcasting's game, by broadcasting's rules, on broadcasting's home turf. And the game is still tied. But just when it seemed cable's bright promise would end, not with a bang, but a whimper . . . just at that moment . . .

❖ BANG!

March 1991, New Orleans. All the talk at the annual convention of the National Cable Television Association centered on digital compression technology. John Malone, president and chief executive officer of Tele-Communications, Inc., America's largest cable company, announced that the industry had passed the *if* stage of compressional evolution and had now entered the *when* stage. The only question remaining was, "How do we turn the influx of hundreds of new channels into something beneficial?"

One benefit was obvious to all. With all those channels—estimates ranged from 150 to 750—the cost of air time for original programming would drop like a rock. But what about disadvantages? At a CableLabs press conference Malone himself, in what must go down as the understatement of the conference, allowed that there may be some difficulty in coming up with attractive programming options.

Later observers would elaborate on Malone's theme. Said Matt Roush, TV critic for *USA Today*, "It's hard to be cheered by the idea of a 500-channel future, as some major cable moguls are promising. We got plenty of nothing as it is."

John J. O'Connor of *The New York Times* put a cap on it: "The nation's largest cable television company plans a 500-channel service, perhaps as early as 1994. Honey, pass the eyedrops."

Still, TCI, along with others, has persevered in the development of video compression. If predictions hold, the Big Bang should, indeed, take place sometime in 1994 with aftershocks lasting until at least 1997. The only question left to answer is this: "Will the events of 1994–1997 truly represent a Big Bang, a beginning, an opportunity . . . or just another whimper?"

❖ THE PARADIGM SHIFT

In the early days of television advertising, the sponsor was king. This was the legacy passed on from radio. As time passed, however, the magazine format became the standard method of remuneration. Advertisers no longer controlled programming. That function passed on to the networks. The archetype, or paradigm, of cable programming has until now resembled network programming in that it is audience based. Network programming, since the adoption of the magazine format of remuneration, has been designed to appeal to the *largest possible* audience. Hence broadcasting. Cable programming has been designed to appeal to the *most interested* audience: narrowcasting. So . . . which comes first, the audience or the advertiser? Under current conditions, with both broadcasting and narrowcasting, the answer is clear: the audience.

Therein lies an opportunity. With a little intellectual tinkering, it is possible to construct a totally original view of the programming function. A paradigm shift. The creation of a new entity which totally replaces the familiar archetype. For example, if the archetypal method of program development today is to base it on assumptions concerning audience preferences—for example, entertainment— what happens if we are asked to develop programming that is *not* meant merely to entertain? What happens, instead, if we explore the development of *marketing-based* programming, that is, programming designed to help viewers make informed buying decisions on purchases near and dear to their pocketbooks—like cars, computers, or even vacations?

Imagine, if you will, that you have just been named marketing manager of Channel 397. In a universe of five hundred channels, your odds of attracting any given viewer are at least one out of five hundred. Tough odds? You bet. Tougher than anything the television industry has ever experienced before. Obviously, you need to set yourself apart. If programming is indeed the issue, your programming would have to be entertaining, or different, or useful. Let's look at your options. If you decide to market Channel 397 conventionally, based on preferences in entertainment alone, you have choices.

Audience preferences, after all, are relatively easy to determine. Ratings services provide a quick object lesson for program development; if six of the top ten rated programs are Westerns, it's a pretty good bet that Westerns are safe. Movies, too, provide guidelines. Napoleon Solo (*The Man from U.N.C.L.E*) and Maxwell Smart (*Get Smart*) would not have made it to the small screen had not James Bond, Agent 007, been such a success on the big screen. And, of course, there are certain formats that seem to have universal appeal: poking fun at the rich (*The Beverly Hillbillies, Roseanne*), broad physical comedy (*I Love Lucy, Three's Company*), complex sociosexual intrigue (*Dallas, Dynasty*), simple morality tales (*Father Knows Best, The Brady Bunch, The Cosby Show*), and mystery puzzles (*Perry Mason, Murder, She Wrote*).

The trouble with broad-based entertainment programming is that it is limiting. If a program has broad audience appeal, it will be forced to compete with other such programs on other broadcasting channels. If it is interesting to a specific audience, it must compete with programs on similarly slanted cable channels. In other words, the channel is at the mercy of the programs it presents. Looked at from a pure marketing standpoint, this isn't good enough. In a spectrum of five hundred channels, most carrying entertainment programming, if you are a good marketing manager you won't submit Channel 397 to the vagaries of entertainment-based programming. But what else is there?

Maybe the answer lies with the companies that are producing such programming. Let's book a flight to the newest, fastest-growing center of entertainment communications in America—Orlando, Florida. If you're looking for entertaining, competitive program development, here it is. You want to lose a ratings fight? Go up against Disney. It's been that way ever since an animated character named Steamboat Willie changed his name to Mickey Mouse. Generations of people around the world have loved the products of Disney imagineering, from *Bambi* to *Aladdin*, from *Snow White* to *Sounder*, from Uncle Remus (*The Song of the South*) to *Mary Poppins*. Clearly, Channel 397 would be foolhardy to take on that crowd.

Discouraged, you spend the next day at The Magic Kingdom and Epcot Center. Hmmm, interesting. Here is programming designed especially for its own unique environment: spectacular 360-degree films; staged "audio-animatronic" programming that passes by fixed audiences; seating arrangements from small cars to entire movable seating sections that plunge viewers inside and through the programming itself.

Outside the Disney World of the tourist is a busy production complex turning out everything from commercials to industrial and corporate communications to fully mounted television shows. A few miles away, in St. Petersburg, the massive *Home Shopping Network* with the world's largest single bank of phones broadcasts by satellite 24 hours a day (72 hours of nonstop programming on three channels). In 1993, *HSN* was bought out by Liberty Media, a company that also owns 25 percent of *QVC*, the nation's other leading shopping channel. Liberty Media, incidentally, is a holding company established by Tele-Communications, Inc., America's largest multiple-system operator.

Liberated from looking at programming only as television entertainment, we see that it is ubiquitous in today's world. Automobile dealers from Longa Toyota in Los Angeles to Arenson Chevrolet in Center Point, Iowa, have a library of videotapes delineating various model selections and explaining the mysteries of fuel injection and antilock brakes. Travel agencies are supplementing their brochure racks with video brochures extolling the virtues of popular destinations. Computer stores offer program disks enabling prospects to experiment before they buy. Elaborately programmed sales presentations have replaced Willie Loman's threadbare sample case in conference rooms around the world. Farmers and farm managers receive a steady stream of videotapes in the mail, outlining the latest advancements in seed corn genetics and sidehill combines.

This kind of programming has not been considered proper television fare for a number of reasons. First among these reasons, of course, has been cost. As mentioned in Chapter 2, rising commercial costs continue to shorten commercial length. Back in the 1950s, prime-time shows like the *Dinah Shore Chevy Show* routinely featured 2-minute spots for the sponsor. Today General Motors, like all auto companies, thinks in terms of 30-second spots, and most of them have their agencies exploring the possibilities of 15-second spots. In a five-hundred-channel world, however, prime time will once more be available, in large chunks, at affordable prices. Will "prime time" have any meaning when audience *numbers* are no longer primary?

In 1984, the FCC legitimized the infomercial industry by deregulating commercial length. Following deregulation, however, advertisers of low-involvement products made direct response ads and infomercials available to cable stations everywhere. Cautiously at first, stations began slating infomercials into dead air, where they did well. So well, in fact, that soon more and more unprofitable time periods were used for infomercials. In recent years, the trend has been up. Any time slot that can't hold its own against the omnipresent infomercial is fair game. Today over 90 percent of stations run them.

Still, infomercials worry many high-involvement, blue-chip advertisers. An experimental infomercial—called a "documercial" by Hal

Riney & Partners, the agency that created it for General Motors—told the story of the manufacturer of the new compact Saturn in Spring Hill, Tennessee. General Motors felt the Saturn was so important to the company's future that it should be built in a highly automated, state-of-the-art plant. They conducted an extensive site search coast to coast, looking for a combination of component availability, friendly tax environment and, especially, the kind of workers who still take pride in doing a good job. The documercial, called *Spring in Spring Hill,* was invested with high production values and successfully transferred the quality workmanship of the proud craftspeople in Spring Hill to the quality of the new Saturn.

Still, the fact remains, a major problem with long-form commercials is their nonschedulability. They are lumped together in the local TV guide under the generic label of "paid programming." Nobody sits down with the intent of watching an infomercial. Viewers select infomercials quite by accident while "channel surfing." Companies in some product categories have come to use and even appreciate that situation—diet plans, kitchen and cleaning aids, cosmetics, hair restorers, music cassettes and CDs, life-style plans, money-making schemes. But the traditional advertisers, complete with all the trappings of the full-service agency including the comforting accountability of pretesting, posttesting, a computerized media department and database, well ... they just can't live that way. They feel the need for schedulability and accountability.

So, as marketing manager of Channel 397, what are you going to do about all this? Well, the first thing you do is identify the competition. Undoubtedly, today's entertainment-based programming will continue to fill network and conventional cable systems. As will programming from sources such as Bloodworth/Thompson, Marcy Carsey, Orion, Fox, Disney, or Desilu. The programming opportunity presented by the 500 channel television paradigm lies instead with a wide variety of public relations sources: corporate training tapes; direct mail video brochures; product demonstration tapes; new product introduction tapes; video product catalogs; in-pack instruction tapes; video newsletters; video annual reports; and tapes developed for trade shows, showrooms, and sales and motivational meetings. High-involvement, blue-chip advertisers of the world are sitting on libraries of already-produced materials—material they would love to expose to a national television audience. An audience bored and disgruntled with today's entertainment-based programming, looking for a change. And what a change! Imagine, programming capable of contributing to one's life rather than numbing it. Indeed, the opportunity lies not with the entertainment status quo, but in a refreshing form of alternative programming. What we'll call marketing programming. And your touchstone? Your model to pattern this programming? It is not conventional entertainment broadcasting, but rather direct marketing. The stuff of marketing channels is not tears and laughter, it is useful information. And it is not exclusively product information. Brand and corporate messages also interest today's consumers who, as we'll see in Chapter 6, often pay as much attention to the reputation of the manufacturer as they do to the quality of the products. You have a lot to offer these marketers, including low-cost time slots in prime time. The only thing you can't offer them is consistent scheduling and accountability.

Or can you? After all, consistent scheduling and accountability are audience-based concepts. And you're into marketing-based thinking. And marketers don't recognize the word "can't." Then, suddenly, it all becomes clear.

❖ TA DA! THE WORLD'S FIRST MARKETING CHANNEL!

If you were to select a product category, say, automobiles, and dedicate Channel 397 to that category, the schedulability problem would be solved. You could offer automobile advertisers their choice of time slots, just like a conventional, entertainment-based channel. Good.

Now, as to accountability. It's a known fact that people who are not at the moment interested in buying a new car tend to ignore automobile advertising altogether. On the other hand, once every three or four years when they *are* in the market, they suddenly become voracious consumers of automobile advertising in all its forms—television, radio, print, literature. Studies indicate that at any given moment 37.6 percent of baby boomers are thinking seriously about trading in the old beater on a sleek, new model. And since the cable audience in general is, in terms of income, upscale compared to the national average, that number may be higher. So while Channel 397, *The Car Buyer's Channel,* may not be able to offer advertisers the relatively static audiences (in terms of numbers and demographics) of a network top ten show, what it *can* offer is a fluid audience actively looking to buy. And while the potential audience may be fluid, it is consistently somewhere in the 37.6 percent plus range. That's efficient!

Now then, if you're a really smart marketer—if you're as smart, say, as Ted Turner or Barry Diller or maybe Michael Eisner at Disney— you'll acquire a whole batch of channels, say, a block of 390 to 410, and think big. You'll probably need at least one additional automobile channel, maybe more depending on volume of response: maybe *The Luxury Car Buyer's Channel* or *The Truck and Van Buyer's Channel.* In addition to corporate-supplied programming such as new model introductions and demonstrations of new features and technologies, your automotive channels will carry related, independent programming such as comparative reports from magazines like *Consumer Reports, Road & Track,* and *Car and Driver;* panel discussions with automobile executives and design engineers; interviews with industry experts; programs on automotive specialty items; and much more.

And then, of course, there are other high-involvement product categories in addition to automobiles. At any given moment, 47.1 percent of baby boomers are mulling over their next vacation destination.

Nearly 40 percent are looking for home furnishings of one sort or another.

Nearly 30 percent are in the market for a major appliance.

One in four is thinking about stereo equipment, a TV, or a VCR. One in five is getting serious about a new computer.

What we have here is a fluid audience of shoppers. Fluid, yet solid. Consider this: entertainment-based programming develops programs in search of an audience (ratings), while marketing-based programming develops audiences in search of programs (results). Nor are these audiences composed of passive viewers who tuned in for entertainment and who regard commercials as so much chaff with the wheat. No, these are people predisposed to buy, actively seeking out enough information to make an informed decision. They're looking for information that once was available from the friendly sales clerk. With so many brands and choices, these are difficult decisions, and it's always hard to admit one's ignorance—especially if the sales clerk is an ill-informed, part-time employee who can't help. Wouldn't it be nice to learn about a product selection in the comfort, privacy, and convenience of your own living room? But most important, if I learn before deciding, really study to make the best buy, I won't be saddled with a bad purchase for years following. The important thing about these buying audiences is not their size, but their purity. Running a 30-second image spot on an entertainment channel is like fishing with a small hook in a big pond, and there may not be any fish in that pond likely to take your particular bait. Running a 30-minute demonstration commercial on a marketing channel, on the other hand, is like . . . well . . . shooting big fish in a small barrel. CPM (cost per thousand) will, after lo, these many years, be displaced by CPB (cost per buyer).

The result is a win-win-win situation.

The sponsor wins because he has a cost-efficient way to deliver an entire sales message, product introductions, or feature demonstrations to an interested, ready-to-buy audience. No more fishing with spots in an entertainment ocean.

The advertising agency wins because it has a specific location to place advertising that interested viewers seek out . . . not just stumble across while channel surfing over five hundred waves.

The customer wins because he has a place to find an abundance of information that he can use to make informed buying decisions: the Yellow Pages and consumer's guide of television—all wrapped up in a single channel.

Such is the promise of marketing channels.

❖ ENDNOTE

1. Rajeev Batra and Rashi Glazer, eds., *Cable TV Advertising: In Search of the Right Formula* (New York: Quorum Books, 1989).

5

THE ROOTS
OF MARKETING
PROGRAMMING

If you were a compulsive shopper living in the New York area during the 1930s, you might have noticed something curious. A number of enterprising New Yorkers had discovered they could beat the Great Depression by talking their way out of poverty. Fast-talking. Fast-fast-fast-talking. You'd see them in department stores, usually in kitchen-wares, extolling the myriad wonders of the most remarkable gadgets. At least they looked like gadgets. But by the time these glib gentlemen of gadgetry finished their demonstrations, conducted with all the dexterity of a magician, that ordinary kitchen gadget had been transformed into an absolute household necessity. They made you wonder how you'd gotten along all those years without it. You bought it, took it home, put it in the drawer or on the shelf . . . and never used it again.

What true shopping aficionados may have noticed that others did not, was that the man demonstrating potato peelers at Macy's looked and sounded just like the man hawking hand-held vegetable blenders at Bloomingdale's. And for that matter, both looked a lot like the guy selling salad choppers at Gimbel's. They seemed to be everywhere, these fast-talking, quick-fingered pitchmen. The fact is, one family had the distinction of providing Manhattan with pitchmen in record numbers. America was already being drawn, as the cobra to the charmer, to the amazing Popeil family.

These early department store pitchmen, along with their compatriots operating from Atlantic City's boardwalk to the Malibu pier, are generally thought of as the grandfathers of marketing programming. They are, in fact, the scions of a proud tradition thousands of years old. Walk through any Oriental market or African bazaar even today and you will see them glibly transforming the most mundane wares into treasures. Before your very eyes a tin pot becomes a family heirloom, a jar of snake oil a miracle cure.

In the 1940s the Popeil brothers, Raymond and Samuel, were among the first of these pitchmen to take their peculiar art form off the boardwalk, out of the department store, and onto the television screen. The new medium brought them a larger audience with fewer paid pitchmen. Retaining a few of their most talented *spielers*, they took to the airwaves. In 1964 Samuel Popeil's son Ronald, who had been plying the family trade in the department stores of Chicago, formed his own company, called Ronco, and the rest is, as they say, history.

❖ DIRECT RESPONSE COMMERCIALS: THE "B" MOVIES OF ADVERTISING

Early direct response commercials, those intended to stimulate an immediate order, differed from conventional commercials in a number of ways. They were far more personal in tone—some would say intrusively personal. Style—the *way* a thing is said—was rightfully considered more important than *what* was being said. But the biggest difference, perhaps, was one of budget. Until deregulation in the 1980s, direct response commercials were characterized by minimal production values. They were shot in studios, often with only two stationary cameras—one set for medium shots and the other set for close-ups of the product demonstration. Talent came in three forms: celebrities, professionals, and accidental amateurs who were so bad they were good.

Celebrities included sports figures like quarterback Frank Gifford, popular announcers from radio days like Dennis James and Don Wilson, and singers and musicians like big-band singer Helen O'Connell, whose appearance in a direct marketing commercial revived her sagging career. Professionals were no-name veterans of the department stores and boardwalks, usually the best of the best (the slickest of the slick?) who could be counted on to deliver every word and make every gesture in *precisely* the right style.

Every now and then an accident made a temporary legend out of a totally nongifted amateur. Direct response pioneer Al Eicoff tells of a client who came to him with a promising product at the right price. The hitch was, the client insisted that his wife, a completely untrained and rather clumsy woman, deliver the commercial. More to prove a point than anything else, Eicoff talked the client into running a live test commercial over a single station in Pennsylvania. For 15 agonizing minutes the poor woman stumbled over the words, lost her place in the copy, dropped the product, and kept wandering off camera. Finally, it was over. Just as Eicoff began explaining the importance of using professionals as on-air talent, the phones began to ring, and for the next several hours the inadequately staffed switchboard took three thousand orders. Flabbergasted, Eicoff arranged to put the woman on film, carefully editing out most of her mistakes. Another test market was selected, but this time the commercial produced almost no response. Eicoff put the mistakes back in and tried again. Again, nothing. No matter how he tried, he couldn't recapture the magic of the woman's first appearance. Maybe it's true . . . everybody is famous for 15 minutes. For this woman, it was 15 minutes stumbling through a commercial in a television studio somewhere in Pennsylvania. John Witek, in his book *Response Television*, draws an analogy between direct response commercials and B movies, and it fits perfectly.[1] A staple of the film scene of the 1930s and 1940s, B movies were made to fill out a double bill, the top half being the A movie. The "B" didn't stand for "Bad," not at all. If it stood for anything, it stood for "Budget," something the B movies lacked in comparison to the A's. They were made on a shoestring by B movie studios like RKO and Republic. The writers, directors, and actors employed by these studios were, although less well known than their counterparts in the A's, good, competent, talented individuals. Thus every now and then magic happened, and a B movie turned out to be better than the A movie it was intended to support. Or the B movie actors did a better job than the highly paid A movie actors. In 1944, for instance, B movie actress Clair Trevor snagged a supporting role in the Bogart-Bacall classic, *Key Largo* . . . and won herself an Oscar. Lucille Ball, tired of her role as "Queen of the B's" at RKO, went into television. She and her husband Desi Arnaz, one of Hollywood's true business wizards, ended up buying RKO and calling it Desilu.

Like the B movie studios, direct response agencies are staffed with people every bit as bright, talented, and dedicated as those in the big "A" agencies. Challenged with limited budgets, direct response writers and producers occasionally hit one out of the park by producing a commercial so compelling it stops the most dedicated channel surfer. You've seen them yourself, usually late at night when you're all alone. You're checking out the late movie selections when you find yourself stopped dead, fascinated beyond all reason by a man and a Chinese wok.

❖ THE SNAKE OIL STIGMA

> *"My old Pappy always said you can fool some of the people all of the time, and all of the people some of the time . . . and those are pretty good odds."*
>
> BRET MAVERICK

Unfortunately, there was a dark side to early direct response commercials, perhaps not surprising when you consider their roots. Remember Dr. Brinkley, impeached governor of Kansas, who marketed worthless nostrums on early radio? With the government on his tail, he began advertising goat-gland transplants as a cure for sexual dysfunction over unregulated Mexican stations. At $750 per operation, Brinkley kept his calendar as full as his coffers. Following a number of cases in the 1950s (sorry, true believers, but the famous Veg-A-Matic didn't chop, slice, and dice as well at home as it did on the television demonstration, which used tricks like cooked carrots and unripe tomatoes to enhance the cutting and slicing effect), the Federal Trade Commission went to work protecting consumers from unscrupulous direct marketers. Today, a host of rules and guidelines defines deceptive advertising and deceptive pricing as well as all the traditional accoutrements of direct marketing commercials such as guarantees, trial offers, warranties, testimonials, endorsements, sweepstakes, and the use of words like "free" and "new." Another trick of the early 1950s, that of advertising nonexistent products to determine if the market potential was there, has also been regulated out of practice.

Still, the memory lingers on in satire. One of the first classic parodies on direct response commercials aired on *I Love Lucy*. Lucy (Lucille Ball), always anxious to get into show biz, manages to get hired as a television spokeswoman for a miracle elixir called VitaMeataVegeMin, which stood for vitamins, meats, vegetables, and minerals. She showed up at rehearsal and was handed a bottle of the product. Taking a large swig she grimaced broadly, signaling a high alcoholic content. During subsequent takes, she grew more and more fond of the product. By the time she was to go on the air, she was giggling, swigging, staggering drunk.

During the early days of television's long-running *Saturday Night Live*, Dan Ackroyd—in regulation loud, plaid sports coat and sleazy mustache—holds up a fish and sets out the problem: What do you do when you catch a nice bass like this, but don't know how to clean it? Instead of throwing it back, Ackroyd suggests, why not invest a few dollars in the Super Bass-O-Matic 76 by Robco, which is clearly an ordinary food blender. With supreme aplomb, Ackroyd proceeds to drop the fish into the Bass-O-Matic and blend it into an odious brown purée. Holding the disgusting concoction to the camera he announces, "We've got bass here, ready to pour." The camera cuts to Laraine Newman who takes a satisfying swig and proclaims "Wow, that's terrific bass!"

Included in this genre is Johnny Carson's running sketch *Art Fern and the Teatime Movie*. Fern (loud, plaid sports coat, sleazy mustache) hawks retail businesses using every trick in the handbook of unethical advertising. He is assisted in his endeavors by the

"Matinee Lady," a stereotypical Hollywood "dumb blonde." Purists argue that Art Fern was not technically a direct marketer as he didn't ask for a call-in response, but rather a visit to the business which was located in a labyrinth of freeways. Always included in the *spiel* were the same set of instructions, which eventually became so familiar the audience chanted them in unison: "Take the Slawson cut-off . . . get out of your car . . . and cut off your Slawson." And then, at the sight of a huge table fork on the map, "Take the Santa Monica Freeway until you come to . . . (UNISON) . . . *the fork in the road.*"

❖ THE LAW OF SALES RESISTANCE

Early direct marketers were known for incredibly creative media buying. Most eschewed network buys as being too expensive, preferring instead to develop elaborate, tightly negotiated arrangements locally and regionally. The reason was results. As early as the mid-1950s, clever direct marketers had begun to notice that there was something unique about sales resistance vis-à-vis television. Pioneers like Al Eicoff were puzzled by the fact that there seemed to be little correlation between ratings and results.2 Logic, and indeed the entire rationale behind network television remuneration, tells us the more people watching, the more people likely to buy. Yet direct response commercials, with call-in or write-in sales providing relatively immediate results, showed no such correlation. Eventually, a pattern emerged. Sales resistance, it was learned, could be plotted by time of day and day of week. In other words, there were certain times on any given day when sales could be made easily and other times on that same day when almost nothing could be sold. Furthermore, these times and days bore no relation to television ratings.

The rules for overcoming sales resistance are as follows:

- Sales resistance is lowest the hour after waking, the hour before going to sleep, and all day Saturday and Sunday.
- Sales resistance is relatively low on Monday, peaks on Wednesday, and then begins to drop to its weekend low.

These rules, formulated as the *law of sales resistance,* make it possible for direct marketers to make the most efficient use of each media dollar. It is this law, not the availability of cheap air time, that explains why today's infomercials avoid prime time, preferring nights and weekends.

❖ THE 1970s: DIRECT RESPONSE BECOMES RESPECTABLE . . . SORT OF

In 1970, Madison Avenue was rocked by a bombshell. Cigarette advertising was abruptly banned on television. Broadcasters began scrambling for clients to replace the loss and suddenly much-maligned direct response marketers began to look more respectable. For thirty years mainstream television executives had looked down their patrician noses at these marketers. Now, however, if one looked just a little further down, just past the sleazy mustache and the garish clip-on bow tie, one noticed that the pockets of those loud, plaid sports coats were full of money. It was definitely time to talk.

As for the direct marketers, they could deal with the best of them. Desperate to fill the time vacated by cigarettes, the stations were willing to be flexible; sufficiently flexible, in fact, to make that time efficient enough to meet the demands of direct response.

It was about this time, too, that direct marketers began to show up in sincere ties and three-piece gray flannel suits, figuratively speaking. Production values began to improve. More and more celebrities were drafted to add prestige to commercials. The urbane British actor John Williams sold classical records, Glenn Ford and Robert Stack sold life insurance, and pop star Kenny Rogers sold a song book. High-volume pitchmen of the past were replaced by low-key men (and sometimes women) with the sincerity to add much needed credibility to the genre.

The genre itself was changing. Direct response pioneer Lester Wunderman perfected a technique he called the "Judy Wrap." The commercial opened on a personable young woman wearing an operator's headphones working in a busy fulfillment setting. Behind her other operators could be seen taking orders. The young woman, called "Judy" only because that was the real name of the actress who portrayed the original operator, explained that an amazing offer would be coming up, and that if the viewer hung on until after the offer, she'd be back with details on how to get a valuable free item . . . which she showed. These free items were usually inexpensive, but quite nice—a cordless phone, perhaps. (Remember, these were the 1970s.) The advertiser would then come on with a pitch of his own describing the quality of his product, perhaps a subscription to *Time* magazine, and finish with a bargain rate saving the viewer money. And at the end, Judy would return and explain that if the viewers called immediately, they would receive not only big savings on the advertised product, but a free item as well. The Judy Wrap was and is a successful direct response technique. Since it works best in a 2-minute format, the availability of time following the cigarette ban was fortuitous indeed.

Another direct response–related technique developed in the 1970s was support advertising. Here, the role of the television commercial is to promote a response from advertising in another medium. The original support program was run in 1972 by *Reader's Digest* magazine. The commercial itself was created and produced on a big budget by J. Walter Thompson, one of America's leading agencies. It encouraged viewers to watch for a sweepstakes offer coming in the mail, and in looks and style it matched any agency-produced commercial of its time. The real difference, of course, was the call to action: not "Call now," but rather "Watch your mail."

This incredibly successful breakthrough commercial changed the face of direct advertising. It was the first support commercial. It was the first commercial to command a production budget equivalent to that of agency-produced, mass-market commercials. And, interestingly, it was perhaps the first commercial that proved, once and for all, that direct response advertisers looked at television differently from mass audience advertisers. It called into question the firmly held belief that direct response commercials were in competition with other commercials. It was the first, faint impression of the *paradigm shift*. Although few saw it at the time, the commercial indicated that direct response marketing was not simply competing in the relatively narrow sphere of television commercials, but rather in the wide, wide world of direct marketing itself.

Mainstream television commercials seemed to address a crowd. They addressed the Pepsi Generation and all those Coke drinkers who went so far as proclaiming "We Are the World." Wow! Direct marketing, whether on television or in print or through the mail, ignores the crowd. Direct marketing is personal: one person talking to another. The commercial selling big band songs of the 1940s asks, "Where were you when you first heard the Glenn Miller Orchestra play this unforgettable song?" No Pepsi Generation here. It talks to *you*. Prewar, sentimental, fiftyish *you*. Direct marketing mail used to address "Dear Friend" back in the days before today's technology. Now it comes addressed to "Dear Craig Evans." How's that for personal? Direct response commercials, like mail brochures, demonstrate the product in words and pictures. And the call-in phone number in each serves the same purpose: "Hey, friend, give me a call."

❖ ENTER THE VCR: THE NEXT LOGICAL STEP

Especially today, videotapes make sense. A study by the Wharton School of Business indicates that business communication on tape is understood and retained at a rate 50 percent greater than printed material. Add to this the fact that baby boomers, as a group, aren't comfortable reading. As average reading levels in America fall past the fifth grade level, video rental and television viewing in general continue to climb. Information coming from the tube is much more acceptable to these people than the same information on the printed page.

So, if video provides the audience involvement and entertainment value only possible with words, music, and moving pictures, and if mail provides personal accuracy to the point of mentioning the recipient's name, the ideal method of effective communication would seem to be the videotape sent in the mail. This technique, of course, requires that the recipient have easy access to a VCR. Common today, direct marketing *via* VCR had its roots, appropriately enough, down on the farm. Agricultural advertising is a multibillion-dollar business. Look at it this way. The average family farm is actually a small business. The farmer, as chief executive officer, spends tens of thousands of discretionary dollars *each spring* on equipment, seed, and agrichemicals. Almost all these purchases are made on credit, a subject that today's farmer understands as well as any Wall Street banker. The farmer's recent counterpart, the multifarm manager, spends even more . . . often well into the *hundreds of thousands* each spring. An entire culture of magazines is edited especially for farm audiences; and from January through April millions of dollars are spent advertising on television. No, you won't see agricultural commercials in New York, Chicago, or Los Angeles, but spend a weekend watching television in Peoria, Fresno, Cedar Rapids, or Lubbock, and you'll see them wall to wall.

Since farm families frequently live beyond the cable lines, they were early purchasers of VCRs, and later of satellite dishes. Agrimarketers were quick to capitalize on this situation. In fact, it was ideal for them. Most agricultural products are technical in nature. And at $200,000 a unit, a grain combine can definitely be considered a high-involvement product. Videotape is ideal for showing exactly which weeds and insects need controlling, how nitrogen fertilizer works underground, how to rig a new model sprayer or planter, and dozens of other things impossible to show in 30 seconds. CMF&Z, the Young & Rubicam agency in Cedar Rapids, Iowa, handling the majority of American agribusiness advertising, creates, produces, and mails thousands of videotapes to a database of farmers each year.

In other spheres, videotape mailings are beginning to catch on. With VCR ownership currently at 80 percent of TV households—and even higher among middle- and upper-class Americans—mass database mailings are possible. Chevrolet and Audi have each mailed out more than a million tapes introducing new models. More often, however, videotapes are mailed in response to requests from other media. On high-involvement products especially, the old tagline "For more information write or call," is

quicklybeingreplacedby "Forafreevideotape,writeor call." Figure
5-1 is an example of how Apple Computer very effectively uses print
and video to present the Macintosh, upfront and personal, as the
ideal computer for small (and large!) businesses.

❖ VIDEO BROCHURES, VIDEO CATALOGS, VIDEO ANNUAL REPORTS, VIDEO PR, AND VIDEO PRESENTATIONS

What we've discussed so far—videotapes featuring new models of cars and combines—fall into the category of video brochures.
They demonstrate features, detail advantages, and clarify benefits.
All very successfully. Studies show that people watch video brochures from start to finish, as opposed to print brochures that they
tend to thumb through, scanning at best, skipping pages at worst.
Here again we see the influence of marketing on video communications. While some are the products of traditional advertising agencies, most come from the same places nonvideo brochures, catalogs,
and presentations come from—public relations agencies, specialty
shops, and internal client communications departments. Among
marketers who have successfully used video brochures are Compaq,
Apple, Estée Lauder, Air France, Soloflex, Avon, Dupont, Chris
Craft, Pontiac, American Tourister, and Royal Viking Line. There are
dozens of others (see Figure 5-2).

Obviously, the difference between the video brochure and the
video catalog is that the brochure highlights one product or service
in detail, while the catalog features all or part of a company's entire
product line. The death knell of the print catalog has already been
heard. In 1992, Sears, Roebuck announced that, after more than a
century, its famous mail-order catalog was being discontinued. The
wave of the future is represented by Sears' Chicago neighbor, Spiegel, which in its experiments with video catalogs has experienced
sales increases as high as 50 percent. Video communications have
also become an important part of the marketing process for retail
marketers Marshall Fields and Neiman-Marcus.

Figure 5-1

Apple Computer Ad

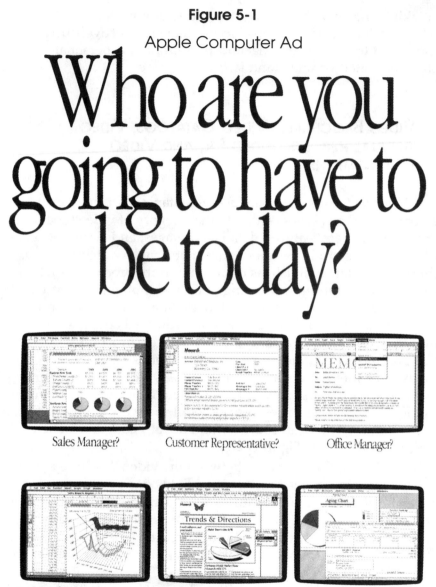

Who are you going to have to be today?

Sales Manager?   Customer Representative?   Office Manager?

Marketing Director?   Advertising Manager?   Accountant?

What do you do when your story is just too complex to cover adequately in an ad?
More and more, manufacturers of high-involvement products like Apple are offering
a videotape as a replacement for the conventional product brochure. Courtesy Apple
Computer, Inc.

As the manager of a small business, you never know what you'll have to do next.

At a moment's notice, you may need to be an accountant, sales manager, marketing director, or even an office manager.

That's why you'll want to look at a business tool that can keep up with you every step of the way.

It's the Apple® Macintosh® computer. The business computer that lets you choose from more than 3,500 different software programs, including programs that will help you track your customers, manage your payroll, create a newsletter, and plan your business.

In fact, there's almost no business task that Macintosh won't make quicker, simpler, and more efficient.

By now, most people have heard about how easy Macintosh is to use. And how you don't have to spend a

lot of time and money on training, whether it's training for yourself or for the people who work with you.

That's because Apple designed Macintosh to work in a simple, intuitive manner. Instead of memorizing complicated commands, all you have to do is select what you want from a menu on the screen.

With Macintosh, unlike other computers, the menus are similar in all software programs. So when you learn one program, you're well on your way to learning them all.

The flexibility of Macintosh even extends to sharing information with other kinds of computers, including those running MS-DOS, because Macintosh is compatible with virtually any system.

And with the introduction of our new Macintosh models, all of these advantages are

affordable for any business of any size.

If you're versatile enough to guide a small business to success, introduce yourself to the computer that's as versatile as you are. Call for our free video, and see what a terrific team you and Macintosh can make. Because whoever you're going to have to be, Macintosh will provide you with one thing more. The power to be your best®

Free small business video.

Our videotape, "In Business with Macintosh," is yours free for the asking. It will show you how Macintosh has helped other small businesses run smoother and more efficiently, and how it can do the same for you. The video also demonstrates specific software programs.

For your complimentary copy, call this toll-free number:

1-800-441-3001, ext.805.

Figure 5-2

A Sampling of Companies Using Video Brochures to
Market Products/Services

Air France	Hartmarx
American Tourister Luggage	Kingsford Company
Amway	(Charcoal Briquettes)
Apple Computer	Lexus
Audi	Lincoln Continental
Avon	Marshall Fields
Brown University	Nieman Marcus
Cadillac	NordicTrack
Chevrolet	Oster Hair Clippers
Chris Craft Boats	Pontiac
Citibank	Ricoh
Compaq	Royal Silk
Dow Chemical	Royal Viking Line
Dupont	Soloflex
Estee Lauder	Spiegel
General Foods	Toyota
Hagerty Marine Insurance	Varitronic
(Classic Boat Collector's Policy)	White-New Idea Tractors
	Yamaha Snowmobiles

Industrial marketers, whose products are almost by definition high-involvement, considered purchases, are also beginning to turn to video brochures and catalogs. One such marketer has even gone further. The author helped John Deere Power Systems Group develop an interactive computerized catalog aimed at design engineers of off-the-road machinery and featuring the company's line of engines and transmissions. This computerized catalog, naturally, has the advantage over video in that designers could actually position Deere's equipment in their drawing board designs. And, unlike a linear video program, which one has to watch from beginning to end, a computer disk offers selective interaction.

Most *Fortune* 500 companies have entire libraries of video PR—public relations footage covering a variety of content in a variety of forms: video newsletters, trade show reels, video news releases and training tapes. Much of this footage, creatively produced on low budgets, makes interesting programming. This year McDonald's is introducing McVideo—a 16-minute videotape of annual report highlights to interested investors. "More shareholders will watch a taped discussion than will read the text of editorial for 16 minutes," comments Jack Greenberg, chief financial officer.

Commonplace in today's video arsenal are video presentations. These are essentially sales aids. Amway, for example, arms its door-to-door salespeople with videos of its more expensive, more complex products—products, in fact, that can't be demonstrated any other way. The program has been extremely successful. Amway's water treatment systems, for example, have become one of its best-selling items, a fact Amway credits to video presentation. Again, video presentations are becoming a part of almost every industrial sale. Manufacturer's reps love them. Sales managers love training their reps with them. It's one thing to *tell* prospects (and salespeople) how a product stacks up to competition, but it's quite another to *show* them. And it's one thing to say how satisfied customers are, and quite another to let the satisfied customer speak for himself or herself.

What we have here is television programming intended to interest more than to entertain, to show more than to tell, narrow in interest rather than broad in appeal. It is generated not by conventional commission-based advertising agencies, but rather by project-based public relations agencies, direct marketing agencies, video boutiques, and client communications and sales training departments. It is not an end in itself, but rather a part of an overall marketing program.

Richard Bencin, writing in *Telemarketing* magazine, summarizes the characteristics of today's commercial videotape.

- It features high-ticket products/services.
- It is aimed at upscale buyers.
- It is used to uncomplicate a complicated selling process.
- Demonstration is usually required.
- Products are not portable (e.g., exercise equipment, travel packages).

- Prospects are not usually accessible by other methods (e.g., doctors, top executives).

- Quality production and image enhancement are required.

- Credibility needs supporting by studies, reports, and testimonials.

Among the products he lists as meeting the foregoing criteria are "furniture, designer clothing, luxury cars, yachts, condos, computer systems, airplanes, financial services, and franchises." He could have added automobiles, travel plans, toys and games, and many others.

❖ DOES ANY OF THIS SOUND FAMILIAR?

Does any of this sound familiar? It does indeed. It sounds a lot like a list of product categories, each suitable for supporting an entire marketing channel as defined in Chapter 4.

As things stand now, this sort of programming is not, technically, programming. It is hit-and-miss, here-you-are, hope-you-like-it tapes distributed through dealer organizations and sales organizations or to individuals through the mail. Occasionally, it is actually run on television, usually with spectacular results. Soloflex, for example, got the idea for its successful infomercials by running its video brochures on cable, where sales rose dramatically. Figure 5-3 shows how existing video messages, with some television programming influence, can be used as marketing programming.

Marketing channels offer marketers an efficient, low-cost alternative to mail. Furthermore, they can guarantee a more interested audience. The snowmobile division of Yamaha recently mailed 45,000 video brochures promoting their 10 new, 1994 models to current snowmobile owners. Dealer visits and resulting sales are being closely monitored to gauge the program's success. One early statistic: at least 50% of the person's receiving the video view it. How many more would watch if the program were broadcast nationally on a marketing channel dedicated to sports and recreation? In 1989, Toyota mailed tapes introducing its new Cressida to 150,000 Toyota owners. Admittedly, the tape influenced owners ready to trade, but

Figure 5-3

Lineage of Marketing Programming

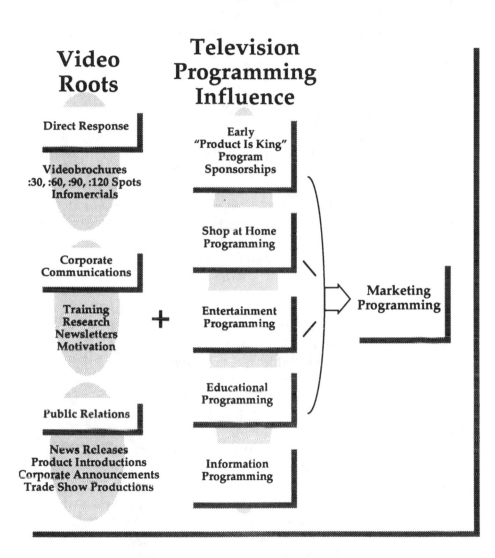

Marketing programming has its roots in the back shop, where the serious, nuts-and-bolts aspects of the selling process get done. This material, when enhanced by the glamorous trappings of the television milieu, takes on new and added importance.

given a three-year turnover, only one in three was currently in the market. How much more cost efficient it would have been for Toyota to put its tape on *The Car Buyer's Channel* (good old Channel 397) playing exclusively to those Toyota owners in a buying mood, as well as owners of competitive cars, some surely dissatisfied and persuadable.

❖ INFOMERCIALS: COMMERCIALS IN DISGUISE

In 1984, the Reagan administration, still in its deregulation mood, rescinded 1973 guidelines limiting commercial time to 12 minutes an hour. Free at last, free at last, direct marketers quickly developed new formats that, collectively, have come to be called infomercials. These commercials, usually 30 minutes in length, mimicked conventional entertainment programming. Some resembled game shows, with an incredulous host being pulled through graphic demonstrations of the wonders of the product by deft pitchmen to the cheers of an enthusiastic, well-paid audience. Others resembled talk shows, with actual celebrities discussing the benefits of the product in comfortable living room sets. Still others retained the original format of the genre—the boardwalk pitchman, although all dressed up for today's market. Depending on the product, the pitchman might be a pitchwoman, and the tone, while still personal, was lower in key.

Madison Avenue's initial reaction to these odd commercials was predictable. Paring knife and potato peeler stuff. Not for us. *Our* clients have images to think about. Besides, with these oddball time slots on these oddball cable channels, with no way of determining audience size, budget accountability is clearly impossible. What about reach? What about frequency? What about, God help us, CPM?

Then, a year or two later, a funny thing happened. After a relatively slow start, probably corresponding to the time it took audiences to adjust to this new phenomenon, sales began to pick up. And up and up. All this without logic or reason, without psychographic or demographic profiles, with none of the time-honored techniques of modern media placement. Infomercials were floating around the dial and around the clock . . . who knew where or when?

... and yet audiences were finding them, watching them and buying from them. So successful were these aberrations that they soon began to provide programming and revenue in quantities large enough to encourage the introduction of new cable channels.

Nor were infomercials appealing only to the Great Unwashed. A talk show–style infomercial featuring quarterback-businessman Fran Tarkenton and promoting a set of personal motivation tapes audaciously priced at $179.95 sold half its offering to Americans in the top 20 percent income range.

It was all very confusing and getting more confusing every year. As we'll see in Chapter 7, there was more to this strange, new commercial format than anyone knew. Or knows.

❖ ENDNOTES

1. John Witek, *Response Television* (Chicago: Crain Books, 1981).
2. Al Eicoff, *Eicoff on Broadcast Direct Marketing* (Lincolnwood, IL: NTC Business Books, 1988).

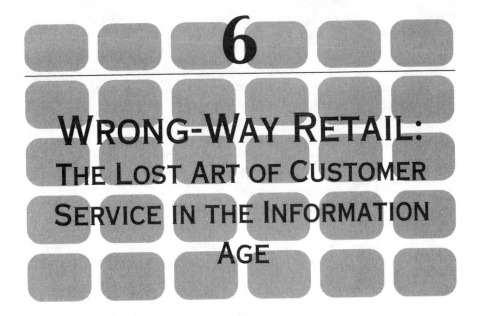

6

WRONG-WAY RETAIL:
THE LOST ART OF CUSTOMER SERVICE IN THE INFORMATION AGE

"Customer service means adding another cash register."

Attributed to SAM WALTON,
founder, Wal-Mart

It hasn't been easy, but the River City Downtown Retailer's Association still fights the good fight. Its members point proudly to the maze of overhead walkways that make it possible for coatless citizens to stroll in heated or air-conditioned comfort through stores, hotels, and office buildings. They point to the former J. C. Penney store, now coyly converted into a minimall of shops offering cards, curios, and locally produced crafts. They point to the 13,000-seat Civic Center and its parade of rock concerts and rodeos, to the elaborately renovated Odeon Theater, now home to the River City

Community Players. And they point with special pride to the new high-rise office buildings that fill the downtown area to overflowing . . . at least from nine to five. Every year's Christmas decorations seem to outshine those of the year before.

As Ed Smith, local jeweler and president of the association, says when soliciting contributions from the membership, "We're in a war against the suburban malls, and wars cost money." There's only one flaw in his logic. He's one war behind, at least. Today, the malls themselves are in trouble. According to a Maritz Ameripoll conducted in 1989, 32 percent of those interviewed reported less mall shopping, while only 14 percent reported more. The big national chain department stores which were lured out of the downtowns in the 1960s to "anchor" suburban malls stand practically empty most weekdays. Shopping habits have changed radically, even since the decade of the 1990s began. Current students of these trends have identified at least five different types of shoppers. Before we examine today's ever-changing retail scene, let's look at the shopping habits of the past half century.

❖ HOW WE SHOPPED: 1930s–1990s

The 1930s—The Waltons

In the depths of the Great Depression, extended families with elderly relatives were common. What money came into the family was reserved for necessities. There was no such thing as discretionary income. The Waltons, like most Americans, tended gardens, made their own clothes; they handed down and made do without. Staples were bought at Ike Godsey's store and paid for in cash.

The 1950s—The Cleavers et al.

The Cleavers, Ward and June and the two boys, Wally and the Beaver, represented the most affluent and comfortable society the world had ever seen up to that time: white, middle-class Americans. They lived in a spacious, centrally heated home, drove a new car, sent their children to college, saw their dentist twice a year, and vacationed at the lake. No Roman emperor ever had it so good. Ward was the breadwinner and June the homemaker. Despite their affluence, Ward and June were children of the Depression. Discretionary income was banked for a rainy day or for retirement. June clipped coupons from grocery ads, watched for sales in the big department stores downtown, and darned socks. Demographically, the Cleavers are identical to their neighbors the Andersons (Jim and Margaret, children Betty, Bud, and Kathy) and the Stones (Alex, Donna, and children Mary and Jeff). All these couples seem to live in the Midwest—Ohio, maybe, or Illinois. Things are different in California with the Nelsons. While Ozzie seems to be the bread-winner and Harriet the homemaker, Ozzie never actually works. It's difficult to imagine Harriet at the market. And while Wally Cleaver, Bud Anderson, and Jeff Stone drive jalopies left over from the 1930s, David and Ricky Nelson drive brand-new fin-tailed convertibles. Ah, California.

The 1970s—The Bunkers and the Bradys

The Bunkers (Archie, Edith, Gloria, and son-in-law Michael "Meathead" Stivic) are the children of the Waltons' distant cousins who went to the city to find work. The Bradys (Mike, Carol, six kids, and maid, Alice) are the 1950s children all grown up. Mike Brady could have been Jeff Stone's college roommate. Or Wally Cleaver's. (One never really felt Bud Anderson was college material.) These families were the first indication, on television at least, that America operated under a class system. The Bradys had discretionary income to burn. Mike was an architect, Carol a homemaker. Yet one cannot imagine Carol clipping supermarket coupons. Alice did the shopping. Carol and Mike and all six kids dressed in designer-label clothes. Things were different at the Bunkers. The concept of paying double or triple for a shirt emblazoned with an Izod alligator was incomprehensible to Archie Bunker and a capitalistic hoax to Mike Stivic. While the Bradys were mall shoppers, the Bunkers were discovering the plebeian joys of the latest fad, the discount store.

The 1980s and the 1990s—The Huxtables and the Connors

While on television the Huxtables are black and the Connors are white, in the real world it's much more likely to be the other way round. Still, color aside, each represents a socioeconomic segment that expanded during the 1980s. The Huxtables (Cliff, Clair, and children Denise, Sandra, Theo, Vanessa, and Rudy) are Haves. The Connors (Dan, Roseanne, and children Becky, D.J., and Darlene) are Have Nots. The Huxtables are rolling in dough: Dad's an obstetrician, Mom's a lawyer. They are mall people. They wear expensive clothes, live in an expensive home, and drive expensive cars. Cliff and Clair (well, Clair for sure) are among the first of the baby boomers, born shortly following World War II. They are, shocking as it may seem, in the same age group as Beaver Cleaver. Thus, despite their present affluence and high level of spending, they frequently find themselves at odds with the flagrant spending habits of their children, who represent post–baby boomers. These kids are totally out of control, the natural food of such predators as Calvin Klein, Benetton, and Liz Claiborne. The mall has become their hangout, shopping their recreation. Vanessa Huxtable has a sweatshirt emblazoned with the motto "Shop Till You Drop."

Just as the Haves, as a class, grew during the 1980s, so did the Have Nots. When the economic bubble burst early in the Bush administration, it was, as always, the Have Nots who took it on the chin. Dan Connor lost his job and his family benefits and has worked at a variety of occupations since. He is occasionally out of work altogether. Roseanne also joined the work force, usually in minimum-wage service jobs. The result has been a dramatic shift in the shopping habits of America that began in the 1980s and continued to accelerate into the 1990s. Roseanne Connor may have hung out at the mall as a teenager, but her shopping was done exclusively through windows. Denise Huxtable's jeans might have come from Bloomingdale's, but Roseanne's came from Sears. By now Roseanne has left the mall altogether and buys clothes for her kids at Target or K-Mart. Clair Huxtable might read grocery labels for nutritional and environmental information, but Roseanne looks for quantity, not quality, and low prices. She patronizes discount grocery stores and shopping clubs. She buys private-label products . . . in bulk. She saves coupons. She makes every penny count, and she teaches her kids to do the same.

But if the malls lost the Connors, there is worse news from the Huxtable kids. Riding the crest of the recession into the adult world, the value of money finally begins to dawn. Extravagant tastes and entry-level salaries don't match up. Then there are time problems. Long hours spent on challenging new jobs leave little time for malling. In 1987, 62 percent of shoppers patronized two or more malls. By 1991 that figure had dropped to just 52 percent. In 1987 only 12 percent of Americans said they never went to malls; by 1991, that figure had risen to 18 percent. All this before the recession had even seriously set in. Although not altogether willing to give up the good things to which they have become accustomed, the new shoppers now place a premium on convenience and value. Catalogs, they find, offer a convenient alternative to shopping trips. Their mailboxes fill with those of Land's End, Eddie Bauer, Neiman-Marcus, and dozens more. They also discover places like outlet stores, where Guess jeans and Red Door perfume can be purchased at discount prices. Theo Huxtable stretches the envelope a little when he buys his used BMW, but does all his own maintenance. He buys his oil and antifreeze at the Venture store out on the parkway (a "cross-shopper").

Thus, as was pointed out earlier, while the River City Downtown Development Committee continues its quixotic battle with the suburban mall, it is truly one battle behind. At least.

❖ THE ROLE OF TECHNOLOGY

Ike Godsey's General Store, snuggled at the foot of Walton's Mountain, was what today's retailer nostalgically refers to as a "Mom and Pop" store. Usually, most of the goods they sold at retail were wholesaled locally. Customer service was at its peak. Ike Godsey wasn't an impersonal shopkeeper, he was a neighbor. And he knew his limited line of merchandise forward and backward. Retail outlets exactly like it had been in operation for more than ten thousand years. There were stores just like it snuggled at the foot of Mount Ararat, the foot of Mount Fuji, and the foot of Mount Kilimanjaro.

The big downtown department store patronized by June Cleaver and Donna Stone had a much shorter history, only a little more than a hundred years. Customer service was one more step removed. The clerks were not owners, but paid personnel, usually with knowledge of a single product line only. The shopping malls so beloved by Jan Brady and Vanessa Huxtable didn't begin to appear until the 1960s, discount stores in the 1970s, factory outlets in the 1980s. These last innovations basically signaled the end of customer service altogether. Sales clerks are just one of the overhead costs exchanged for low prices. Clerks for high-involvement items such as television sets or wristwatches are few and far between, and often not terribly knowledgeable about their product lines.

The two driving factors behind these changes seem to be (1) technology and (2) the state of the middle class. Until the nineteenth century, cities were small and distances between them long. The middle class (always the backbone of retailing) could travel neither fast nor far on shopping trips. Each Mom and Pop–type store served an area within walking distance of its customers. They were small, and there were millions of them.

In the nineteenth century, major cities began to grow, largely because of technological changes in public transportation. Thanks to horse carts, grocery stores could serve larger areas. Combined with horse-drawn cabs, elevated railways, and subways, a variety of stores could concentrate in a single downtown area. In places from Manhattan Island, the Chicago Loop, and downtown River City, shops proliferated and department stores rose to dizzying heights.

In the twentieth century, the arrival of the automobile, combined with the unprecedented growth of the middle class, eventually doomed the downtown areas as people favored suburban shopping.

And today, as we prepare to enter the twenty-first century, technology again is changing the way we shop. The middle class, more and more single-parent households and working wives, has even less shopping time. Technology like catalogs and television shopping and computers and overnight delivery companies and fax machines are beginning to fill the gap. As marketers, we are entering an exciting new age.

❖ FROM CARTER TO CLINTON: THE NEXT GREAT RIDE BEGINS

Following more than thirty years of unprecedented prosperity, the likes of which we had never seen before and won't soon see again, Americans received a jolt: Mr. Carter's recession. John Boy Walton, 60-year-old professor of literature at North Carolina State, chuckled at the panic he sensed in his fellow citizens. "You call *this* a crisis?" he laughed. "This is nothing. Now in '29, *there* was a crisis." But he was talking to a generation who had never known anything but upswings and bull markets. They were people who had come to believe that this economic aberration, from the late 1940s to the late 1970s, was actually the norm. And suddenly all the lines leveled and then, horror upon horror, began to drop. Lines like housing starts, GNP, balance of trade. The only lines that seemed to be going up were unemployment and inflation. And the Misery Index. And if that wasn't bad enough, the Ayatollah Khomeini was holding our diplomatic staff in Iran hostage. Everybody was miserable. Everybody, that is, but the Republicans.

In the 1980 election, Carter suffered the worst political defeat since . . . well . . . Hoover. The Democrats had had a bad four years and were about to have an even worse decade.

The recession politely acted like such recessions had always acted. A sharp downturn, a brief period in the trench, then a steady upturn that accelerated as the economy began to stabilize once more. Buoyed by the recovery and Ronald Reagan's cheerful optimism, Americans happily watched the lines turn upward, and began forming long lines of their own at cash registers. Happy days were here again. The 1980s became the most free-spending decade in history.

Like all good things, the boom finally came to an end. As did the Reagan presidency. Vice President George Bush handed Democratic candidate Michael Dukakis the worst presidential defeat since . . . well . . . Mondale. Then suddenly, downturn again. Mr. Bush's recession had begun. Spending eased. Americans sat back, decided the old jalopy had one more good year in her, and waited for the recession to snap out of it. There was the sharp downturn, just as in Mr. Carter's recession . . . the time in the trench, just as in Mr. Carter's recession . . . and then more time in the trench . . . and more time . . . . and more time. Something was wrong. Mr. Bush's recession was not acting politely like Mr. Carter's had. It was stuck in the trenches.

During the next few years, discretionary spending, by the middle class at least, virtually ground to a halt. The extent of the mess was revealed. People who never heard of a deficit studied economics with the fervor of John Kenneth Galbraith. Erosion and declines begun in the early 1980s resumed in the late 1980s: housing starts were down, unemployment rose.

The trauma of Mr. Bush's recession, along with its long, long aftermath, changed shopping habits forever. With new technologies at hand, and with typical American ingenuity, buyers and sellers found new and different ways of conducting their business.

As for George Bush, he suffered the same fate as Jimmy Carter's. In America, recessions just aren't popular.

❖ CAREER GIRLS AND WORKING WOMEN

Let's face it: when you're talking shopping, you're talking women. More and more, you're talking working women. But working women with a difference. The goal-oriented career women who went boldly out into the male-dominated workplace of the 1970s were mostly well-educated, well-qualified Yuppies with well-placed husbands and few or no children.

As the 1990s approached, however, a new type of working woman came on the scene. Unlike her working sister, this woman never had any intention of joining the work force. She expected to get married and raise a family, just like her mother and grandmother before her, and for a while, she did. Then one day her world turned upside-down. First, Charlie got laid off and then the company shut down the plant altogether. The family income dropped from Charlie's $11.50 an hour to a meager welfare stipend. Instead of paying by check she was reduced to paying with food stamps.

Up against it, she checked the want ads and went to work. And as the economy shrank, her numbers grew. Today, you see her everywhere: checking groceries at the market, cooking burgers at Chubby Chuck's, dishing up Jell-O in the school cafeteria, waiting tables at the Korner Kafe. Her employers love her. Unlike the high school kids against whom she competes for her job, she is steady, she won't graduate or move away, she definitely won't get married, and she probably won't get pregnant.

So, what we have here is two different kinds of women; hence two different kinds of shoppers—with only one thing in common, time, or rather lack of it. These women are busy; almost always busier than their husbands. In addition to their jobs, they do most of the cooking and cleaning and parenting and practically all of the shopping. There isn't much they can do to reduce the time it takes to work, parent, cook, or clean, but there are ways to save time shopping. And the good old free enterprise system has responded in spades.

While both these women are too busy to waste time shopping, each solves the problem in a different way. The low-paid working woman is willing to give up what might be called shopping amenities, mainly service, to save both time and money. The high(er)-paid career woman is willing to give up some (but not all) service to save time, and while less concerned with money than her lower-paid sister, she is extremely concerned with *value*, which she defines as the best quality for the money.

Responding to these new women, the retail shopping scene of the 1990s is changing fast. According to *Research Alert*, in its 1990 issue, *Life-styles America*, as well as other sources, these changes include the following:

More Discount-Type Stores

The big discount chains of recent years, stores like Target, K-Mart, and Venture, are flourishing. Once exclusively the domain of working women in search of bargains, these stores now attract more affluent career women in search of value. Some stores are emphasizing their service functions and branding policies, moves that will stand them in good stead in the 1990s. A new level of discount-type stores has moved into the niche once occupied by these giants— warehouse stores and shopping clubs. While not particularly attractive to the career woman, these stores have caught on with low-income women and their families. If you're willing to pack your own groceries and buy in bulk, these stores offer appealing price savings.

More Specialty-Type Shops

Exactly the opposite of discount stores, these shops offer affluent shoppers relief from the burden of too many choices. Shoppers who might be daunted by the prospect of finding a lemon reamer at Target or fireplace tongs at Venture can find help, for a price, at a kitchenwares store or a fireplace shop.

More Factory Outlets

Factory outlets offer something for everyone. Bargains for the price-conscious working woman, value for the brand-conscious career woman. The newest trend in retailing is the "outlet mall" where several such stores are encamped together at a short distance from population centers.

More Off-Price Retailers

These chains, like Marshall's and TJ Max, specialize in name brands, but with a twist. Their merchandise is advertised as being "imperfect" with unspecified flaws. Usually the flaw, if one can find it at all, is ludicrously minimal, often fixable. At savings of 50 percent or more, these stores are attractive to both high-income and low-income shoppers.

More Super Malls

It's called the Mall of America and its 445 stores on four floors, along with its spacious parking lots, occupy 78 acres south of Minneapolis. Skeptics looked down their noses; it's just too much, they said. But they were wrong—or so it appears. At the time of this writing, sales have been running 45 percent ahead of projections, with the average weekday shopper spending $65 and the average weekend shopper spending $140. Weekend traffic is running at about 200,000 people. We can expect more such super malls, but instead of offering an assortment of strictly retail stores, they will also feature fitness centers, theme parks, fine dining and entertainment, senior centers, hotels, concert halls, day care centers, possibly even condominiums. The super mall will become, in reality, a minicity.

More Catalog Shopping

Perhaps more than any other form of retail, the shop-by-mail segment, in all its many aspects, has been getting its act together. Okay, you could always trust shopping from a catalog that was merely a division of a respected retail store such as Sears, Wards, or J. C. Penney. After all, if you had a quality problem or a size problem, you could always take it back and receive instant gratification. And even if you didn't live anywhere near a Neiman-Marcus store or a Marshall Field's, their reputations for quality assured catalog shoppers. But what about those catalogs-without-stores, the mail-order houses like Spiegel? And what about all those other catalogs that came in the mail? The thin ones, the 5"-by-7" booklets, what about them? In 1987, complaints about shop-by-mail merchandise constituted America's leading consumer grievance. Two years later, in 1989, such complaints had fallen by 42 percent. Today, 21 percent of all Americans shop from catalogs. Many of these from marketers such as L. L. Bean, Land's End, Brookstone, and Hammacher Schlemmer set the standard for retail quality.

More Television Shopping

Improvements in the production quality of direct response commercials have been accompanied in recent years by increases in the quality of the products being offered. Taking a leaf from the catalog industry's book, TV marketers today understand that their biggest asset in the future will be credibility. Also, as more and more blue-chip marketers explore the possibilities of direct response television, image . . . totally dependent on product quality . . . is claiming a higher and higher priority. Television, with the advent of marketing channels, can serve as a substitute for the knowledgeable sales clerk, assisting the potential consumer in his or her buying decision. Where once only low-cost, low-involvement merchandise was considered grist for the direct response television mill, today the ante is being raised. As marketers of big-ticket, high-involvement products from Saturn cars to Soloflex fitness equipment include television in their marketing mix, the rules change. As in all forms of today's merchandising, the subject of *brand* comes up.

More Computer Shopping

Today, 35 percent of American families own computers and 8 percent of those subscribe to on-line services (see Figure 6-1). While few in number, patrons of these services are America's most affluent consumers. These are young (40 plus) families earning big bucks ($70,000–$199,000). On-line services currently offer limited shopping (airline tickets, hotel reservations, etc.) and are lightly patronized. But before writing off this unique method of retailing, take a look at the messages going back and forth, from coast to coast via on-line. Mostly it's kids asking questions about computer games. "How do I get my *SimCity* past 100,000 population?" "I'm thinking about buying *Wolfpack* . . . has anybody got any tips?" "Forming an *NFL* league in Chicago area . . . need player interested in managing either the *Chargers* or the *Seahawks.*" Computer literacy starts early. As these kids grow up, and raise kids of their own, computer shopping will truly come of age.

Figure 6-1

Computer Facts

**Nationwide
Cross Section**

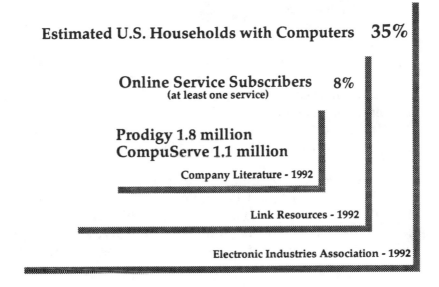

Estimated U.S. Households with Computers   35%

Online Service Subscribers   8%
(at least one service)

**Prodigy 1.8 million
CompuServe 1.1 million**

Company Literature - 1992

Link Resources - 1992

Electronic Industries Association - 1992

The smallest slice of America's shopping pie will never be the largest. But as the Nintendo kids grow up, the category is projected to grow 28 percent per year. Courtesy Link Resources and the Electronics Industries Association.

More Brand Buying

*"Hey, Mom! Our group had 35 percent
fewer cavities . . . with Crest!"*

Remember that? It was the 1960 battle cry of one of the most successful marketing campaigns ever staged. Teamed with the endorsement of the American Dental Association, featured in every ad and commercial, Crest's dollar sales jumped 60 percent during the first month of the campaign, 34 percent due to brand switching. Within five months, Crest picked up a full five points in market share.

Although long and clumsy, the endorsement was indelibly etched on the minds of a generation, most of whom can recite it till this day:

> *"Crest has been shown to be an effective decay-preventive dentifrice that can be of significant value when used in a conscientiously applied program of oral hygiene and regular professional care."*

The case of Crest is even more impressive when you consider that it is a low-cost, low-involvement product, usually bought out of long habit. Here were people—mothers, mostly—switching themselves and their families to Crest and sticking to their guns through the period of adjustment:

> *"Mom, this doesn't taste like our old toothpaste . . . I don't like it!"*

Low-involvement or not, the *Crest* case drives home the most important point of brand building: credibility. Credibility comes from third parties with no ax to grind, in this case the Council on Dental Therapeutics of the American Dental Association. In the 1990s, more than ever before, effective branding will be critical to marketing success.

❖ THE CASE FOR BRAND BUILDING: CREDIBILITY VERSUS CLUTTER

If you see it in an ad or commercial, you might be convinced.

If you read about it in a newspaper item or magazine article, you're more likely to be convinced.

If you learn that recognized authorities are recommending it, you're even more likely to be convinced.

If you hear good things about it from a friend or neighbor who has used it, you're still more likely to be convinced. But if you've used it yourself and liked it, none of the above is necessary.

Brand recognition enhances every one of the processes outlined here. Add the phrase "If you have a preconceived favorable impression of the product and . . ." to each of the foregoing statements and the effectiveness of the sources is much greater. In the 1990s, that can make an absolutely critical difference for two reasons: first, the disappearance of the sales clerk, and second, the proliferation of brands. Both these conditions exist in your average discount store. The shopper is faced with aisles and aisles of branded products from kitchen appliances to automotive supplies. There are dozens of brands of TV sets alone. It's all very confusing, and there's no one around to help.

Buying an item is a process (see Figure 6-2). In order to make a selection, if you're like most people, you fall back on your knowledge of brands. You buy the one with the most brand credibility, the sum total of all the third-party information you've collected. According to *The Yankelovitch Monitor 1992*, brand buying simplifies decisions, guarantees quality, and reduces surprises. If it's a low-involvement item, say, a case of motor oil or box of aspirin, you take it home with you right away. If it's a high-involvement item, a sound system, perhaps, or a dishwasher, you might check prices on the same model in two or three different stores, looking for the best value. In some high-involvement product categories, brand loyalty is so intense that shoppers will go elsewhere if it's not immediately available. These include cameras (68 percent would search elsewhere), cosmetics (62 percent), men's apparel (61 percent), consumer electronics (60 percent), and hardware (59 percent).

Sam Walton became one of America's richest men by implementing exactly the right idea at exactly the right moment. At a time when the majority of consumers decided they were willing to give up service for price, Wal-Mart was there. Today, that consumer is still in the majority and, barring an unlikely outbreak of unprecedented prosperity, is likely to remain so, but there's another group of consumers gaining in importance. It's that 1.4 percent of Americans who buy 11 percent of the products. They're professional, upscale, family people. Although they insist on quality, they're impatient with the rigors of shopping and wary of the retail system with its markups and middlemen. More and more, they're turning to the most viable alternative, catalog shopping.

Figure 6-2
The Stages of a Buying Decision and Use of Commercial Advertising Messages

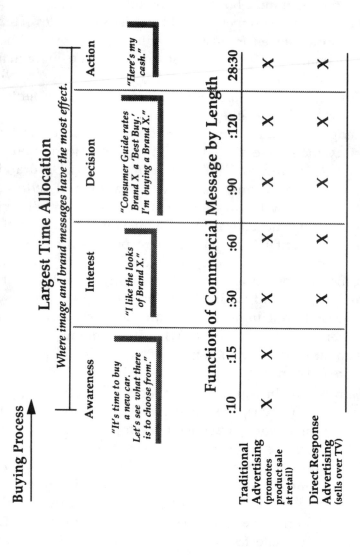

Buying Process →

Largest Time Allocation
Where image and brand messages have the most effect.

	Awareness	Interest	Decision	Action
	"It's time to buy a new car. Let's see what there is to choose from."	"I like the looks of Brand X."	"Consumer Guide rates Brand X a 'Best Buy.' I'm buying a Brand X."	"Here's my cash."

Function of Commercial Message by Length

	:10	:15	:30	:60	:90	:120	28:30
Traditional Advertising (promotes product sale at retail)		X	X	X	X	X	X
Direct Response Advertising (sells over TV)			X	X	X	X	X

Notice how buyers, moving closer to a sale, seek out more and more information from longer and longer commercials. Direct response advertising plays an increasingly important role as interest turns to decision leading to action.

112

❖ CATALOG SHOPPERS: THE MOTHER LODE

Compared to noncatalog shoppers, catalog shoppers are better educated and more likely to work in the professional-managerial sector (see Figure 6-3). Individually, they earn more and spend more than any other economic group. Half of them are between 26 and 44. They read more, shop more, travel more, attend more movies, exercise more, have more hobbies, make more home repairs, and are more likely to work on their own cars. They are more likely to buy familiar brands and prefer conservative, traditional styles. They are more likely to have two incomes, patronize the same supermarket, and own a pet, a microwave oven, an answering machine, a cellular phone, a CD player, and a computer. They are more likely to use the Yellow Pages, ATMs, and credit cards. For the big-ticket, brand-conscious, high-involvement marketer, they are truly the mother lode. And they have one more peculiarity that relates directly to the subject of this book. It has to do with their relationship to television.

You'd think, with such busy schedules, they wouldn't have much time left for television viewing. Yet compared to noncatalog shoppers, more of them have remote controls, cable TV, and VCRs. They rent more videos and spend more time watching television in general.

Perhaps most interesting of all, *13 percent of them, as compared to only 1–3 percent of noncatalog shoppers, buy from shopping channels.* The catalog shopper of today, it would seem, is the television shopper of tomorrow. And marketing channels, with their brand and quality emphasis, would seem to be the ideal way to mine the mother lode.

Figure 6-3

Catalog Versus Noncatalog Shoppers: 1992 Facts and Demographics

Nationwide Cross Section		Catalog Shoppers **21%**
	Non-catalog	Catalog
Earned income		
$30,000 - 90,000	33%	50%
$50,000 - 75,000	11	18
Education		
Attended college	52	67
Married	45	57
Own house	56	66
Age		
18 - 24	16	11
25 - 34	22	27
35 - 44	17	25
45 - 54	12	16
55 - 64	12	11
65 +	21	11
Buy from TV shopping shows	1	13
Leisure time spent watching TV	68	71
Own home computer	22	36

Deloitte & Touche - 1992

Catalog shoppers, like cable subscribers, are knowledgeable, progressive, pre-ferred customers, exactly the kind of customers who buy most of the upscale brands and high-involvement products likely to be advertised on marketing channels. Courtesy Deloitte & Touche.

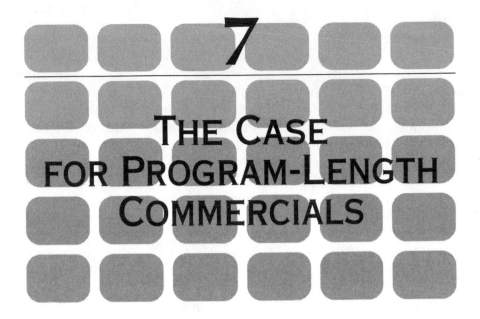

7

THE CASE
FOR PROGRAM-LENGTH
COMMERCIALS

*"Rating points don't buy products . . .
people do."*

SUSAN COHAN, Monarch Marketing

We have seen the decline of the sales clerk and the subsequent importance of brand recognizance. Faced with a wall of similar products, and without the presence of a sales clerk to influence decision making, the average consumer will fall back on the reputation of the brand. And as the cost and complexity of a product rises, so does reliance on brand. The decades-old slogan, "You can be *sure* if it's Westinghouse," often reviled by the trendy creatives of the 1960s, would seem to be spot-on in the 1990s. The evolution of the retailing process has more than justified the millions upon millions Westinghouse has paid promoting that slogan and placing its brand name high on the "dependability" ladder in the consumer mind.

Thus, as brands continue to proliferate and in-store service continues to deteriorate, it is those companies who own strong, well-known brands that are the winners. There have been other winners, too, most notably the infomercial industry, which has become a sort of substitute sales clerk. The sales clerk of old had enormous influence on decision making. He could, with a smile and a nod of encouragement, confirm your decision to buy the name-brand product. But he could just as easily, with a look of quizzical disapproval and a flurry of competitive sales literature, steer you toward a different brand (called "selling off") or a different product ("selling up").

He accomplished these feats by first establishing a benchmark product—the one you saw advertised at a sale price in the newspaper, perhaps. Having reassured you that the benchmark product is very good, he then began to compare it with other models, more expensive models with more attractive features. If he was good, he could sell you up to a more expensive model or, despite decades of expensive advertising, sell you off one brand and onto a new one. This process takes more than skill, it takes time—such a transaction is virtually impossible within the time confines of a 30-second television spot. But with 30 *minutes* at your disposal, results have proved that in many product categories it is not just possible, but probable.

In 1984, in line with the Reagan administration's efforts to get government off the collective backs of business, the Supreme Court overturned a 1973 Federal Communications Commission and industry regulation that had limited commercial time to 12 minutes an hour. Henceforth, commercials could take as much time as advertisers felt they needed. The result was the reintroduction of the long-form 30-minute commercial after an absence from the small screen of more than eleven years. In their latest incarnation, these long-form commercials were called infomercials. First on the airwaves, as might be expected, were infomercials for low-cost, low-involvement products. These commercials continuously assure viewers that "operators are standing by" and urge them to "call this number now." The Popeil brothers and Ronco, among others, relied on their tried-and-true boardwalk pitchman techniques. Sets were simple, the mood highly personal, the demonstrations impressive.

These were followed by the "commercials in disguise" mentioned in Chapter 5—the 30-minute commercials designed to look like game shows, talk shows, and variety shows. Both these types—true infomercials with the objective of immediate sales—are with us today and new variations continue to evolve. Bell Atlantic, for example, merged the infomercial with the family sitcom and came up with "The Ringers," promoting a variety of consumer phone services.

The fact that revenues from infomercials have risen from $350 million in 1988 to $750 million in 1992 is testimony to their effectiveness. In 1993, sales are expected to top the 1 billion mark. *Megatrend's* John Naisbitt predicts sales of $10 billion within 10 years. The following figures tell the story:

Infomercials Generating Revenues of $100,000,000 Plus

1. Tony Robbins's self-improvement programs
2. Victoria Jackson's cosmetics
3. Richard Simmons's diet programs
4. John Ritter, Michael Landon, and Burt Reynolds's "Where There's a Will There's an A"

Commercials Generating Revenues of $50,000,000–99,000,000

1. Wally Nash's "Great Wok of China"
2. Bruce Jenner's stair climber

Typically an infomercial has a life span of 12–18 months. If the product is still selling well, a new infomercial is made. Most of those mentioned here are in their second or third incarnation. "Where There's a Will There's an A" was still generating sales at the time of Michael Landon's death, and the spot is currently being revised featuring Burt Reynolds.

The undoubted effectiveness, not to mention efficiency of infomercials, has had its effect on big-ticket, high-involvement advertisers as well. Reluctant to use the name "infomercial," perhaps tainted by the boardwalk hustler image, Hal Riney called them "documercials." They have also been called program-length commercials and advertorials. Whatever you call them, they differ from the infomercial in a number of ways. First, they feature a product offering from a blue-chip, national brand advertiser or global company like General Motors, Volvo, Volkswagen, American Airlines, Kodak, McDonald's, Braun, or Redken. Second, documercials are high-budget spots featuring the same high production values seen in short-form network spots. But most important, documercials differ from the infomercial in intent. The documercial, because of the high-priced, high-involvement nature of the product being featured, usually doesn't ask viewers to "Call in and order now." With some exceptions, the objectives of documercials are usually image or quality enhancement, brand reinforcement, lead generation, dealership traffic building, and so on. Their objectives are to force a buying decision at retail rather than immediate call-in sales.

Whether you run an infomercial, a documercial, or no "mercial" at all depends on what you have to sell. Because the fact is, people buy different products in totally different ways.

❖ SALT, CUTLERY, WOKS, CARIBBEAN CRUISES, AND COMPUTERS

How many brands of kitchen salt can you name? You can count them on one finger, right? Morton. And what does Morton's salt do when it rains? It pours. Everyone knows that. Is this "pourability" relevant to you in any way? Have you ever tried a different brand of salt and found, to your horror, that when it rained it *didn't* pour? Other than to learn about its relationship to blood pressure, have you ever sought out information on salt? Salt is a low-involvement product category, with few (no?) brand differences. In fact, brand differences are nonexistent to the point where *Consumer Reports* has never done a brand comparison. Any information you have received about branded salt has been received *passively*. The only reason you know about Morton is that the company has been running the same basic ad campaign for more than fifty years. It is name identification, pure and simple. As a result, few grocery stores are without Morton's salt on their shelves. But if Morton, for some reason, were not there, you wouldn't go elsewhere to buy it. Salt, in the minds of most Americans, is salt. As Morton has proved, advertising works on these kinds of products, but an infomercial would be overkill in the extreme.

How about cutlery? Here is a relatively low-involvement category with many differences between brands. Buyers can find high-priced brands like Chicago Cutlery in the finest kitchen boutiques, and they can find plastic-handled brands on their supermarket shelves. Cutlery ranges in quality from the set used to carve the Thanksgiving turkey to the collection of odds and ends in the cupboard drawer. A buyer in the market for a set of "everyday" cutlery, a newlywed perhaps, makes a selection from the many brands available at the discount store. He or she then evaluates the purchase *after the fact*. If the knives hold an edge, they are pronounced excellent. If they don't, or if the handles fall off, the evaluation places them in the junk category. As far as marketing is concerned, one can see the importance of "brand" in these low-involvement categories. Morton's has bought and paid for its brand leadership at a cost of millions of dollars over many decades, which is why most people reach for the familiar blue container. While consumers may not be able to judge the steel quality of cutlery or the optical quality of sunglasses, they assume the brand they know, the advertised brand, the brand that comes to mind first, has an investment in that brand's quality, which takes the risk out of purchase. They reach for the familiar. Which is why cutlery is advertised in print—catalogs and direct mail programs, mostly. The only exception to traditionally promoted cutlery is a brand that has been advertised for years on television, in a series of impressive demonstration commercials asking for call-in orders. It's probably the nation's most recognized brand name in cutlery: Ginsu knives. Because advertising messages about this category of products (low involvement/many product differences) is received passively, Ginsu's success at gaining name recognition must have something to do with the fact that it is aggressively advertised in a direct response format.

While Ginsu has traditionally used short-form commercials, usually 120 seconds, another low-involvement advertiser with an oriental connection has found success with the long-form infomercial: Wally Nash's Great Wok of China. And while Ginsu prefers the high-powered, quick-fingered, hyperactive style, Wally Nash prefers a laid-back style more suitable to his unflappable British personality. You might think 30 minutes is a lot more time than one needs to describe the simple wok, which is, after all, nothing but a high-sided sauté pan. Yet Wally proves it can be done. Smooth and distinguished despite his apron, he stands turning out dish after dish while describing his wok in minute detail. He covers its history, notes its hand-made manufacture, and explains how it differs from machine-made woks. This last ploy is a clever attempt to keep interested buyers from simply picking up a knock-off wok at the discount store. And while Wally has sold more than $50 million worth of his woks, still local retail sales of woks increase whenever the infomercial runs. Is it possible this format can turn passively received information into information actively received? More about that later.

The examples just cited fall into the low-involvement category. Because of their relatively low cost, there is little risk involved in their purchase. Salt is salt, and even if the cutlery you buy is poor quality, still it's no big deal. Surviving knives simply end up in the odds-and-ends drawer. Advertising for such products is received passively, if at all. High-involvement products, on the other hand, involve risk. They cost a lot of money. In some cases, the purchase is something that will have to be lived with for a long, long time. It is not something to be taken lightly. Information is eagerly sought from any and all sources: word of mouth, newspaper and magazine articles, friends and neighbors, salespeople, advertising, brochures, and literature. Let's take a look at two high-involvement categories.

While cruises in general fall into the last category, we'll discuss (high involvement/many brand differences), when we limit the category to *Caribbean* cruises exclusively, they fall into the third category, which is that of high-involvement products with *few* brand differences. Unless you're an experienced "cruiser," you probably don't perceive many differences between the various cruise lines serving the Caribbean. There are Princess, Carnival, Norwegian Caribbean, Royal Caribbean, and many others. They make approximately the same ports of call: Nassau, the American Virgins, Aruba, San Juan, and so on. All the ships have all the amenities, and the food is universally superb. And with all sorts of price deals available, cost isn't really a critical factor. With little perceived difference between brands, most people pick the cruise that looks like the "best bet" and make their evaluations later. But because of the costs involved, information about these cruises is actively sought, which explains why they are heavily advertised in all media and have discovered, like more and more high-involvement products, the explanatory and comparative advantages of the documercial. Not just on television, but as a video brochure supplement to literature found at the travel agency.

Finally, let's take a look at products in a high-involvement/many-brand differences category: personal computers. A Caribbean cruise is over in ten days, but you'll be living with your PC for years to come. There is no such thing as an impulse buy in this category. Information is actively and aggressively sought. There are dozens of brands, many quite well known. One hears good things about the IBM, but what about an IBM clone? Would it be just as good at a fraction of the cost? And what about the reputed friendliness of the Apple? Would I be happier with that? Because of their products' complexity, computer marketers have largely shunned commercial television; there just isn't much you can explain in 60 seconds, let alone 30. The medium of choice for this category is magazine advertising, where long copy can carry at least part of the story. Here again, as in the automobile category, videotapes are a staple at the dealership level. It is expected that these marketers will soon be on television with documercials.

Apple, through a third-party affiliation, has developed a cutting-edge television show called *Mac Today*, which it has limited success in placing. As with infomercials, the show has accountability and scheduling problems. As of this writing there is simply no national channel in the entire cable spectrum suitable for a quality program on computers.

The key to all these buying decisions is perceived differences. If a category is one where there are many perceived differences between brands, shoppers follow a think-before-you-act scenario. They study up, as it were, looking for the brand that has the product differences they want, for whatever reason. Once the purchase is made, these buyers end the analysis process, revel in everything good about the product, and tend to overlook any shortcomings.

If a category is one in which few product differences are perceived, the prospect buys a product to relieve an uneasy state of mind, which Henry Assael has called "dissonance reduction."[1] With nothing upon which to base a rational decision, the consumer buys first and then experiences what Assael calls "postpurchase doubt" during which the product is analyzed for strengths and/or flaws. The state of dissonance experienced by people buying products in these categories increases in direct proportion to the ultimate cost. Chocolate chips is one thing; carpeting is quite another.

❖ INFOMERCIALS: LOW-INVOLVEMENT BEGINNINGS

Infomercials for high-involvement products like computers are tailored to the product. In the low-involvement arena, however, products are tailored to the infomercial. Some products naturally fit the long-form format, while others don't. The following is a list of criteria that indicate potential product success:

1. It should have a markup of 5 to 1 or better.
2. It should have previously demonstrated mass market (particularly blue-collar) appeal.
3. It should lend itself to visual demonstration.
4. It should have proven retail or direct sales.
5. It should have an attractive price-value relationship.
6. It should be priced lower than $49.95.
7. It should make life a little easier or appeal to fundamental desires such as wealth, sex appeal, or success.
8. It should be supported by impressive testimonials.
9. It should have back-end sales potential.

Companies like Popeil and Ronco actively seek out products that match the infomercial format, buy the product rights, script the pitch, produce the spot, and offer it to broadcasters. Whether the program is aired locally, regionally, or nationally, in some cases a percentage of profits from resulting sales are passed back to broadcasters. Results, of course, are immediate: within 48 hours it is clear exactly how well the infomercial worked. Latest figures indicate that today over 90 percent of stations broadcast some infomercials. As noted earlier, these infomercials are usually simply produced with glib standup presenters skillfully demonstrating the product. The product is king. They were the original direct response commercials and survive successfully today. For the right product, nothing works better.

❖ INFOMERCIALS: THE LOW-INVOLVEMENT PRESENT

After 1984, other marketers with seemingly workable products in their line began to experiment with the format. The marketing arrangements for these products, however, differed from earlier arrangements in a number of ways. The owning company kept the product rights and thus media control over the spots. The spots themselves were upgraded, often disguised as game shows or talk shows. They often employed celebrities as spokespersons. With the possible exception of the $49.95 price limit, however, this new generation of infomercials resembled traditional infomercials on all points mentioned earlier. While the spots themselves may be genteel—say, an attractive group of women discussing cosmetics or hair care with a celebrity hostess—they can also retain the rock 'em, sock 'em demonstration styles of the forerunners. In a commercial for Auri car wax, for instance, the presenters actually start a fire and fry a hamburger on the hood of a Rolls-Royce to demonstrate the product's protective qualities.

Today, the infomercial is still very much with us, but a new genre of long-form programming—we'll call it "marketing programming"—is on the rise.

❖ MARKETING PROGRAMMING: THE HIGH-INVOLVEMENT FUTURE

In the 1990s, marketers of high-priced, high-involvement products began to experiment with the 30-minute, long-form commercial format, among other techniques—all of which fall into the broad category of marketing programming rather than strictly direct response. Perhaps the impetus for this kind of experimentation came from a landmark direct marketing campaign conducted by Lincoln-Mercury in the mid-1980s. This campaign featured direct mail exclusively, with no media advertising involvement. The Lester Wunderman Company, a subsidiary of Lincoln-Mercury's advertising agency Young & Rubicam, developed an idea for selling Lincoln's top-of-the-line models exclusively with direct mail, something never before done. Armed with a list of luxury car buyers, Wunderman developed a handsome, tastefully designed mailing containing a flattering letter and a questionnaire that took about 20 minutes to complete. It asked the recipient, as "someone interested in fine automobiles," to take a few minutes from his or her busy day and fill out the questionnaire. The letter apologized for the length of the task, but explained that information thus gathered would be used to aid future designers with an eye to the improvement of the luxury car. To their delight, the response percentages went well into the double digits, which is remarkable when you consider most mailings with questionnaires—even simple ones—average returns of less than 2 percent, often less than 1 percent.

Depending on the answers they gave, respondents received a second mailing consisting of literature and a second letter—again very classy and personalized. "Dear Mr. Smith," it said in essence, "as a person who indicated concern about comfort, you might like to see what Lincoln has to offer by way of comfort features." Or safety features or mechanical features or design features. Mailings continued, many with requests for more opinions, creating a great deal of dialogue between Lincoln and the luxury car buyers.

Among the successful features of the campaign was a separate mailing program aimed at keeping nonrespondents in the loop, as well as a lead-sharing program with local dealers. Among the built-in devices found in the questionnaire itself was a one-two punch: the first question asked how often the car owner traded for a new model, and a later question asked when the last model was purchased. This, of course, enabled local dealers to call about a demonstration ride at precisely the time when potential customers were in the market and ready to buy.

The results? Not only did sales go up, but Lincoln established a database of luxury car owners who still participate in the marketing dialogue with the company. In the late 1980s, Lincoln added video brochures to its mix, notably a beautifully produced production featuring the 1990 Town Car hosted by golfer Jack Nicklaus. Imagine how much low-cost exposure a marketing channel could provide for these expensively made long-form commercials.

The Lincoln campaign proved to other high-involvement marketers that traditional media advertising wasn't the only game in town and that, with a little imagination and daring, other effective sales methods might yield viable results. Sales methods like long-form commercials.

Like Lincoln's mail campaign, marketing programming for high-involvement products are not simply direct response vehicles. Nobody ever bought an automobile by calling an 800 number. Such infomercials, or rather documercials, have different objectives than just immediate sales. Lead generation, perhaps. Or as a device to bring prospects to a local dealership. Or as an inexpensive way to explain a complex product or feature to potential buyers loyal to competitive brands, people who aren't likely to visit the local dealer. Or quality reinforcement. Or image and brand building.

This is not to say such documercials don't ask for an immediate response of one kind or another.

"For the address of the dealer nearest you, call . . ."

"For a copy of our product video brochure and price list, call . . ."

"For a coupon worth $100 off the printer with your PC purchase, call . . ."

"If you'd like to be on our mailing list, call . . ."

"For a free computer disk you can use to determine your individual needs, call . . ."

❖ MARKETING PROGRAMMING: POLITICS AND CAUSES

Perhaps one of the most interesting innovations in the infomercial field were the long-form political commercials run by third-party candidate H. Ross Perot in the presidential election of 1992. Using plain language and plain production, along with a host of rather crudely designed charts and graphs, Perot explained the complexities of the troubled economy along with his solutions for dealing with them. While Perot claimed to eschew sound bites, he used them masterfully, but his devotion to long-form commercials proves he felt he needed more than a 30-second campaign to do the job. In July of 1993, McDonalds, looking to build trust with African-Americans, launched a documercial spotlighting the company's commitment to the black community. As with Perot, the 30-minute format proved ideal. With the lure of cheap time in a five-hundred-channel world, people with causes, from politicians to environmentalists, will be hitting the long-form trail more and more often.

❖ MARKETING PROGRAMMING: AUDIENCE AND BUYING DYNAMICS

In a 1992 study of nearly two thousand individuals nationwide, Roper found that only 6 percent of the sample has bought merchandise via direct response television, while only 3 percent buy from shopping channels (see Figure 7-1). Still, infomercials generate millions, with millions being added every year. A recent TV Guide survey to determine the popularity of infomercials found 72 percent of viewers have watched an infomercial with 78 percent reporting seeing them once a month. During the same period, 17 percent watched 2-5 infomercials and a dedicated 4 percent tuned in 5 or more. Of those watching, 29 percent purchased products. One reason for this is the fact that people who buy from infomercials are, like the catalog buyers profiled in Chapter 6, younger, busy, educated spenders with kids, cars, and often two incomes. Faced with an infomercial or documercial that has relevance to their situation, they have both the inclination and wherewithal to buy. In fact, the overlap between television buyers and catalog buyers is highly correlative (see Figure 7-2).

❖ THE EFFECT OF MARKETING PROGRAMMING ON THE RETAIL SCENE

One of the most remarkable findings about infomercials is their effect on retail buying. One would expect most retailers to consider in-

Figure 7-1

People Who Buy from TV

Nationwide Cross Sections
U.S. Adult Consumers

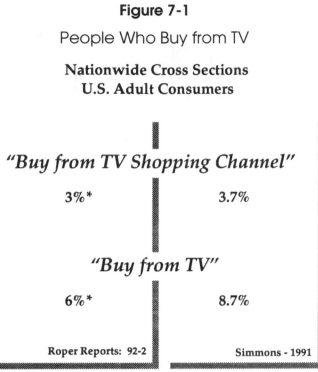

"Buy from TV Shopping Channel"

3%*   3.7%

"Buy from TV"

6%*   8.7%

Roper Reports: 92-2   Simmons - 1991

* **Purchased in last 3 months**

Several major-market research organizations report that 1–3 percent of viewers buy from TV shopping channels and 6–9 percent buy from television in general, which includes direct response commercials. Courtesy Roper Reports and Simmons.

fomercials tough competition. In fact, just the opposite has occurred. Whenever an infomercial runs in a given market, sales of products in the same category increase at a ratio of 5–8 to 1 (see Figure 7-3). In other words, for every hand mixer, dental care unit or fruit/vegetable juicer sold by infomercial, as many as eight units carrying as many different brand names are sold by local retailers. (Infomercials historically move categories of products, not just single brands.) It would seem that infomercials have a residual effect: people watch them, are sold on the advantages of the product they feature, and, rather than call in, reveal credit numbers, or pay postage, pick one up at the local Target store. Remember, only 6–9 percent of viewers buy via direct response; more than 90 percent still patronize local retailers.

Figure 7-2

Catalog Shoppers as TV Buyers

Nationwide Cross Sections

"Buy from TV Shopping Shows"

Non-Catalog Shoppers	Catalog Shoppers*		Boomers 25-44
1%	13%		Regularly 2.8% Occasionally 19.7%
	Deloitte & Touche - 1992		Impact Resources - 1991

* 21% of U.S. Consumer Population

As a group, when compared to the public at large, catalog shoppers and baby boomers are much more likely to occasionally buy from television. Courtesy Deloitte & Touche and Impact Resources.

More and more, infomercials are becoming a sort of electronic product catalog. While product selection on infomercials is necessarily limited, the amount of persuasive information on those products is greater. And whether the message is "Call in now" or "Stop by Target," both seem to attract a similar upscale audience, affluent and eager to buy. These facts alone are enough to bring blue-chip advertisers into the long-form genre; after all, if that's the direction in which their prime audience is moving, that's where they'll be. As can be seen by the adoption-diffusion scale (see Figure 7-4), that is clearly the direction in which their prime customers are headed.

While both catalog shopping and infomercial shopping seem well into the early majority and early adapter stage, accordingly, there are two other methods of home shopping still in the innovator stage: computer shopping and home shopping channels. Let's take a brief look at both.

Figure 7-3

Effect of Infomercials on Retail Sales of Juice Extractors

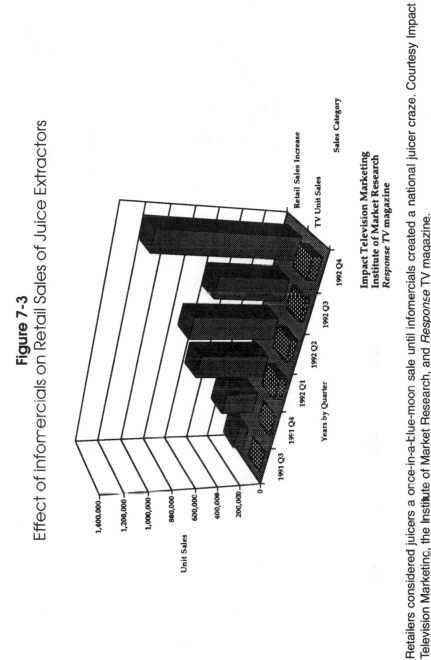

Impact Television Marketing
Institute of Market Research
Response TV **magazine**

Retailers considered juicers a once-in-a-blue-moon sale until infomercials created a national juicer craze. Courtesy Impact Television Marketing, the Institute of Market Research, and *Response* TV magazine.

Figure 7-4
Adoption/Diffusion of the Long-Form Commercial by National Brand Advertisers

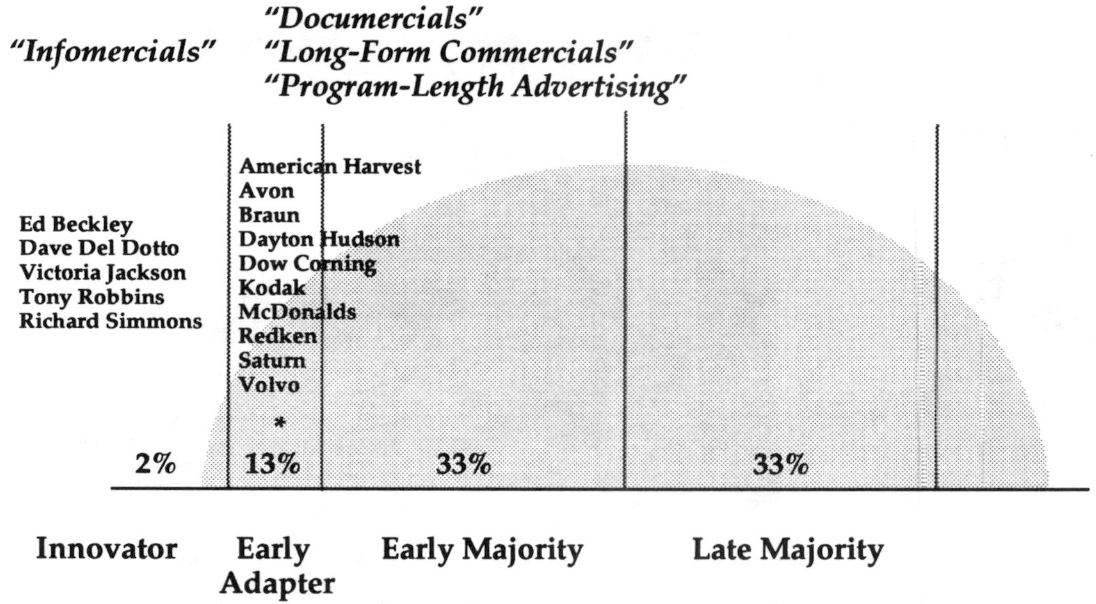

"Infomercials"

"Documercials"
"Long-Form Commercials"
"Program-Length Advertising"

	American Harvest Avon Braun Dayton Hudson Dow Corning Kodak McDonalds Redken Saturn Volvo		
Ed Beckley Dave Del Dotto Victoria Jackson Tony Robbins Richard Simmons	*		
2%	13%	33%	33%
Innovator	Early Adapter	Early Majority	Late Majority

* **You are here! Today's development probably places us somewhere between 9 and 11% into the long-form commercial's life cycle**

While the technique is still a playground for innovators and early adapters, companies like Braun, Saturn, Kodak, American Airlines, McDonald's, Dayton Hudson, and Avon are currently experimenting with long-form commercials. Each year the genre moves toward the early majority.

❖ THE COMPUTER MALL

As mentioned in Chapter 5, computer shoppers represent a small but extremely promising retail presence. Their most attractive feature, in terms of advertising, is their affluence. They resemble catalog shoppers (indeed, 82 percent of them are), but their demographics are even better. For example, 69 percent of subscribers to CompuServe have completed at least four years of college, their median age is 41 plus, and 38 percent have household incomes in excess of $75,000. Furthermore, they are more apt to buy: the buying response rate for catalog users is 1.5 percent, while shoppers on the computerized electronic mall respond at a rate of 2.5 percent.

Services such as CompuServe and Prodigy, as well as local computer shopping services, are growing and multiplying along with America's increasingly computer-savvy population. CompuServe's electronic mall features more than 100 merchants, including nationally known retailers, plus access to 71 different catalogs. Among the interesting services offered by these systems is "insider's information" such as automotive pricing and special deals on airfares. In the case of automobile-buying infoseekers, car companies describe this group of consumers as "highly qualified prospects"—they've researched the car via on-line services and are now in the door, ready to buy.

Sales on these systems have grown at a rate of 28 percent annually and continue at an ever-increasing rate every year. The computer mall, probably as part of a communications megasystem combining broadcast television, cable, and telephone technology, will play a large part in the twenty-first-century retail scene, as we'll see in Chapter 12. Meanwhile, the telephone serves to provide today's direct response marketers with interactivity.

❖ HOME SHOPPING: SHOP WHILE YOU FLOP

She's 45 plus years of age, a high school graduate, married to a relatively well-off ($40,000 plus) breadwinner. She now finds herself with nothing much to do: with all the kids off on their own, the house pretty much takes care of itself. With just the two of them at home, cooking is easy, and besides, they seem to eat out a lot more than they used to. So . . . what does she do for fun? Well, unless she has something else pressing to do, she may shop. The change is, more and more, she shops on television. It's fun, it's recreational, she doesn't have to fight traffic, and she can do it whether the stores are open or not. All she needs is a telephone and a credit card. And if she becomes truly addicted to home shopping, buying zircon rings and porcelain dolls that she has to hide in the attic to keep her husband from learning how much she spent . . . well . . . she can probably get a booking on Oprah. (Granted . . . this is an extreme case!) The point is, people in this group regard shopping—at the mall or on the shopping channel —as pure entertainment.

These people aren't the same people buying on the computer. Computer shopping is like going to a mall, finding the store you want, and making a purchase. The shopping channel is like a mall, only someone else determines which store you may visit. Despite the fact that shopping channels offer what they choose to, when they want to, at a price they set, still, they work. The industry was shocked when Barry Diller, former head of programming at the *Fox Network*, surfaced as a partner in the leading shopping channel, *QVC* (which stands for Quality/Value/Convenience, the battle cry of the 1990s consumer). Diller, like other visionaries, is able to see the shopping channels for what they are: an incredibly low-cost way to put more merchandise in front of more shoppers in less time than any other retail technique in history. Unlike their major competitors, discount stores and factory outlets, shopping channels like *QVC* and *Home Shopping Network* have brought back the sales clerk: personable, knowledgeable people, often celebrities, who lay on the persuasion as thick and rich as the Popeil brothers ever did. For example, comedienne/talk show hostess Joan Rivers appeared on a series of weekend showings. After just five weekends, sales of her jewelry products had reached $10 million. Actress Morgan Fairchild sold a million dollars' worth of jewelry with simulated Diamonique gem-stones in just three hours. As they could with actual sales clerks, some lucky callers get to talk with the celebrities. So here is Clara Clapsad-dle of East Akron, Ohio, chatting it up with Carol Channing, En-gelbert Humperdinck, Omar Sharif, or Suzanne Somers.

While celebrity presenters doubtless add a little extra oomph to the sale, still the vast majority of sales are made without them. Many of the congenial presenters on *QVC* and *HSN* have become pseudocelebrities in their own right, on a first-name basis with frequent callers. Some even get fan mail. The merger between *QVC* and *HSN* portends even greater use of television for retailing. The combined assets of the two will allow for exploration and exploitation of teleshopping's interactive potential.

Not to be left out, the networks are attempting shopping programs of their own. ABC's Nitecap with Robin Leach didn't quite measure up (cancelled after the pilots fizzled), but NBC's new direct marketing division is teaming up with the Mall of America for a one hour game show featuring brand name goods from the largest shopping/entertainment complex in the U.S.

Saks, in its first hour of televised merchandising on *QVC*, sold its entire inventory of private label clothing—$570,000 worth—contributing to the observation that as merchandise quality continues to improve and as more national brands come on board, audience composition will undoubtedly move beyond the early adapter stage to the early majority stage.

The future for shopping channels looks bright. In July of 1993, the televised home shopping industry received a vote of confidence from the FCC. FCC officials found full-time home shopping channels "in the public interest" and that denying them the right to be carried on cable systems would raise other complicated issues. FCC "approved" programming offers news, public information and diversity. As you'll see in Chapters 9 and 10, marketing channels, more easily than shopping channels, meet and surpass these criteria.

Shopping channels have the advantage of bringing enormous quantities of merchandise to enormous numbers of people. Their major disadvantage is the fact that the channel, not the shopper, calls the scheduling tune. Except for the few addicts, who watch all the time, most viewers stumble on shopping channels by accident, while looking for something else. If the product-of-the-moment happens to be of interest, the channel surfer stops and watches. If not, she or he surfs on. As we'll see in the next chapter, marketing channels feature many of the good points of shopping channels with none of the weak points. Instead of a mall where someone else determines which product categories to feature, marketing channels offer a number of malls, each specializing in a specific product category.

It stands to reason that consumers naturally pay more attention to product categories in which they have an immediate interest, particularly big-ticket, high-involvement categories like automobiles, computers, ocean cruises, and refrigerators. Passive attitudes change to active when they find the kind of information that takes the risk out of risky decisions. High-involvement shoppers, as the name implies, become highly involved in such programming. And while the kind of programming one is likely to find on a marketing channel may be entertaining, its informational aspect is of primary importance. Entertainment is the frosting on the informational cake.

Unlike long-form commercial programming scattered among conventional cable channels, such programming on marketing channels is sought out by design, not stumbled upon by accident and that makes all the difference.

❖ ENDNOTE

1. Henry Assael, *Consumer Behavior and Marketing Action* (Belmont, CA: Kent, 1981).

8

THE PARADIGM SHIFT BEGINS

A paradigm shift is no small thing. Sometimes it is an enormous thing. Perhaps the classic example occurred in the sixteenth century, when astronomer Nicholas Copernicus challenged the archetypal human belief that the sun revolved around the Earth. In fact, Copernicus said, the Earth revolves around the sun. The only thing that revolved around the Earth, he claimed, was the moon. To self-centered man, who had always believed himself to be the primary concern of God, the idea that he was not the center of the universe was heresy. Which brings us to the second characteristic of a paradigm shift: they take some getting used to. Old ways of thinking die hard. While other astronomers and medieval scientists eagerly accepted Copernicus' theory, it took the Catholic Church two hundred years to remove his book from the index of prohibited works.

As mentioned in Chapter 4, we are currently undergoing a paradigm shift in the way we view the most powerful communications medium in history. No, it doesn't alter our view of man's place in the universe; that won't happen again until we make positive contact with life forms on other planets. But its effects will be felt by billions of people around the world, and it will shape the global economy for better or worse.

> *"We are moving away from the decade of entertainment to the age of information."*

LAWRENCE GROSSMAN, former president NBC News

❖ THE ENTERTAINMENT ARCHETYPE

Ever since that day in 1922 when AT&T began to lose faith in its radio-as-phone-booth concept and allowed some of its more talented (?) employees to sing, play instruments, or give dramatic readings on the air, commercial broadcasting has been seen as a medium of entertainment. Pure, overwhelming entertainment. Yes, broadcasting has brought us news. Sometimes spectacularly, as with Edward R. Murrow's broadcasts from London during the Nazi blitz or Peter Arnett's eyewitness accounts of the bombing of Baghdad in the opening moments of Operation Desert Storm. While not technically entertainment, certainly these moments must be categorized as riveting and involving. In the absence of such gripping subject matter, news programming is characterized by smiling, brightly clad presenters, quick video clips, lots of human interest features, and all the other accoutrements of "happy news."

And yes, broadcasting has brought us education. But with the exception of college-credit programming on public access channels, even education is entertaining on television for a very simple reason. If it isn't, nobody watches. Most educational television is aimed at children, and most parents and educators consider it very good. But the fact remains, the reason it is so good is that it is so entertaining. Programs like *Sesame Street* make potentially dull subjects like math and English fun. And for exposing preschoolers to their first view of the mysterious ways of the great big world, what better guide than Mister Rogers?

As for adult documentaries, cable has brought them to their various audiences. There are people who love documentaries and people who don't. Very little middle ground exists. To people who don't, they are cloying and pedantic. To people who do, they are pure entertainment. And there are a few—Walt Disney's *True Life Adventures* and the Jacques Cousteau documentaries, for example—which were picked up by the networks and run in prime or early prime time. Proving that even documentary haters like documentaries sometimes.

When we sit down to watch television, we expect to be entertained. We expect programming that delights and involves us, that takes us out of our humdrum lives to beautiful places we have never been, to see fascinating things we have never seen, and meet interesting people we have never met. We expect programming that makes us laugh, that makes us cry, that gives us something to talk about at lunch the next day. That's entertainment!

Now we have infomercials. The proliferation of entertainment formats, the appearance of celebrities, and the heightened production values bear testament to the fact that the producers of infomercials are disciples of the entertainment archetype. More precisely, it proves the marketers behind them have paid homage to the gods of entertainment.

❖ THE STATE OF TELEVISION TODAY

From the marketer's standpoint, long-form commercials and shopping channels offer new and exciting directions to explore. As such, to existing cable and broadcast networks, they represent a threat to conventional entertainment-based television. Dollars once automatically spent reaching the mass audience are now being diverted to the smaller but more involved audiences watching the new direct response programming. The fact is, and the archetype notwithstanding, indications are that television's image as an entertainment medium is at an all-time low.

While viewership figures prove otherwise, most Americans *claim* they watch television less than in the past. Regardless of the reliability of these claims, the *reasons given* are interesting. In a recent survey, 71 percent of Americans claim they watch less television because of what they consider objectionable programming; 64 percent deny that programs represent their personal values; 69 percent feel it has a negative effect on children. Out of fifty products rated on a good buy/bad buy survey, cable was rated the forty-fourth worst buy, while pay cable was rated fiftieth. In a separate survey, cable was rated a worse value than movie tickets and pay cable was ranked worse, even, than credit card fees, lawyers' fees, and hospital charges. The majority of watchers today worry that they watch too much television. Not that it affects *them*, mind you, but they feel it affects *others* negatively, mainly children.

❖ OUR ENDURING FASCINATION WITH VIOLENCE

> *"I wish you would come up with another device other than running the man down with a car, as we have done this now in three different shows. I like the idea of sadism, but I hope we can come up with another approach to it."*

> Memo from QUINN MARTIN, producer, *The Untouchables*

Funny thing, violence. We go to great lengths to make sure it doesn't happen to us, yet we're fascinated, as moths by a flame, when it happens to someone else. Media violence is especially fascinating, since we know deep down that no one actually gets hurt. We can enjoy the thrill, without the guilt.

The thing about the media, however, is that they keep evolving, so that violence keeps coming at us faster and faster with each new technology. The Bible is full of violence, as was Europe's first widely circulated work of fiction, *The Romance of the Rose*, from the thirteenth century. At that time, however, few people could read. Popular theater first brought media violence to the masses. Shakespeare's love of violence is with us today—*Hamlet*, *Othello*, *Macbeth*, and *Richard III* run red with blood. In France the *Grand Guignol*, originally the French version of Punch and Judy, existed for hundreds of years, while Punch's simple beatings of Judy gradually evolved into gory on-stage special effects, including garrotings and guillotinings.

In America, with the rise of the public school system and middle-class literacy in the nineteenth century, the penny press provided young and old alike with "penny dreadfuls," cheaply printed accounts of the violent exploits of Western desperadoes. The first silent movie with an actual plot, *The Great Train Robbery*, was based on such exploits, and the violent trend continued in films until today when Freddy Kreuger stalks dreamers on Elm Street and dinosaurs lunch on lawyers in *Jurassic Park*. While newspaper comic strips remained relatively free of violence, comic books didn't. In the 1950s, public outrage caused violent comic books to be banned. Radio violence was relatively puerile, depending as it did on sound effects, but television corrected that.

Early television violence was usually mixed with humor. The masters of pain in those days were Jackie Gleason and Sid Caesar. Gleason, for example, would drop an anvil on his foot. For several seconds he simply stared wide-eyed into the camera, until finally he would roar in pain—over and over, clumping from one end of the set to the other, for several minutes. Caesar's technique was the opposite. Accidentally hitting his thumb with a hammer, Caesar would register no emotion whatsoever. Calmly he would put the hammer down and walk off the set. Seconds would pass, then screams of agonizing pain from offstage.

Before we discuss the introduction of movie-type violence to television with the advent of *Cheyenne* in 1956, let's take a look at the *volume* of violence, the level at which people have been exposed to it. The kid growing up in Cleveland *circa* 1870 probably read one "penny dreadful" a week at most. He could participate vicariously as Billy the Kid or John Wesley Hardin dispatched ten or fifteen citizens per issue. His great-great-great grandson, growing up in the 1940s, was receiving violence at a much faster rate. Because of the proliferation of titles and growing sophistication of distribution, plus an elaborate swapping system with his buddies, he could read perhaps ten comic books a week, as role models from Batman to Plastic Man to Dick Tracy "Ka-Powed!" and "Rat-tat-tatted" various evil-doers. On Saturdays he went to the double feature at the Majestic Theater and saw a cartoon wherein Daffy Duck gets sliced, skewered, and shot; a short subject where the Three Stooges perform various acts of mayhem on each other; a war picture where John Wayne mowed down row on row of fanatic Japanese suicide troops; and a Western where Hopalong Cassidy gunned three rustlers from their horses with one shot.

With television, the volume of violence reaches incredibly strident levels. Where his grandfather went to the movies only once a week, today's kid has movies and cartoons in his family room, maybe even his bedroom, on at least thirty-six channels, twenty-four hours a day. A survey by *TV Guide* ("Is TV Violence Battering Our Kids?" August 22, 1992) counted 1,846 individual acts of violence over ten Washington, D.C, stations in a random 18-hour viewing day. Of these, 175 resulted in one or more fatalities, 389 featured serious assaults, 362 involved guns, 673 depicted slapping, pushing, dragging and other hostile acts, and 226 involved people menaced with deadly weapons. Cartoons, with 471 incidences, featured the most violence, followed by TV promos with 265, movies with 221, toy commercials with 188, music videos with 123, ads for theatrical films with 121, TV dramas with 69, news with 62, reality shows with 58, sitcoms with 52, and soap operas with 34.

According to a 1992 study by the American Psychological Association, by the time children enter the seventh grade, they have seen on TV an average of 8,000 murders and 100,000 other acts of violence. The volume of violence today is deafening. Critics claim this causes a numbing effect; violence loses its power to shock.

The broadcasting industry is of two minds when it comes to the question of how seriously television actually influences viewers. On the one hand, it is felt that television advertising can actually change the buying behavior of the audience. In fact, it is felt that such advertising is largely responsible for the cars we buy, the laundry soap we use, the soft drinks we consume, the supermarkets we patronize, and all the many other ways we spend our money. And yet while broadcasters are quick to point out the power of 30-second and 60-second commercials, they are loathe to attribute the same power to 24–48 minutes of programming. Their detractors argue that if television can influence teenagers to buy Guess jeans or Pepsi Crystal, then it can also influence them in their feelings about the legitimacy of violence as a solution to every-day problems.

A study begun in 1960 by Leonard Eron, chairman of the APA's Commission on Violence and Youth suggests that children—especially boys—who watch television violence tend to be more aggressive in school, and that this aggression leads them to watch more violent television. Furthermore, he found a strong correlation between the violence exhibited by boys at 8 years old and boys at 18 years old. It seems that the heaviest viewers of television at age 8 became those most often convicted of violent crimes, and who were most likely to use violence in disciplining their own children.

Given the fact that Americans clearly include violence under the category of entertainment, and that Americans consider entertainment the main reason to watch television, and that Americans seem more concerned about watching television than ever before, it would seem the industry is in trouble. It would also seem that the prospect of five hundred channels, filled with more entertainment and more violence, has little appeal to these Americans.

Despite all this, we watch as a nation more television than ever before. Do we love it? Or do we hate it?

❖ TELEVISION: WATCHING IT MORE . . .

Consider this. According to Nielsen data, Americans watched basic cable 7.5 more hours a week in the 1991–92 season than they did in the 1985–86 season. That amounts to an increase of more than sixteen days a year. And three more years spent watching over a television lifetime of sixty-five years.

Male baby boomers watch slightly more than fourteen hours a week, with their wives averaging about an hour less. Apparently, it takes longer to cook dinner and clean the kitchen than it does to take out the garbage. If there are children in the home (any number, any age), both Mom and Dad watch about an hour a week less. Well-educated boomers watch less than do poorly educated boomers. People who work long hours, as we might expect, watch less television.

All this tallies to an average daily viewing time—home use—of 7 hours and 41 minutes.

Indeed, television viewing has become an all-day activity. In the 1950s, 45 percent of all viewing took place during prime time and another 32 percent during evening fringe hours, with the remainder in daytime. In most markets, of course, there was no overnight programming. Today, 30 percent of viewing is done during the prime-time hours, 36 percent fringe-evening, 23 percent daytime, and 11 percent in other periods. In many homes, television has become "background noise" or an "electronic nightlight." It goes on at breakfast and doesn't go off again until Dad wakes up at 3 A.M., turns off the set, rolls over, and goes back to sleep.

Of course all viewing in the 1950s, with a few oddball cable exceptions, came into the home compliments of the networks and their programming sponsors. Today, cable households split their viewing with networks capturing only 36 percent of viewing time, cable capturing 30 percent, independents capturing 21 percent, and local affiliates showing nonnetwork programming (local news, etc.) capturing 17 percent.

The increase in viewing time is, of course, largely due to the abundance of new cable programming. Or is it the other way around? At any rate, both have grown with astonishing speed in the decade 1980–1990 (see Figure 8-1).

The appearance of cable has also split the audience. While it's true that better-educated people tend to watch less television overall, it's also true that the cable-watching audience is better educated and more affluent than is the noncable-watching audience. Three factors would seem to account for this anomaly. First, older viewers with proportionately less education, often with fixed retirement incomes, are less likely to subscribe to cable. Second, low-income/low-education families often can't afford cable. And, finally, people with less education tend to exhibit less curiosity; hence, even if cable is available, they tend to limit their viewing of cable channels to movies and sports channels.

So, watching television has become the third most time-consuming activity we indulge in, next to sleep and work. We spend a third of our lives in front of the tube. We love it . . . right? Well . . .

Figure 8-1

Cable Grows While Pay Plateaus, 1980–1992

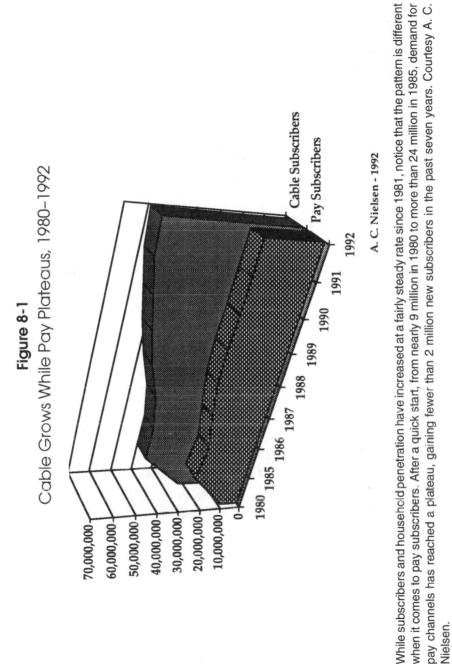

A. C. Nielsen - 1992

While subscribers and household penetration have increased at a fairly steady rate since 1981, notice that the pattern is different when it comes to pay subscribers. After a quick start, from nearly 9 million in 1980 to more than 24 million in 1985, demand for pay channels has reached a plateau, gaining fewer than 2 million new subscribers in the past seven years. Courtesy A. C. Nielsen.

❖ Television: Enjoying It Less

According to *Life-styles America, 1990s,*[1]

- Americans care more about "whether or not they should watch TV" than what they actually choose to watch once the tube is turned on.

- Americans rate television viewing as one of the most pleasurable parts of the day and one of the most anticipated, yet feel they shouldn't watch so much.

- Americans complain there are too few quality, educational programs on television, but they don't support them when they appear.

- They subscribe to cable to get better programming, yet the networks still command the majority of viewing time.

- While cable penetration is increasing, it seems to be reaching saturation.

- Satisfaction with service is low and staying low.

- Satisfaction with pay cable is even lower, has plateaued, and is considered a poor value for the money.

We don't seem to love it, but we do seem to watch it. Have we entered the world described by George Orwell in *1984* where television sets are always in sight, always on? One early observer thought so. Rolf Meyerson in his article "Social Research in Television" published back in 1957, issued a chilling prediction which may have come true:

> The entertainment that is TV is not simply an accretion of entertainment programs, it is the television set and the watching that entertains. Viewers seem to be entertained by the glow and the flow . . . Television succeeds because it is there![2]

And the proof? It's right there in your hand. It's called a remote control.

❖ The Grass is Always Greener on Another Channel

"Grazing is the sweet revenge of the underestimated viewer."

TODD GITLIN, Professor of Sociology
University of California at Berkeley

A torpedo putters up the lagoon, coming to rest on the beach. Mary Ann and the Skipper, who happen to be fishing nearby, observe the event, awestruck. "Look, Skipper," squeals Mary Ann, "it's a little tiny submarine." As she starts to run toward the object the Skipper, horrified, restrains her. "N-N-No, Mary Ann," he shouts, "it isn't a little tiny submarine . . . it's a great big t-t-t-torpedo!" The Professor makes a closer examination and discovers that the torpedo is an experimental model that must have been accidentally fired during naval maneuvers somewhere nearby. Furthermore, he says, it contains a homing signal that is still operational. The Navy is bound to come looking for it. Unless some idiot detonates the torpedo by touching the bowl-shaped aluminum nose cone, the castaways are saved! Cut to Gilligan back at camp, cooking over an open fire. His soup bowl, made from half a coconut shell, suddenly catches fire, causing him to drop it, putting out the fire. "Darn," he says, sucking his burnt finger, "if only we had a decent set of aluminum cookware."

You grab your remote control. *Clickety-clickety-clickety-click.*

"By now the lioness is desperate," says the smooth, British-accented narrator. "She hasn't eaten since giving birth to her cubs and she is weak with hunger." The lioness waits, still as death, while the herd moves closer . . . and closer. Suddenly, she springs from the tall grass and gives chase. "This time she's in luck," intones the narrator. "An old wildebeest has apparently broken its leg. And in nature's kingdom, that's a sentence of death."

Same old lioness; same old gnu. Doesn't this look familiar? *Clickety-clickety-clickety-click.*

Most people, about one in three, graze, zap, or channel surf because they are dissatisfied with the channel they are watching, wish to avoid a commercial, or are afraid that they are missing something better on another channel. If, by the time the first commercial rolls around, the end of the show is obvious, viewers are convinced that something less predictable is running elsewhere. Away they go, usually upward, usually one complete revolution of existing channels. Unless, of course, they encounter something so powerful they are stopped in their tracks.

Not everyone, however, grazes out of dissatisfaction with the programming. Previously identified as a "zapper," about one in four grazes to avoid commercials, although this technique easily fails as most channels run their commercials at approximately the same time. Ted Turner's Superstation *WTBS* cleverly attracts these people by programming five minutes behind everyone else. Of course *WTBS* runs the risk of someone becoming engrossed in another channel's offering and never reaching the Turner channel, but given the incidence of dissatisfaction this seems increasingly unlikely.

❖ SUPERSURFERS: HERE COME THE KIDS

> *"The attention span of today's average American is that of a ferret on espresso."*
>
> DENNIS MILLER, comedian

Then there's the younger generation, the kids who grew up with a remote control in their hand. Many of them, about 11 percent of the total viewing audience, use grazing as a method of watching two, or sometimes even three programs at once. Not sports freaks who spend all weekend grazing from one game to another, but *MTV* kids who can actually follow two plotlines without feeling they are somehow missing out. And if they miss the climax, so what? Music videos often feature a definite plot, but then simply drift off, unresolved, at the end.

Even more detached from dramatic consequence than these people are a younger generation who graze with the intent of creating a sort of video mosaic. Plot, game scores, whodunit, character development, cartoons . . . all are irrelevant to these television abstractionists. They are perfectly happy just grazing along, looking at all the pretty pictures like visitors to an art gallery whose exhibit has no theme. These people are watching *television*, not programs. They call it "zoning out."

What conclusions can we draw from this? For one thing, it seems clear that inadequate programming, not commercials, is responsible for the majority of grazing. For another, we must conclude that grazing is a trend on the upswing. People over 50 are much less likely to graze. The biggest segment of grazers most advertisers are interested in reaching is the 18- to 34-year-old group. It is unlikely their habits will change as they age, and it seems the next generation grazes even more.

While the young graze more than the old, and while men graze more than women, studies indicate that seven out of ten viewers enjoy television less while grazing is in progress. One suspects this figure is so high because on any given commercial break, about three out of ten dedicated grazers are clicking away, contributing to the anger of others in the room who aren't.

What all this really tells us, on careful analysis, is that grazing is caused largely by programming dissatisfaction. Good, quality programming, the top ten network shows, for example, has proven itself relatively resistant to grazing. The problem is, as grazing proves, traditional entertainment programming works when it's good, but it isn't good very often.

And then there's the whole issue of the increase in the volume of violence. As its very pervasiveness reduces its power to shock, programming goes further and further in its portrayal of murder and gore. The baby boomers, while they watch violence, seem to worry about it more than their earlier generations. While they don't necessarily believe it will affect them, they worry about what it's doing to their kids. Today Americans *say* they either zap the channel or shut off the set if things get too violent. True or not, observers like Michael Medved in his book *Hollywood vs. America: Popular Culture and the War on Traditional Values*, provides evidence that a revulsion with violence is already taking place, and the entertainment industry will have to change its ways or lose its audience.[3] Even the much ballyhooed "violence warning notices," proposed by the networks and the entertainment community to advise viewers of problematical program content, do little more than provide a band-aid solution to what many consider an arterial bleeder problem. Faith in the entertainment community's ability to self-regulate notwithstanding, in time, stricter federal regulation will likely be called for.

Combine this state of affairs with the fact that television has lost its novelty—nobody watches puppies in a box anymore—and the fact that a new generation of Nintendo-playing, *MTV*-watching, channel-surfing kids is coming of age and the message is clear: there's no way traditional, entertainment-based programming can effectively load up forty channels, let alone five hundred.

The fact is, television has become so pervasive because it distracts, relaxes, and amuses us at very little cost and with very little effort. The problem is stagnation. Nothing is happening. Cable, by aping network programming, has reached saturation. Subscribers to pay cable channels have subscribed; nobody else seems to want on the bandwagon. Pay-Per-View has come to be viewed as an expensive yawner. Every new television season seems to bring us more of less. In short, we're bored.

Yet there are signs, even today, that the entertainment-based paradigm is beginning to shift. It has begun, as always, with the appearance of anomalies. The first was *Spring in Spring Hill* for General Motors' Saturn. And there have been others.

❖ ENDNOTES

1. *Life-styles America, 1990s,* (Long Island City, NY: Alert Publishing, Inc., 1991).

2. Rolf Meyerson, "Social Research in Television," from *Mass Culture: The Popular Arts in America* (The Free Press of Glencoe, 1957, Bernard Rosenberg and David White, eds.).

3. Michael Medved, *Hollywood vs. America: Popular Culture and the War on Traditional Values* (New York: HarperCollins, 1992).

9

ANOMALIES:
SIGNS OF THE SHIFT

American musical theater began with the minstrel shows of the ante bellum period. Up until then, what little theater was available appealed to the few, not the many. In the late eighteenth century, just before the disciplined and rigid Victorians led the attack on the bawdy freedom of the Restoration movement, theatergoers were treated to fare ranging from the classics of Shakespeare to the comedies of Sheridan and Fletcher. In those days, theater was for the few, not the many.

Then along came Christie's Minstrels, a happy-go-lucky amalgam of slave music and broad, corny, often racist jokes and routines performed by Mr. Bones and Mr. Interlocutor, white men in blackface speaking in Negro dialect. Christie's Minstrels were an anomaly, something totally unique, something that went against everything that had gone on before. Suddenly theater became popular, leading to the formation of more minstrel shows that traveled the length and breadth of the land. Where thousands had attended theaters before, now millions in big cities and small towns alike flocked to see the minstrels in theaters and on riverboats in both the North and the

South. In the 1840s, Edwin Christie the impresario met a young composer named Stephen Foster and paid him a few dollars for a tune he had written, a silly little ditty called "Oh, Susannah." Within months the whole nation was whistling the tune. Christie's Minstrels had become the nation's first mass entertainment medium. For the next several years, Christie proceeded to rip off the rights to Foster's greatest songs. Foster died young and impoverished prior to the Civil War, while troops of both persuasions sang his sentimental songs around their campfires.

For a century, the minstrel-type revue was the archetype of American musical theater. The format—touching solos, big production numbers, jokes, and stories—evolved. Eventually, blackface disappeared. The Ziegfeld Follies were essentially an amalgam of the minstrel shows without the racism, and with more glorified production and comedy numbers. Still, the Follies were a revue, a sequence of individual star acts from Eva Tanguay to Will Rogers interspersed with lavish production numbers featuring the scantily clad, statuesque Ziegfeld Girls. On occasion, the revue pattern was broken with a fully plotted production. Operettas like Sigmund Romberg's *Student Prince* and Franz Lehar's *The Merry Widow* became popular among the upper classes. On the popular stage, shows like Jerome Kern's *Show Boat* combined plot and music. Yet because the plots of these musicals seemed built around the songs, they were still reminiscent of the old minstrel show. Songs like Kern's "Old Man River," haunting and lovely as it is, did little to advance the plot of *Show Boat*.

Thus, for a century, musical theater resembled musical theater of the past. Then came the night of March 31, 1943. The crowd of first-nighters filled Broadway's St. James Theater to overflowing. The pit band finished the overture, then fell silent. The curtain opened to reveal an old woman churning butter on the porch of a farmhouse. From somewhere offstage came the deep baritone voice of John Raitt (yes, Bonnie's father).

> There's a bright golden haze on the meadow;
> There's a bright golden haze on the meadow;
> The corn is as high as an elephant's eye,
> And it looks like it's climbin' clear up to the sky.

The audience was confused. Where was the big production number to open the show? Was this a play or a musical? It was quickly evident that the song, "Oh, What a Beautiful Morning," was setting up a story. It was performing a sort of opening monologue, only instead of being spoken it was being sung. The show ended with a standing ovation, curtain call after curtain call. And the critics loved it as much as the audience. Composer Richard Rodgers with his new partner, lyricist Oscar Hammerstein, had a hit on their hands.

The play *Oklahoma!* was an anomaly in musical theater. It wasn't a revue, but rather a story with a definite plot, like conventional drama, except that parts of the plot were presented musically. Rodgers and Hammerstein, of course, followed up with similar productions from *Carousel* to *The King and I*. Their success encouraged others to follow until today, with few exceptions, all American musical theater fits the musical-play pattern. As so often happens, the anomaly has become the norm.

❖ ON THE NATURE OF CHANGE

Skip Weitzen in his book, *Hypergrowth,* explains the significance of the anomaly not in show business terms, but in strictly business terms.[1] He defines hypergrowth as the act of capitalizing on an abnormally high rate of growth for a period of a decade or more. Furthermore, he contends that hypergrowth doesn't normally just happen; it is a process that must be understood, anticipated, and carefully orchestrated.

The first step is understanding the norm. One must be thoroughly steeped in the culture of the existing state of any business or industry. It is only then, Weitzen says, that we can recognize an anomaly when we see one. In other words, if we don't understand the norm, how can we recognize something that doesn't conform to it? Anomalies come in two forms: those created when the market changes on its own, thereby creating a new demand, and those created when a new product drives market change. Among the examples cited by Weitzen is that of Compaq, which in just eight years grew to become a giant with annual sales of $2.9 billion. In the case of Compaq, the anomaly was created by a new product: a truly portable computer. The product itself was capable of driving the market change which would then create a demand. Rod Canion, the founder of Compaq, realized that the ability to take a computer home after work would have so much appeal to so many people that the ensuing demand would support a new industry niche. The next job was to get shelf space for portables in the dealerships. One tactic he used to accomplish this was to hire the sales manager of IBM's PC team. Very quickly revenues from portables outstripped revenues from both mainframes and minis, and as the first and biggest player in the new portable market, Compaq reaped the biggest benefits.

How do you spot an anomaly? Because they're something new, they're also news. They are written up in newspapers and trade/industry magazines. Weitzen suggests looking for certain key phrases that may indicate the emergence of an anomaly, phrases such as

> "For the first time . . ."
>
> "In an unusual turn of events . . ."
>
> "In an unprecedented move . . ."
>
> "A unique situation . . ."

If you've spent much time reading lately, from the national news magazines to TV/cable, and advertising industry trade magazines, you have seen such phrases associated with infomercials, documercials, direct response television, and other uses of the media that fly in the face of the strictly entertainment archetype. And those who properly read the signs, who correctly analyze the direction of this fluid situation, and who act on it stand to experience hypergrowth in the decade ahead.

❖ THE SHIFT TO TELEVISION

The first great paradigm shift in commercial broadcasting was, of course, the advent of television in a radio world. Not just television—that had been around almost as long as radio; rather, it was the advent of *affordable* television that drove the market change. Individuals and corporations who correctly read the situation—who had spotted the earlier anomalies—were poised to earn millions, and many of them did. The networks shifted to television with ease, as did most of the radio set manufacturers who soon shifted production to accommodate the demands for affordable sets. Individual fortunes were also made by aggressive television set retailers who had the wisdom to advertise their products on, of all things, television. Eccentrics like the redoubtable Mad Man Muntz pleaded with viewers to hurry down and buy a set because "when my wife sees the price tags on these sets she'll think I'm crazy, and I'll have to raise them. So don't wait!"

But despite the changes wrought by television on society, one thing hadn't changed: television, like radio, was considered primarily—overwhelmingly—an entertainment medium. For more than forty years, this has been the archetypal way of looking at television. It was the reason we bought our first sets in 1948, and it was the reason we subscribed to cable in 1981. And it's the reason why most proposals aimed at satisfying the requirements of a five-hundred-channel world remain entertainment based. Among the channels either existing or proposed are a *Cartoon Channel, History TV Network, Sega Channel, Sci-Fi Channel, Crime Channel, Military Channel, The Talk Channel, How-to Channel, Romance Classics*, and *TV Macys*.

The problem with such approaches is, as always, the availability, or rather lack of availability, of programming. At first glance it might seem that there is plenty of existing programming for, say, a *Sci-Fi Channel*. It might begin with Georges Melies's 1902 film *A Trip to the Moon*; then offer the episodic serials of the 1930s featuring the adventures of Buck Rogers and Flash Gordon; and the kinescopes of early live television sci-fi programs like *Captain Video* and *Tom Corbett, Space Cadet*, and *BEM* (Bug-Eyed Monster); films of the 1950s and 1960s such as *The Creature from the Black Lagoon* and *The Blob*; television series from *Star Trek* to *The Outer Limits*; black-and-white classics like *Them, The Thing*, and *Invasion of the Body Snatchers*; modern classics like *2,001: A Space Odyssey* and *Star Wars*; and even the film most critics consider the worst movie ever made, Ed Wood's incredible affront to the cinema industry, *Plan 9 from Outer Space*.

Put all that end to end, run it twenty-four hours a day and how long can it last? Two months? Three months? Six months, even? Even taking the generous figure, six months, the problem is clear. Repetition. Even the most avid science fiction buff will see everything he cares to see in a year, maybe two. Of course the channel might innovate with interviews with authors and stars, the Ray Bradburys, Steven Spielbergs, Leonard Nimoys, William Shatners, and Patrick Stewarts. But the fact is, the longevity of such a channel depends less on new programming than on new fans coming into the market. It's the same problem faced by the other single-interest entertainment channels from *Crime* to *Military*. This is not to condemn these channels; new buffs are constantly entering the genre, and new material is always being generated, however slowly. And there just aren't many such single-interest themes that can attract the kinds of audiences even these channels attract—certainly not five hundred channels worth. What these channels truly represent are more of the same. And even if we manage to viably fill a hundred channels with entertainment programming of various kinds, which is doubtful, we still have a lot of channels going begging. And as we noted in Chapter 3, with the percentage of the American public interested in patronizing Video-On-Demand (2 percent), it's hard to fathom the cable industry's prediction of four hundred plus movie channels.

So the question becomes, where do we look for new programming? Easy. We look for anomalies. We look for headlines and articles using words like "new," "unique," "for the very first time," and "recently announced." These articles began to appear in the mid-1980s, talking about a strange new kind of commercial called infomercials, commercials designed to look like conventional entertainment programming. Exhibiting the same confusion felt by the audiences watching the cowboy, Curly, sing the opening number to *Oklahoma!* we asked ourselves questions. Is it a program or a commercial? Why is it so long? Where did that studio audience come from, and why are they applauding so much? Isn't that Martin Sheen? What's a big star like Martin Sheen doing in a 30-minute commercial?

But in the manner of twentieth-century man, people whose experiences embrace both Kitty Hawk and the Sea of Tranquillity, we adjusted quickly to this curious new thing. So quickly, in fact, that when

GM's documercial *Spring in Spring Hill* was shown, we recognized it as still another anomaly. Comparing it to the "conventional" infomercial—it was as if they'd been around for decades—we asked more questions. Is it a commercial or a documentary? If it's a commercial, what are they selling, exactly? And if it's an infomercial, why is it so expensively produced? Where are the phone numbers? Why aren't they asking me to send money, or call in for something? It seemed for all the world like another anomaly. There was more to come.

❖ OH, WHAT A BEAUTIFUL MORNING: THE DAWN OF MARKETING CHANNELS

Early in 1993, The Providence (R.I.) Journal Company announced *The Television Food Network*, scheduled to begin operation before, appropriately enough, the Thanksgiving holiday. Not technically a network, a channel actually, *TVFN* was designed from the start to appeal to gourmet and gourmand alike. Among the programming ideas discussed: celebrity cooking shows, recipe programs, recipe reviewers, live call-in shows, discussions and demonstrations on food and health plus a weekly half-hour show called *How to Feed Your Family on $75 a Week*. *TVFN* believes that it is the perfect environment for food advertisers, who constitute a multibillion-dollar annual advertising budget. Like the *Sci-Fi Channel* (even more so), *TVFN* has a problem finding adequate programming to fill a twenty-four-hour channel. Initial planning includes the idea of running the same eight hours of programming three times a day. One can't help but feel the success of *TVFN* is problematical. Still, it's an interesting idea, and another anomaly.

Another interesting idea, mentioned earlier in Chapter 7, comes from The Syndication Group which offers *Mac Today*, introduced late in 1992 (see Figure 9-1). Aimed at "the Mac person and non-Mac person alike," these programs include "cutting-edge subjects of interest such as virtual reality, desktop publishing, video, medical applications, human interest stories, celebrity user and company profiles, product reviews, and current Mac-related news." To distribute the programs, the Group came up with a novel idea: subscribers

Figure 9-1

A Series in Search of a Channel

This unusual ad offers a series of Macintosh short subjects; readers are urged to participate in a movement aimed at convincing cable channel operators to dedicate time to them. (Courtesy The Syndication Group.)

to CompuServe were invited to visit The Syndication Group on-line. Then, "If you cannot find us on a local station, E-MAIL us and we can explain how you or your group can assist us with affiliating with a TV station in your area."

And, finally, another promising anomaly: an article in *Mediaweek* quotes GM advertising head Phil Guarascio as saying, "We're going from in-your-face marketing to down-your-throat marketing. We need to get up close and personal with the people buying our products."[2] He went on to announce that GM was developing a long-form video brochure for distribution to consumers. (Obviously, this video brochure could easily serve as a televised infomercial . . . *if* there were a cost-efficient place to air it. A place, perhaps, like *The Car Buyer's Channel*.) Apparently even traditional-minded giants like General Motors are reassessing their advertising methodology.

❖ *E!*—EVOLUTION!

Throughout this book, we have insisted that entertainment-based programming cannot possibly be created fast enough or good enough to fill five hundred channels. Instead, we have suggested that information-based marketing channels offer the most logical programming addition to entertainment. Which makes it all the more ironic that the closest thing we have to a single-interest marketing channel today is *E!*, whose single interest is—you guessed it—entertainment.

E! is a revamped version of a channel called *Movietime*, launched in 1987 as a movie-trailer service. For a number of reasons, *Movietime* was a money loser from the get-go. Four cable companies bought in at the beginning, but the fact remained the channel was seriously undercapitalized. To make matters worse, *Movietime* didn't receive any per subscriber revenues from MSOs, a situation remedied, too late, in 1990. The channel relied on advertisers for revenue flow, and advertisers were slow in coming. Despite this faltering start (or perhaps because of it), *Movietime*'s franchise, movie trailers, was soon expanded to include television promotion. Several other ventures were spun off the channel, including a magazine, but within three years it was clear that *Movietime* was floundering.

Enter *HBO*, which assumed management control in return for a tidy $45 million shot in the arm, and set out on a complete makeover. The transition team consisted mainly of three bright youngsters: Sheri Herman, 35, retained from *Movietime*'s staff; Fran Shea, 32, brought in from *HBO*; and as president and chief executive, 38-year-old Lee Masters, one of the guiding lights behind *MTV*. In fewer than six months an entirely new format was in place, subject to experimentation, but with plenty of thinking behind it. The program parts were split into hours, with news at the top and various programming segments following. These segments came and went for about a year, as research determined which ones were working and which weren't. Segments today provide a wide, constantly changing look at the entire world of entertainment, not just movies and television, but theater and music as well. Viewers are treated to interviews with movie, rock, and country-western stars, interspersed with programming such as behind-the-scenes action on movie sets, plus features on soap opera plotting or what's been really embarrassing on this week's daytime TV talk shows. A careful balance is maintained between news and celebrity gossip. Celebrities, it is felt, may stop the channel surfers momentarily, but it's news that keeps them coming back. Presenters and interviewers on *E!* are bright, cool, smooth. Perhaps the key to the differences between *Movietime* and *E!* is the amount and type of advertisers the channel attracts. One of Lee Masters's first directives explained that the channel would no longer accept advertising for products like contour chairs and hearing aids, red ink be damned. Today, advertisers on *E!* completely reflect their new demographics—young, active, acquisitive.

E! has many of the characteristics of a marketing channel. Most obvious, perhaps, is its emphasis on information. The fact is, of course, much of the information on *E!* is entertaining, due to its subject matter, but as Lee Masters says, "Famous faces will make people feel good about the network, but information is what keeps them coming back." Another similarity between *E!* and a marketing channel is the wide variety of related programming available on the channel.

The difference between the two is one of commercial involvement. Someone viewing *E!* is involved, all right, but in the program segments, not the commercials or film promotions. Or at least not much. Despite the fact that everyone complains about the price of movie theater tickets, they aren't exactly a considered purchase. Nor are most of the advertised products on the channel—chewing gum, soft drinks, blue jeans, cosmetics, and so on. In this respect, *E!* is no different from the networks of old: the programming is expected to attract and keep the audience watching, while the commercials are necessary, but not necessarily appreciated. On marketing channels, due to the fact that they advertise high-involvement, big-ticket, considered-purchase items, it is the commercials themselves that attract and hold the audience. For the first time—more of those words indicating an anomaly—the commercials *become* the programming, not the other way round.

❖ PROFILE OF A MARKETING CHANNEL

To achieve "must carry" status from the FCC, a channel's programming content must be "in the public interest;" described as offering "news, public information or diversity." The elements that make up a marketing channel are, not surprisingly, based on the needs of the market and more than satisfy the FCC criteria. For purposes of illustration, let's take a look at the market we'll be serving through Channel 397, *The Car Buyer's Channel.* Research tells us that at any given time one out of every three Americans has car buying on his or her mind. Interestingly, women today actually buy more new cars than do men. So, borrowing a technique from Marketing 101, let's draw a single-individual profile to represent the entire market. In other words, as marketers of *The Car Buyer's Channel,* who, exactly, are we talking to? And what do they currently think/feel/believe about buying cars?

Our prospect is a recently divorced working woman with a school-age child at home. Her job, while it pays well, takes more of her time and attention than she'd like. She feels a little guilty about not spending what she feels is the proper amount of quality time with her child. She is a cable subscriber and occasionally shops from catalogs. Her only experience in buying a car came shortly after her marriage when she accompanied her husband from showroom to showroom, through the process of wheeling and dealing until the transaction was finally concluded. It is not a fond memory. Now she faces the prospect of buying a new car alone. Like most Americans, she is not looking forward to the experience. She has conducted a miniresearch survey among her officemates to determine relative costs, compare appearances, and catalog likes and dislikes. She has three or four models in mind. And while she doesn't know much about cars, and dreads the time all this will take away from her already-crowded schedule, she is determined not to let some slick car salesman rip her off.

That's not all we know about her, of course. For example, we know she shares characteristics in common with others in her age and income group.

- We know that the greatest scarcity she feels is not money, but time.
- We know that, to her, convenience is more of a necessity than a luxury.
- We know she is likely to have ordered merchandise out of catalogs or in response to call-in television.
- We know she is less impressed with a bargain price than with value, which she defines as the best quality for the least cost.
- In the face of more new products and too many choices, we know she is a "brand buyer," placing her confidence in the familiar rather than buying from strangers.
- We know she places great store in reliability and service.
- We know she is sophisticated in the ways of the world, especially regarding shopping, advertising, the media, and hype.

Put in terms of car buying, what she really wants is

1. to make an educated buy of the best quality/value car
2. in the most convenient and efficient manner
3. in the least amount of time
4. for the smallest amount of money

Automobile retailing today offers none of the above. Making an educated buy on something as complex as a new car is a time-consuming process, which involves research in special interest car magazines as well as automobile editions of magazines like *Consumer Reports*. As for the shopping process itself, shoppers must spend literally days going from dealership to dealership, talking to salespeople, test-driving cars, watching videos on selected models and features, and reading product literature. Rather than feeling good about getting the best value, the customary price haggling leaves us confused and wondering. Even "one-price" buying is failing to simplify the process, since most consumers (58 percent) feel they're not getting the best possible deal. In terms of fun ways to spend your time, our busy working mother ranks buying a car right up there with dental surgery.

Given all that, how does the programming on Channel 397 meet those marketplace needs? Let's take a look at the kind of programming our busy mother might find on *The Car Buyer's Channel*.

1. Product-Specific Long-Form Commercials

Long-form commercials designed to highlight either a single model or a full brand offering will play an important role on *The Car Buyer's Channel*. The 30-minute format allows advertisers to explain fully even the most complicated features, advantages, and benefits. These commercials take the place of the knowledgeable salesperson, perhaps with a great deal more credibility and certainly with more consistency as far as message is concerned.

Another advantage these commercials offer the advertiser is an opportunity to get your model on the viewer's short list. Since watching a long-form commercial requires little time and no effort, viewers who wouldn't take the trouble to seek out the local dealership and kick the tires are more likely to move the car from the "no way" category to the "worth a look" category.

Finally, because these commercials do double duty as a dealership point-of-sale item, production costs can be amortized. They are something the advertiser needs anyway, and putting them on Channel 397 represents a simple usage extension.

Product-specific commercials offer the car buyer an alternative to the time-consuming shopping process, satisfying the need for

convenience. They provide viewers with a no-effort, no-commit-
ment, no-gas-and-no-shoe-leather way to shop. Instead of running
all over town, prospective buyers can sit in their easy chairs and get
the lowdown on every car on or off their short lists without confess-
ing their ignorance to a car salesman. Once they've narrowed (or
expanded) their choices, *then* they can go test drive the contenders.

2. Brand/Corporate Image Long-Form Commercials

Saturn, Volvo, and Volkswagen were pioneers in the documercial,
and given the car buyer's penchant for brand buying, the documercial is likely to become an important part of the programming day.
As Ries and Trout pointed out in their landmark treatise *Positioning:
The Battle For Your Mind*,[3] and again in their latest work, *The 22
Immutable Laws of Marketing*,[4] communication of your product position is crucial. And the long-form commercial is an ideal vehicle for
making your brand the benchmark against which your competitors
are measured. The authors cite the safety-oriented documercial produced by Volvo as a part of its ongoing positioning campaign; at this
writing, when it comes to safety, Volvo owns the franchise. To
safety-minded consumers, Volvo comes first to mind, and is the
benchmark against which all other cars are compared. Volvo's infomercial has reportedly accrued over 29,000 dealer leads. Given the
effectiveness of the long-form commercial in communicating a
product's position, these documercials will comprise the marketing
programming seen on Channel 397.

3. News

In today's automotive world, things are changing constantly. Prices
fluctuate, rollbacks and rebates come and go, engineering and design
groups come up with innovations, recalls are issued, lawsuits are
instituted and settled. *The Car Buyer's Channel* will cover the industry
on a daily basis with complete reports and updates.

In addition to providing listeners with the latest information
and news on price changes, deals, and rebates, the programming can
help satisfy the viewer's sense of value, defined as the best quality
at the fairest price.

4. Model-to-Model Comparisons

One of the objectives of *The Car Buyer's Channel* is to serve as a sort of *Consumer Reports* magazine. Every year when new models come out, the automotive press conducts comparison tests within category groups. Throughout the year, comprehensive road testing of individual models provides viewers with objective, third-party information. By making arrangements, or buying out these independent testing units, the results of these comparisons will be broadcast in detail on Channel 397.

Again, such programming allows the viewer to comparison-shop from an easy chair, without the deliberately confusing competitive chatter of anything-but-objective car salesmen. Imagine the appeal this kind of programming has for our working mother with her limited knowledge and a strong determination not to get ripped off. Research that would have taken weeks of digging and reading is all there, with the results made clear.

5. Interviews and Talk Shows

Any major industry is driven by and surrounded by remarkable, charismatic individuals and the automobile industry is certainly no exception. Americans like industry spokesmen Lee Iacocca and Phil Guarascio (GM) and industry critic Ralph Nader have their counterparts in Europe and the Far East. And what about the people who design and build our automobiles? Lawyers, politicians, stunt men and women, safety experts, economists, environmentalists, test drivers, futurists, racing drivers, anyone who has anything to do with the course of the industry is a candidate for a Channel 397 interview.

The importance of corporations talking about their goals and aspirations cannot be overstated. The 1990s consumers have made it clear that they not only want to know more about the products they are buying but also about the companies making the products. Are they environmentally responsible? Testing products on animals? Depleting natural resources or exploiting a Third World country? Or are they giving a portion of their profits to a worthy cause? Recycling wastes? Donating products to the homeless? Today, who you are is

as important as what you make. Today's consumers want to patronize corporations that are good world citizens.

Again, this kind of programming helps satisfy the curiosity of
the educated, affluent 1990s car buyer. It helps in the formation of
better-educated decisions.

6. Short-Form Commercials and Direct Response Offers

Long-form commercials are generally constructed with two or three
120-second inserts where advertisers can run short-form commercials or immediate call-in offers. On *The Car Buyer's Channel*, these
offers might include product brochures, price-saving coupons, con-
test and sweepstakes information, free-goods offers, anything the
promotional mind can conceive. Also, these inserts might be offered
to local dealers or regional dealer organizations for market promotions. Other commercials would be sold in the news and talk show
segments for car-related products such as insurance, rustproofing,
aftermarket products and services, security alarms, tires, motor oil,
or whatever appeals to industry media buyers.

7. Miscellaneous Programming

Just as *E!* conducts ongoing experiments and testing of new programming ideas, it is logical that *The Car Buyer's Channel* will do the
same. Thinking up these ideas is a game anyone can play. For
example, what about a program on *Blue Book* pricing of used cars as
a guide to how well various models hold their resale value? Or how
about comparison shows on such things as radios/CDs/tape players, cellular phones, tires, and warranties? What about programs
explaining the ins and outs of financing plans? Or call-in shows on
specific topics or specific brands or models? Or a consumer panel
show covering topics from "How do you like your new car?" to
"What do you like most/least about your local dealer?" Or how
about a sitcom format explaining how to deal with commonly used,
but possibly unethical ploys of car salespeople or auto repair mechanics. The possibilities are endless.

❖ FORCING CHANGE: THE REAL EFFECT OF MARKETING CHANNELS

Does such programming scare off potential advertisers? On the contrary, such programming challenges automobile marketers to improve their product, improve their service, clean up their act at the dealership level, and make themselves competitive. The fact is, the basic format for automobile retailing was established early in the century when brand choices were limited, model selection was often nonexistent, and there was no such thing as an extra. Henry Ford was once urged to offer his famous Model T in a variety of colors. After all, it was the world's first truly mass-produced and mass-marketed motor car, so color selection seemed an obvious extra to offer. Ford replied that people could buy the Model T in any color they liked . . . as long as it was black. Today's manufacturers cannot afford such arrogance.

It was also a more leisurely era, a time when bargaining was an accepted part of retailing, when doctors made house calls and were occasionally paid off with a country ham or a crate of chickens. People who could afford the luxury of an automobile could afford to take all the time in the world to buy it. It was a time when nobody worked on Sundays.

Through the years, as brands, models, features, and extras proliferated, the industry continued to take advantage of the public's inability to keep up. This growing ignorance of the product was met by what can only be called arrogance on the part of the industry. The market changed—where car buying was once the exclusive province of men, it isn't anymore. Yet the process of buying a car hasn't changed since 1910.

Despite the fact that our working mother has no time, is overwhelmed by brand and model choices as well as a vast array of extras, and is tormented by the idea that somehow she is going to come out on the short end of the cost-price stick . . . despite all this she is forced to drive from showroom to showroom, deal with a confusing cadre of salespeople each with a completely different set of facts, and then must either spend uncomfortable hours haggling or simply pay the clearly inflated going rate just to get it over with.

And to top it all off, on the one day when she has a little extra time, Sunday, the showrooms are closed.

The Car Buyer's Channel answers the needs of the market. Long-form commercials provide a clearer, more consistent alternative to salespeople. And because they're on television the credibility factor greatly increases, as has been borne out by two recent studies conducted by Opinion Research Corporation.[5] The first study found that when asked to rank the mass media in terms of believability, Americans ranked television first (34 percent), newspapers second (31 percent), magazines third (13 percent), radio fourth (5 percent), and direct mail last (3 percent). Ironically, consumers also ranked television as the most annoying medium (47 percent), ranking even higher than direct mail (23 percent).

The second report indicates that advertising itself is becoming more believable. Since 1973, the believability of advertising rose from just 51 percent of respondents to a 1989 figure of 62 percent. During the same period, the number of respondents who considered advertising unbelievable fell from 47 percent to 35 percent.

Clearly, objective third-party programming helps determine which features are really important, strengths and weaknesses of brands/models, a certain amount of pricing and financing information, plus advice on how to cope with today's archaic retailing system. In short, the marketing channel helps the viewer beat the system by playing a smarter game. All one needs is a programming schedule and a VCR.

❖ SCHEDULING: MANY PUZZLES, MANY SOLUTIONS

Just as the development of individual programs is a game anyone can play, so is the development of schedules. A full selection of marketing channels will doubtless feature a variety of scheduling formats. Using *The Car Buyer's Channel* as an example, a number of possibilities present themselves. With all the choices available in the automotive spectrum, some kind of scheduling organization is required to help viewers sort out what they're looking for from what they're not.

One way to accomplish this is by dedicating a number of channels, each dealing with a different automotive category. Earlier we mentioned *The Luxury Car Channel* and *The Truck and Van Channel.* Another possibility is a category-a-day arrangement with, for example, "Cars Under $15,000" on Monday, "Cars $15,000–30,000" on Tuesdays, "Cars $30,000+" on Wednesday, "Vans and Campers" on Thursday, "Minivans" on Friday, and so on. Obviously, research and testing is needed to put this intriguing puzzle together, and clearly the solution for *The Car Buyer's Channel* will be different from that used by *The Computer Buyer's Channel.*

One thing we know for sure: scheduling must be solidified and made available to the potential viewer. We already know that the life-style of today's consumers puts a premium on time. That's one reason why more than 80 percent of these affluent cable viewers own VCRs. They will not sit through twelve hours of automotive programming. Most of them will have developed a list of possibilities with certain brands/models listed as "must see," others listed as "take a look," and still others as "dark horses." This type of prospective buyer has absolutely no interest in looking at anything else. If her budget calls for a $15,000 car, she is certainly not interested in looking at a Lincoln Town Car or a BMW. Probably, her list now totals fewer than ten cars. What she wants is to view and or tape only information about those ten. To do that she needs a schedule to find programming appropriate to her budget, tastes, and brand preferences.

❖ HOW TO FIND *THE CAR BUYER'S CHANNEL*

As interactive technology becomes prevalent later in this decade, such schedules will be easy to access. Marketing channels, indeed all cable channels, will be equipped with a "navigator" that will take seekers to whichever categories interest them. It will be a process as easy as following the steps in a computer menu. But for now, scheduling will have to be handled as current technology allows. Schedules will probably be broadcast at the top of the hour. Printed schedules might be made available at car dealerships or other automotive outlets—garages, tire stores, discount stores with automotive departments, franchised muffler and transmission stores, and so on. In return for television exposure, automotive magazines like *Car and Driver* and *Motor Trend* would probably be interested in publishing these schedules. During new car introduction periods or special price promotion periods, industry advertisers from the home office in Detroit or Tokyo to the local dealer organization might be advised to put schedules in magazines like *TV Guide, People, Time,* and so on. Local radio announcements might team up with local newspaper ads in proximity to TV schedules or next to local dealership ads. Finally, the cable companies themselves have a big stake in making marketing channels successful. They should provide cross-channel avails; that is, they should run commercials for *The Car Buyer's Channel* on other channels—"Tune in Channel 397 Sunday morning for the latest in minivans and campers"—not a bad idea, placed in a camping or fishing show on *The Discovery Channel.* Cable channels should also publish schedules in monthly cable magazines or mail them along with the monthly statement.

❖ How Does the Channel Make Money?

Actually, the marketing channel makes money in exactly the same way as any other commercial television channel: by selling time to local, regional, national, and international advertisers. Time for long-form commercials will be paid by national and international sponsors out of annual advertising budgets. This programming has the potential to draw local and regional dealer organizations as well as national advertisers of peripheral products from tires to insurance.

Much of the activity on *The Car Buyer's Channel* will be directed toward promotion of local dealers. This will likely be in the form of direct response commercials built around events and price promotions. If, for example, the Chicago Area Oldsmobile Dealers were featuring a "Rebate Month," what better advertising tool than a long-form commercial promoting the latest model Olds? The same holds true of single-dealer events such as tent days or a showing in a mall parking lot.

The fact is, *marketing channels offer cable operators a rich, new source of commercial sales,* which is why they should be offered free and included as part of the local channel's basic cable service. Marketing channels contribute to the local food chain. They offer local advertisers from car dealers to computer distributors an attractive new advertising alternative. As we have seen, a marketing channel like *The Car Buyer's Channel* is more than just a new kind of television, it's a new kind of retailing, a kind of retailing, moreover, that more comfortably fits the life-style of today's busy, affluent consumer.

So far, we've used the automotive industry to demonstrate how marketing channels might work. But of course there are other industries capable of supporting channels of their own. Fifteen others, for starters.

❖ ENDNOTES

1. H. Skip Weitzen, *Hypergrowth: Applying the Success Formula of Today's Fastest Growing Companies* (New York: John Wiley & Sons, 1991).

2. Phil Guarascio, GM will bypass media with direct-to-consumer video, *Mediaweek*, March 30, 1992.

3. Al Ries and Jack Trout, *Positioning: The Battle for Your Mind* (New York: Warner Books, McGraw-Hill, 1986).

4. Al Ries and Jack Trout, *The 22 Immutable Laws of Marketing: Violate Them at Your Own Risk* (New York: HarperCollins, 1993).

5. Opinion Research Corporation, as cited in *Media Matters*, May 1990.

10

THE SWEET SIXTEEN:
BEYOND *THE CAR BUYER'S* *CHANNEL*

In addition to the automotive industry, what other industries make good candidates for marketing channels? To qualify, four criteria should ideally be met:

1. It must be an industry that spends enough on advertising to make the channel viable.

2. It must be an industry that produces high-involvement, considered-purchase products/services.

3. It must produce products/services that need to be renewed or replaced periodically so that there will always be buyers in the market.

4. The existing retailing system must pose life-style–related problems for prospective buyers.

Applied to the full spectrum of American business, sixteen industries emerge as viable candidates. The first eight (see Figure 10-1) match up to the criteria just listed in either three or four respects. The second eight (see Figure 10-2) don't necessarily fit the established format in all respects, but in one, current ad budgets, they are so formidable they must be considered candidates. In each case we have included the top advertisers in the category only. Figures shown here are taken from *AdWeek's* 1992 supplement "Superbrands: America's Top 2,000 Brands." For a complete list of advertisers and budgets, see the appendix.

Figure 10-1

The First Eight Industries That Make Good Candidates for Marketing Channels

Planned Major Purchases of Baby Boomers*

	Current Ad Budgets (all categories - in millions)
47.1% Vacation/Travel	$ 1,797
38.8% Furniture/Home Furnishings	259
37.6% Car/Truck	4,370
29.5% Home Appliances	302
25.3% Jewelry/Watches	59
24.8% Stereo Equipment	+
24.5% TV/VCR	342
21.5% Computers/Computer Products	595

© 1993 AdWeek Magazine L.P.

Impact Resources - 1991

* Percentage of 100,000+ 24-44 year olds responding "yes, probably, undecided" to "intend to purchase within the next year."

These eight industries have large advertising budgets, market products/services of some complexity, enjoy a great deal of market turnover due to the need for replacement, and in some cases, present a retailing challenge to the average consumer. Courtesy Impact Resources and © 1993 *AdWeek L.P.* used by permission of *AdWeek*.

❖ 1. AUTOMOTIVE

Amount spent on advertising: $4,370,000,000

Those intending to purchase: 37.6 percent

Major Category Advertisers

Media Expenditures: $300–349.9 Million

Brand	Corporation
Chevrolet cars and trucks	General Motors Corp.
Ford cars and trucks	Ford Motor Co.
Toyota cars and trucks	Toyota Motor Sales USA, Inc.

Media Expenditures: $150–199.99 Million

Buick cars	General Motors Corp.
Dodge cars and trucks	Chrysler Corp.
Nissan cars and trucks	Nissan Motor Corp. USA

Media Expenditures: $100–149.9 Million

Acura cars	American Honda Motor Co., Inc.
Chrysler cars	Chrysler Corp.
Honda cars	American Honda Motor Co., Inc.
Mazda cars and trucks	Mazda Motor Corp.
Mitsubishi cars and trucks	Mitsubishi Corp.
Pontiac cars	General Motors Corp.

Industry Health and Direction

American manufacturers, having lost significant market share to foreign manufacturers in the 1980s, got their act together in the 1990s. By placing renewed emphasis on quality and significantly improving and updating manufacturing facilities, share erosion has been stopped and in some cases even reversed. At this writing, the two best-selling cars in the United States are Ford's Taurus and Honda's Accord. As an industry, automotive is extremely sensitive to the general economy.

The automotive industry fits all four criteria perhaps better than any other. Annual media expenditures for the category, including automobiles, vans, campers, motorcycles, and trucks, as well as peripheral advertisers such as tires, motor oil, and gasoline, total more than $4 billion. Clearly, automotive industry marketers aren't going to give up traditional advertising media and put everything into marketing channels. However, this is an industry that has traditionally put the lion's share of its budget into television advertising. Given this, it's not hard to imagine automobile companies and peripherals putting, say, an experimental investment of 20 percent of budget in a marketing channel. Twenty percent of $4 billion comes to $800 million. Every year. A tidy sum by any measurement.

As to the second criterion, we have already seen how brands and models have proliferated beyond the capacity of the average motorist to keep up. Back in the days of the shade tree mechanic, one's choice was limited to a car from one of the Big Three or a few off-brands like Studebaker, Packard, and Hudson. With the influx of foreign brands, beginning in the 1960s and continuing full force thirty years later, the picture has become more muddled than ever. Not even the most dedicated buff can keep them straight. The car buyer of today, perpetually short on time, simply has more choices than can be dealt with.

The third criterion—the need for periodic replacement—makes the automotive industry particularly adaptable to the marketing channel format. We know that at any given time, more than one out of every three Americans is either somewhat interested or already in the market and actively attending to automobile advertising. Does that mean marketing channels will give the entertainment-based channels a run for their money, ratingswise? Of course not. But what it does mean is that when a conventional 30- or 60-second automobile commercial airs on a network or cable show, two out of three Americans are completely uninterested. We also know that one out of three interested buyers are raiding the fridge, making a pitstop, or channel surfing to see what's on the other channels. It also means the closer our prospective buyers come to decision time, the more likely they will turn to the marketing channel for useful information. Remember, marketing channels don't promise to deliver ratings;

they promise an interested audience composed of people actively in the market. The "entertainment" value of the program is relative to the "information" the viewer is seeking. The audience selects itself; they know who they are and they know when they are ready to take advantage of the unique services of the marketing channel. Advertisers don't have to find them, hit or miss. They'll find the advertisers at precisely the right time. Right for them.

We have already dealt with the fourth criterion in detail. Few major industries have managed to operate for so long on such an archaic retailing system. If it ever fit the life-style of the century's first decade, it certainly doesn't fit the life-style of the century's last.

❖ 2. VACATION/TRAVEL

Amount spent on advertising: $1,797,000,000

Those intending to purchase: 47.1 percent

Major Category Advertisers

Media Expenditures: $100–149.9 Million

Brand	Corporation
American Airlines	American Airlines, Inc.
Delta Air Lines	Delta Air Lines, Inc.

Media Expenditures: $50–99.9 Million

Continental Airlines	Continental Airlines Corp.
United Airlines	United Airlines, Inc.

Media Expenditures: $25–49.9 Million

Alamo car rentals	Alamo Rent-a-car, Inc.
Amtrak passenger rail service	National RR Passenger Corp.
Avis car rentals	Avis, Inc.
Carnival Cruise Line	Carnival Cruise Lines, Inc.
Hertz car rentals	The Hertz Corp.
Holiday Inns	Holiday Corp.

Hyatt Hotels	Hyatt Hotels Corp.
Marriott hotels and resorts	Marriott Corp.
Northwest Airlines	Northwest Airlines, Inc.
Norwegian cruise line	Kloster Cruise Ltd.
Royal Caribbean cruise line	Royal Caribbean Cruises Ltd.
Southwest Airlines	Southwest Airlines Co.
TWA Airlines	Trans World Airlines, Inc.
USAir	USAir, Inc.

Industry Health and Direction

The recession of the early 1990s hit the travel industry hard. The wars of the airlines basically wiped out some of the weaker players and didn't help the stronger ones. Discount fares were snatched up by people who had planned to fly anyway, not new fliers. Hotel and motel occupancy rates flattened out at just above 60 percent. Car rental companies maintained, but only by raising prices. As the general economy improves, however, the industry seems to be turning around. The hotel business, for example, is up 11.8 percent from its recession low.

The most obvious reason to assign a marketing channel to this industry is its enormous renewability. At any given time, nearly half of all Americans are planning this year's vacation. And a few weeks after they get back to work, they start thinking about next year. As a result, the industry spends millions in advertising. And the product is the whole wide world.

One unique feature of this category, relevant to a marketing channel, is the availability of programming. There is not an island in the Caribbean, a state in the United States, a country in the world, or a cruise line in existence that doesn't have a battery of videotapes in its marketing arsenal. Such tapes may or may not be available at your travel agency, but even if they are, who wants to stand around the agency watching, or to take a tape home only to have to arrange to return it the next day? What you definitely will find at your travel agency is brochures. Hundreds, nay, thousands, of brochures. Unfortunately, the difference between a brochure and a video is as vast a gap as the difference between a video and actually being there. As with the auto industry, the travel industry is a natural marketing channel candidate.

Also, one has to believe a marketing channel will be a great boon to local travel agencies; all those marvelous videos, all those time-consuming decisions will be made at home, over time. Prospects will arrive at travel agencies with either their minds made up or their choices narrowed. In addition to destinations, the marketing channel for this industry will carry programming on specials, deals, and bargains. Probably no other industry has such constantly changing pricing variety as does travel. A marketing channel provides both travel agencies and consumers with quick-breaking deals on airline tickets, cruise costs, fly-drive deals, railroad tickets, hotel rates, and more.

NOTE: As of this writing, Landmark Communications is airing its own *Travel Channel*, acquired from TWA in 1991. *The Travel Channel*, as currently structured, bears no resemblance to a marketing channel. It is, in fact, based on conventional entertainment channels. For instance, it does not sell programming time: it creates its own programming and sells time in 30-, 60- and 120-second increments. There are no programs offering access to travel bargains such as airfares, hotel packages, or cruise tickets. And, finally, because cable MSOs are required to pay a fee to air *The Travel Channel*, it may become a pay service to subscribers in the future.

❖ 3. FURNITURE/HOME FURNISHINGS

Amount spent on advertising: $259,000,000

Those intending to purchase: 38.8 percent

Major Category Advertisers

Media Expenditures: $25–49.9 Million

Brand	Corporation
Ethan Allen home furnishings	Ethan Allen, Inc.
Stainmaster™ carpets	E. I. du Pont de Nemours & Co.

Media Expenditures: $15–24.9 Million

Contour™ lounge chairs	Craftmatic/Contour Industries
Craftmatic™ adjustable beds	Craftmatic/Contour Industries
Monsanto Wear-Dated™ carpets	Monsanto Co.

Media Expenditures: $10–14.9 Million

Armstrong flooring	Armstrong World Industries, Inc.
Lenox crystal and china	Lenox, Inc.
Sealy mattresses	Sealy Corp.

Media Expenditures: $5–9.9 Million

Corning cookware and dinnerware	Corning, Inc.
La-Z-Boy furniture	La-Z-Boy Chair Co.
Lane furniture	The Lane Company, Inc.
Lorus clocks	Seiko Time Corp.
Mannington resilient floors	Mannington Mills, Inc.
Ortho mattresses	Ortho Mattress, Inc.
Serta mattresses	Serta, Inc.
Simmons Beautyrest™ mattresses	Simmons Co.
Sleepy's mattresses	Sleepy's
Sun Valley waterbeds	Sun Valley Waterbeds
Thomasville furniture	Thomasville Furniture Inds, Inc.

Industry Health and Direction

The furniture industry lives on households, particularly affluent households—the more the better. Because of the predicted reduction in households resulting from the end of the baby boom, the industry will have to work harder to maintain its footing. The key to success in the next decade will lie in catering to baby boomers in their peak earning years, by appealing to their sense of value, meaning good quality for the money. The future looks bright.

U.S. households spend between $25 billion and $35 billion a year on furniture. A marketing channel has two things to offer this industry. First, it is an alternative to magazine advertising, furniture's traditional medium. Television has the potential to bring those still-photo magazine layouts to life. Second, television appeals to the very people who buy the most furniture. Householders under the age of 35 account for one-third of all furniture sales, with the average American spending $310 a year on home furnishings. But when you examine householders under the age of 35 with incomes of over $40,000—affluent cable viewers—that figure rises to $731 a year. The cable audience segment of the population accounts for only 6 percent of households but 13 percent of furniture spending. The figures are even better with householders 35 to 44 who account for almost one-fifth (19 percent) of total U.S. furniture sales. Staying with householders with incomes of $40,000 plus, we find average annual furniture sales of $688 in the years 44 to 55. Once the kids are finally out of the nest, Mom and Dad remodel or move to a small house, if they can afford it. It is not until after age 55 that furniture buying, and coincidentally cable involvement, begin to level off.

❖ 4. HOME APPLIANCES

Amount spent on advertising: $302,000,000

Those intending to purchase: 29.5 percent

Major Category Advertisers

Media Expenditures: $25–49.9 Million

Brand	Corporation
Dirt Devil™ vacuum cleaners	Royal Appliance Mfg. Co.

Media Expenditures: $15–24.9 Million

Braun home appliances	Braun, Inc.
GE appliances	General Electric Co.
General Electric corporate	General Electric Co.
Maytag appliances	Maytag Co.
Whirlpool appliances	Whirlpool Corp.
Windmere™ appliances	Whirlpool Corp.

Media Expenditures: $10–14.9 Million

Carrier air conditioning/ heating products	Carrier Corp.
Eureka vacuum cleaners	The Eureka Co.
Kitchenaid appliances	Kitchenaid, Inc.
Lennox air conditioning/ heating products	Lennox International, Inc.
Regina steamer/carpet cleaner	The Regina Company, Inc.
Trane heating and cooling systems	The Trane Co.

Media Expenditures: $5–9.9 Million

Bissell carpet cleaning system	Bissell, Inc.
Black & Decker appliances	Black & Decker Corp.
Dust Buster™ Power brush and vacuum	Black & Decker Corp.
First Alert™ home safety products	BRK Electronics
Frigidaire home appliances	Frigidaire Co.
Hoover vacuum cleaners	The Hoover Co.
Kenmore™ appliances	Sears, Roebuck & Co.
Magic Chef major appliances	Magic Chef Co.
Presto Saladshooter™	National Presto Industries, Inc.

Industry Health and Direction

The home appliance industry is on a roll. According to the Association of Home Appliance Manufacturers, refrigerator/freezers, washing machines, dryers, and humidifiers have enjoyed record sales every year in the 1990s. And December 1992 was the best quarter ever for ranges, dishwashers, washers, dryers, disposals, and refrigerator/freezers.

Appliances, like automobiles, fit all four of our criteria. The total category budget exceeds $300 million, much of it already committed to conventional television advertising. A proliferation of increasingly complex products puts the consumer at a disadvantage. All those choices serve to confuse prospects, causing them to fall back on brand preference, which is itself becoming risky. Today's global market has, as in the case of automobiles, virtually eliminated favorite old U.S.-made brands, which are now loaded with overseas components. Again, as with automobiles, obsolescence plays a role; nearly one out of three Americans is actively in the market at any given time. And, finally, an appliance marketing channel is a better shopping fit for today's life-style than the existing retail structure. With the help of tape decks and channel schedules, shoppers can comparison-shop from the comfort of their living rooms and work up their short lists before they head for the shopping centers or discount stores.

Given the vast differences in the category (washers and dryers, dishwashers, food processors, blenders, electric toothbrushes, hand mixers, coffee grinders, microwave ovens, stoves, refrigerators, freezers, toasters, can openers, etc.), a great deal of creativity will be required in programming for this channel. One imagines a need for shorter infomercials: while 30 minutes may be required to thoroughly preview a new Lincoln Town Car, the same cannot be said of a microwave, or even a food freezer. Perhaps the schedule will feature more 15-minute commercials. Another solution is to group appliances into logical clusters: coffee machines from hand grinders to espresso makers, laundry items, ranges of all kinds, and so on. One also imagines a great deal of comparison programming for the information-starved viewers of this product-filled channel.

❖ 5. JEWELRY/WATCHES

Amount spent on advertising: $59,000,000

Those intending to purchase: 25.3 percent

Major Category Advertisers

Media Expenditures: $15–24.9 Million

Brand	Corporation
Seiko watches and clocks	Seiko Time Corp.

Media Expenditures: $10–14.9 Million

Swatch watches and accessories   Swatch Watch USA
Timex watches   Timex Corp.

Media Expenditures: $5–9.9 Million

Citizen watches	Citizen Watch Co. of America
Franklin jewelry	Franklin Mint Corp.
Lorus watches	Seiko Time Corp.
Movado watches	Movado Watch Co.
Pulsar watches	Pulsar Time, Inc.
Rolex watches	Rolex Watch USA, Inc.

Industry Health and Direction

The lower end of this industry—costume jewelry and low-cost watches—has been enjoying enormous success on the shopping channels. The higher end has restricted its advertising activities largely to the class magazines. The attention to quality paid by the baby boomers has probably led to a strong resurgence from the recession, with a rise of 5.2 percent in business in 1992.

Prior to the coming of the shopping channels along with long-form commercials, it's probably safe to say that with few exceptions, notably Timex, the majority of products in this category were advertised in print media rather than television. Even without a marketing channel dedicated to this category, a valuable lesson has been learned: that is, when it comes to jewelry, television has become the most involving, most efficient sales medium in history. At present, most of the jewelry sold directly from television is of the zirconium variety, but with more than one in four Americans actively seeking out watches and jewelry at any given time, it clearly behooves the more expensive brands to explore the medium. A marketing channel will give these advertisers schedulability they can't get on shopping channels, plus an electronic black-velvet background to show off their sparkling wares.

Since no true marketing channel actually exists at this writing, it is interesting to speculate on the differences between them. One such difference is certain to be tone. For the jewelry/watch channel, one imagines a quiet, dignified tone in programming, with celebrity-studded infomercials and documercials to match the diamond-studded watches. Here a famous international actress being shown (along with the viewers) a line of contemporary jewelry; there a suave leading man examining (along with the viewers) a line of expensive Swiss- or Italian-made watches. Imagine the contrast in tone between this elegant channel and, say, the home appliance channel. Each channel will reflect its traditional retail outlet—Tiffany's or Target.

❖ 6. STEREO EQUIPMENT

Amount spent on advertising: $342,000,000 (shared with TV/VCR)

Those intending to purchase: 24.8 percent

Major Category Advertisers

Media Expenditures: $50–99.9 Million

Brand	Corporation
Energizer™ batteries	Eveready Battery Co.

Media Expenditures: $25–49.9 Million

Duracell batteries	Duracell USA, Inc.
Sony video equipment	Sony Corp.

Media Expenditures: $15–24.9 Million

Hitachi electronics	Hitachi Ltd.
Magnavox audio/video systems	Philips Consumer Electronics

Media Expenditures: $10–14.9 Million

Pioneer audio/video systems	Pioneer Electronics USA Corp.
RCA televisions	Thompson Consumer Electronics
Texas Instruments electronics	Texas Instruments, Inc.

Media Expenditures: $5–9.9 Million

BASF audio/videotapes	BASF Corp.
Canon camcorders	Canon USA, Inc.
Delco car stereo systems	Delco Products
Emerson electronics	Emerson Radio Corp.
Fuji videotape	Fuji Photo Film USA, Inc.
Goldstar electronics	Goldstar Electronics International
JVC electronics	JVC Company of America
Motorola electronics	Motorola, Inc.
Panasonic camcorders	Panasonic Co.
Philips compact disc players	Philips Consumer Electronics
Rayovac batteries	Rayovac Corp.
Sharp consumer electronics	Sharp Electronics Corp.
Sony color televisions	Sony Corp.
Sony compact disc players	Sony Corp.
TDK audio/videotapes	TDK Electronics Corp.

Industry Health and Direction

The baby boomers who built this category in the 1970s are alive and well and more affluent than ever. Their kids, the *MTV* generation, continue to fuel the fire. As a whole the industry is healthy, and its direction continues to be up.

When baby boomers moved into their first apartment, they bought stereo equipment first and furniture second, a priority that continues today. Also, the fact that this industry supports a massive retail structure tells us it's a true candidate for a marketing channel. Again, this industry meets all the criteria. It offers viable revenues, increasingly complex products, and a proliferation of model choices. One out of four Americans is in the market at any given time, and today's retail structure, which, while not archaic like that of the automobile industry, suffers from similar ills such as poorly trained or nonexistent clerks. Additionally, costs for the same item often vary widely from store to store.

Clearly, a marketing channel offers shoppers a better alternative. But there are advantages to the retailer as well. This is a category prone to sales events. It sometimes seems half the bulk of the Sunday newspaper consists of ads for stereo sales. Commercials promoting local weekend sales on the marketing channel offer the retailer a powerful, involving supplement to his or her newspaper effort.

❖ 7. TV/VCR

Amount spent on advertising: $342,000,000 (shared by stereos)

Those intending to purchase: 24.5 percent

Industry Health and Direction

As we have seen, the time spent watching television continues to increase. Television sets and VCRs are showing up in living rooms, kitchens, bedrooms, and even bathrooms. As an indication of the industry's health, in 1992, unit sales of color TV sets alone rose by 11.6 percent to $22 million.

The same industry features that apply to the stereo equipment market apply to the TV/VCR market. More often than not they share the same dealer and distributor organizations. But with nearly $350 million in total advertising revenues and a constant market of nearly 25 percent, TV/VCR is big enough to support a channel of its own.

❖ 8. COMPUTERS/COMPUTER PRODUCTS

Amount spent on advertising: $595,000,000

Those intending to purchase: 21.5 percent

Major Category Advertisers

Media Expenditures: $25–49.9 Million

Brand	Corporation
Apple computers	Apple Computer, Inc.
Compaq computers	Compaq Computer Corp.

Digital computer systems	Digital Equipment Corp.
Hewlett-Packard computers/ office equipment	Hewlett-Packard Co.
IBM computer systems	IBM Corp.
IBM corporate	IBM Corp.
NEC computer products	NEC Technologies, Inc.

Media Expenditures: $15–24.9 Million

Dell computers	Dell Computer Corp.
Epson computer products	Epson America, Inc.
Macintosh computers	Apple Computer, Inc.
Microsoft computer software	Microsoft Corp.
Prodigy on-line service	IBM Corp./Sears, Roebuck
Sharp information systems	Sharp Electronics Corp.

Media Expenditures: $10–14.9 Million

Intel computer components	Intel Corp.
Lotus computer software	Lotus Development Corp.
Tandy computer systems	Tandy Corp.
Toshiba computer systems/ products	Toshiba America Info Systems
Video Technology learning aids	Video Technology Industries

Industry Health and Direction

While revenues have been tremendous during the brief lifespan of this new industry, confusion has reigned. Computer people have not been good marketers, as a rule. Pioneering corporations have lost share to manufacturers of cheaper clones. Technology increases so fast that prices plummet annually. Standards are either nonexistent or constantly changing. Recently, however, the industry has discovered the advantages of marketing, particularly as regards brand reinforcement. Never afraid to take chances, industry leaders are experimenting with a host of advertising alternatives, notably direct marketing. This need to define their brands, combined with their penchant for experimentation, will doubtless lead them to marketing channels in the future.

Next to automobiles, the computer category fits the marketing channel to near perfection. With an enormous industry advertising budget of nearly $600 million, currently spent mainly in the print media due to the complexity of the products, the television opportunity is evident. The long-form commercial provides computer advertisers with the "room" they need to differentiate their brands/models from their competitors. One can speculate that much of that impressive industry budget will shift to television once a dedicated marketing channel comes into existence.

The very complexity of computers and computer-related products makes them ideal candidates for 30-minute infomercials explaining features, advantages, and benefits of the various models. There are so many different brands to choose from; the equipment is initially expensive, but often obsolete in a year or two; retail outlets range from company stores to discount houses; service can often be questionable; prices skew widely; there is the prevalence of "clones": because of all this, confusion is the very hallmark of the computer marketplace. And as we have seen, where too many choices and too much confusion exists, prospects tend to fall back on familiar brand names. For this reason, one expects to see many long-form documercials stressing brand, quality, and service capability.

In addition to infomercials and documercials, one sees a need for independent comparison programming and, due to the fast-changing nature of the industry, additional news coverage.

Interestingly, perhaps the greatest difference between the automotive and computer industries as related to our four criteria is the fact that while the automobile retail structure is antiquated, the computer retail structure is still evolving. The presence of a marketing channel dedicated to the computer industry can help in the development of a structure that is truly relevant to the life-styles of today. (see Figure 10-2.)

Figure 10-2

The Second Eight Industries That Make Good
Candidates for Marketing Channels

Major Category Advertisers

	Current Ad Budgets (all categories - in millions)
Food/Beverage/Restaurant/Alcohol	$ 8,514
Cosmetics/Apparel	3,424
Pharmaceuticals/Healthcare	1,825
Sporting Goods/Recreation	503
Toys and Games	397
Pet Foods/Supplies	292
Office Equipment/Supplies	169
Photo Supplies/Equipment	165

© 1993 AdWeek Magazine L.P.

These industries, though not necessarily complex or difficult to buy, share two characteristics that make them totally logical candidates for a marketing channel: each industry currently spends enormous amounts of money advertising, and each supplies products that need constant replacement. © 1993 *AdWeek L.P.* Used by permission of *AdWeek*.

❖ 9. FOOD/BEVERAGE/RESTAURANT/ALCOHOL

Amount spent on advertising: $8,514,000,000

Major Category Advertisers

FOOD
Media Expenditures: $50–99.9 Million

Brand	Corporation
Cheerios™ cereal	General Mills, Inc.

Media Expenditures: $25–49.9 Million

Campbell's condensed soups	Campbell Soup Co.
Eggo™ waffles	Mrs. Smith's Frozen Foods Co.
Kellogg's Corn Flakes™	Kellogg Co.
Kellogg's Frosted Flakes™	Kellogg Co.
Kellogg's Pop-Tarts™	Kellogg Co.
Kellogg's Raisin Bran™	Kellogg Co.
Nutrasweet™ sweetener	The Nutrasweet Co.
Post Grape-Nuts™ cereal	Kraft General Foods, Inc.
Total™ cereal	General Mills, Inc.
Total Raisin Bran™ cereal	General Mills, Inc.
Wrigley's Extra Sugar Free Gum™	Wm. Wrigley Jr. Co.

BEVERAGES

Media Expenditures: $50–99.9 Million

Brand	Corporation
Coca-Cola Classic™	The Coca-Cola Co.
Diet Coke™	The Coca-Cola Co.
Diet Pepsi™	Pepsi-Cola Co.
Dr. Pepper and Diet Dr. Pepper™	Dr. Pepper Co.
Folger's coffee	Folger Coffee Co.
Maxwell House™ coffees	Kraft General Foods, Inc.
Pepsi-Cola	Pepsi-Cola Co.

Media Expenditures: $25–49.9 Million

Gatorade Thirst Quencher™	The Quaker Oats Co.
General Foods International™ coffees	Kraft General Foods, Inc.
7-Up™	The Seven-Up Company
Sprite™	The Coca-Cola Co.
Tropicana fruit juices	Tropicana Products, Inc.

RESTAURANTS
Media Expenditures: $850–899.9 Million

Brand	Corporation
McDonald's restaurants	McDonald's Corp.

Media Expenditures: $100–149 Million

Brand	Corporation
Burger King restaurants	Burger King Corp.
Kentucky Fried Chicken restaurants	KFC Corp.
Pizza Hut restaurants	Pizza Hut, Inc.
Taco Bell restaurants	Taco Bell Corp.

Media Expenditures: $50–99.9 Million

Brand	Corporation
Domino's Pizza delivery	Domino's Pizza, Inc.
Hardee's restaurants	Hardee's Food Systems, Inc.
Little Caesars restaurants	Little Caesar Enterprises, Inc.
Red Lobster restaurants	Red Lobster USA
Wendy's restaurants	Wendy's International, Inc.

ALCOHOL (BEER/WINE/LIQUOR)
Media Expenditures: $100–149.9 Million

Brand	Corporation
Budweiser™ beer	Anheuser-Busch, Inc.
Miller Genuine Draft™ beer	Miller Brewing Co.

Media Expenditures: $50–99.9 Million

Brand	Corporation
Bud Dry™ beer	Anheuser-Busch, Inc.
Bud Light™ beer	Anheuser-Busch, Inc.
Coors Light™ beer	Coors Brewing Co.
Miller Light™ beer	Miller Brewing Co.

Media Expenditures: $25–49.9 Million

Brand	Corporation
Coors beer	Coors Brewing Co.
Gallo wines	E. & J. Gallo Winery
Heineken™ beer	Van Munching & Co., Inc.
Miller High Life™ beer	Miller Brewing Co.

Industry Health and Direction

While spending in these categories remains fairly constant—people have to eat and drink—the products of choice constantly change with life-styles. Today's health-conscious consumer is causing massive shifts in buying habits. In soft drinks, Coke and Pepsi continue to lose ground to specialty drinks such as ready-to-drink iced teas and iced coffees as well as fruit juices. Wine sales continue to rise, but at the expense of beer and spirits (with the exception of tequila). The recent concern for value has led consumers to experiment with private-label supermarket brands, with the result that brand-name cereals, among other food products, have lost ground. And, finally, the fast-food chains continue to beat each other to death in a series of price wars. Marketing channels should provide these industries with a valuable forum for introducing new products as life-styles continue to evolve.

No, these aren't complex, expensive, high-involvement, considered-purchase products. And, no, there's nothing about the current retail structure that flies in the face of today's consumer.

Still, what makes them candidates for a marketing channel—perhaps several marketing channels given the depth and breadth of the category—is the availability of $8.5 billion in advertising revenues and the fact that at any given time 100 percent of Americans are actively in the market for products in this category.

Furthermore, advertisers in this category are television-prone to begin with. Most of that powerhouse budget already goes into television. They understand the medium and they like what it can do for them. Given the lack of complexity characteristic of products in this category, one would not expect many infomercials, but given the overwhelming importance of brand, in light of today's massive erosion to generics, documercials should flourish. Then, too, expect a lot more local advertiser involvement on this channel. Commercials for local restaurant and supermarket specials are likely candidates for short-form spots inserted in long-form commercials. Also, much short-form commercial programming exists for products like beer and soft drinks; it is likely that such heavy television advertisers will do a great deal of experimenting on the marketing channel. Scheduling on this channel will obviously be difficult, but with nearly a billion dollars to play with, surely this is a challenge that can be met.

❖ 10. COSMETICS/APPAREL/ACCESSORIES

Amount spent on advertising: $3,242,000,000

Major Category Advertisers

COSMETICS
Media Expenditures: $50–99.9 Million

Brand	Corporation
Cover Girl™ cosmetics	The Procter & Gamble Co.
Sensor™ shaving system	The Gillette Co.

Media Expenditures: $25–49.9 Million

Crest™ toothpaste	The Procter & Gamble Co.
Degree™ antiperspirant	Helene Curtis, Inc.
Head & Shoulders™ shampoo	The Procter & Gamble Co.
Helene Curtis Salon Selectives™	Helene Curtis, Inc.
Huggies™ disposable diapers	Kimberly-Clark Corp.
L'Oréal cosmetics	L'Oréal Cosmetics
Maybelline cosmetics	Maybelline, Inc.
Norelco shavers	Norelco Consumer Products Co.
Oil of Olay™ lotion	Richardson-Vicks, Inc.
Pampers™ disposable diapers	The Procter & Gamble Co.
Rogaine™ men's hair growth products	The Upjohn Co.

APPAREL/ACCESSORIES
Media Expenditures: $50–99.9 Million

Brand	Corporation
Levi's jeans and sportswear	Levi Strauss & Co.

Media Expenditures: $25–49.9 Million

Dockers™ sportswear	Levi Strauss & Co.

Media Expenditures: $15–24.9 Million

Bugle Boy™ clothing	Bugle Boy Industries, Inc.
Cotton, Inc.	Cotton, Inc.
Fruit of the Loom men's/boys' underwear	Fruit of the Loom, Inc.
Fruit of the Loom women's underwear	Fruit of the Loom, Inc.
Haggar apparel	Haggar Apparel Co.
Lee jeans and sportswear	The Lee Apparel Co., Inc.
Polo/Ralph Lauren apparel	Polo/Ralph Lauren Corp.

Media Expenditures: $10–14.9 Million

Fruit of the Loom casualwear	Fruit of the Loom, Inc.
Gitano sportswear and accessories	The Gitano Group
Guess? sportswear	Guess? Inc.
Hanes men's underwear	Hanes Underwear Co.
Hanes Silk Reflections™ hosiery	Hanes Hoisery, Inc.
Jordache apparel	Jordache Enterprises, Inc.
Sheer Energy™ pantyhose	L'Eggs Products, Inc.
Totes accessories	Totes, Inc.

Industry Health and Direction

A mature market that traditionally shows only about 4 percent growth a year, apparel and cosmetics sales dropped dramatically during the recession of the early 1990s. Women, the primary consumers in this market, began to realize that the difference between designer products and less expensive equivalents was one of label and name rather than quality. Sales across the board were up, but only slightly. To the industry's credit, it has been among the first to realize the value of direct response television, and savvy marketers like Diane Von Furstenburg, Calvin Klein, and Revlon are exploring new techniques.

Here is an industry that is rapidly falling in love with direct response television. Revlon has been looking for ways to develop its own exclusive network and is investigating cutting-edge trends in direct response marketing.

The reason for this excitement is the proven effectiveness of direct response television—shopping channels—in moving cosmetics and apparel. As mentioned in Chapter 1, the first real nationwide advertising success on radio was the response to actress Marion Davies's beauty secrets and offer of an autographed photo. From day one, television has proven itself equally capable of generating sales in this category, as demonstrated by the phenomenal success of Revlon sponsoring the big-money quiz shows of the 1950s. In the early days of shopping channels, it was found that the promotion of cosmetics—any cosmetics—caused them to be ordered as fast as they could be manufactured. In the early 1990s, marketers of designer apparel discovered the shopping channels. It was Diane Von Furstenburg, legend says, who convinced Barry Diller, television's maverick futurist, that the shopping channel *QVC* was the single greatest advance in fashion marketing since the runway. Diller reasoned that if shopping channels had appeal to blue-chip fashion marketers, they could appeal to other blue-chip retailers as well. Kim Delsing, president of Calvin Klein, had been investigating *QVC* even before Diller arrived. "Anyone who isn't interested in *QVC*," she was quoted as saying, "is living on another planet."

Very quickly, the industry moved from the shopping channel format to the long-form infomercial format. A line of cosmetics was built around actress Victoria Jackson, whose initial 30-minute spot proved to be one of the biggest revenue producers in infomercial history. Soon others followed, usually using the celebrity format. Singer/actress Cher was asked by a friend to appear in an infomercial for a new line of hair care products. Despite the fact that she had been thinking about bringing out a hair care line of her own, she agreed, out of friendship, to participate. So successful was the infomercial that Cher once commented during an interview on a TV talk show that she made as much money as a guest as she would have as an entrepreneur.

While it's important to remember that the vast majority of these products are still sold at retail, with all the enthusiasm for television experimentation in this category, it is difficult to imagine that a dedicated marketing channel could possibly fail.

❖ 11. PHARMACEUTICALS/HEALTH CARE

Amount spent on advertising: $1,835,000,000

Major Category Advertisers

Media Expenditures: $100–149.9 Million

Brand	Corporation
Nutri/System weight loss centers	Nutri/System, Inc.

Media Expenditures: $50–99.9 Million

Advil™ pain reliever	Whitehall Laboratories
Ultra Slim-fast™ weight loss program	Slim Fast Foods Co.
Tylenol™ and Extra Strength Tylenol™	McNeil Consumer Products Co.

Media Expenditures: $25–49.9 Million

Alka-Seltzer Plus™ cold/allergy medication	Miles, Inc.
Anacin™ tablets and caplets	Whitehall Laboratories
Dynatrim™ diet drink	Lederle Consumer Health Products
Excedrin™ tablets and caplets	Bristol-Myer Squibb Co.
Gyne-Lotrimin™ cream	Schering-Plough Corp.
Jenny Craig weight loss centers	Jenny Craig International
Monistat-7™ cream	Johnson & Johnson
Nyquil™ cold medication	Richardson-Vicks, Inc.
Robitussin™ cough medicines	A. H. Robins Co., Inc.
Tylenol™ cold medication	McNeil Consumer Products Co.
Weight Watchers weight loss program	Weight Watchers Int'l, Inc.

Industry Health and Direction

As age begins to take its toll on the boomers, they react characteristically. They demand information—especially when it comes to their health. Exciting things are happening in this market. The Food and Drug Administration (FDA) is releasing a number of prescription drugs into the over-the-counter arena. Even more exciting, the American Medical Association reversed its blanket policy against advertising branded prescription drugs directly to the consumer. It has agreed to work with the FDA in establishing standards that, among other things, would require a "clear health education message" and that would make it a requirement that advertisers make information on side effects and warnings perfectly clear to the consumer. One expects budgets to increase dramatically in this area as the target audience widens from strictly physicians to the general public.

If there was ever a channel with "ageless" appeal, this is it. From the health-conscious, exercise-crazy boomers and postboomers to the pill-taking, prescription-filling preboomers (the fastest-growing population segment in America), the interest level is high. Again, there have already been remarkable success stories in this category. Probably the most remarkable is the Soloflex exercise machine.

Originally, Soloflex produced a 22-minute video that it distributed by mail request. Management found that an incredible 40 percent of the people who saw the video ended up buying the product. Realizing the need for greater exposure, Soloflex adapted its video brochure into an infomercial and launched it on cable. The rest, as they say, is history.

Aerobic exercise tapes, marketed primarily with long-form commercials, have proliferated to the point where they have become confusing. First came Kathy Smith and Jane Fonda, followed by every workout queen in Hollywood.

But probably the most remarkable player in the health care category to date is the irrepressible Richard Simmons. Originally, Simmons used infomercials to promote a simple, realistic diet plan along the lines of Weight Watchers. Sales went up and stayed up. His next venture, introduced in the fall of 1987, was an easier-to-follow version of his original plan called the Deal-A-Meal. Sales rose even higher. Ever aggressive, the following year Simmons came out with a series of aerobics tapes called "Sweatin' to the Oldies," along with a successful cookbook. Sales continued upward. Finally, Simmons branched out into the infomercial format. Over the years his plan had resulted in a number of impressive success stories—people, usually young women, who had progressed from obese to slim without gaining weight back. Simmons developed commercials in which he arrived at the subject's home, unannounced, wearing his trademark "Sweatin' to the Oldies" shorts and tank top. The subject, totally flabbergasted, was then interviewed. The subject would invariably end up in tears, as would Simmons. Inserted in the documercial, of course, were short-form commercials for various Simmons products. Simmons—engaging and frenetic—has made millions in direct response television for himself and his investors. Today, his stock of products includes two cookbooks, four "Sweatin' to the Oldies" tapes, one "Sweatin' to the Classics" tape, plus two cassettes—one for walking and one for hiking. And when you consider all those sales came at the expense of conventional diet programs, some of which were basically identical to his Deal-A-Meal, the value of direct response television becomes obvious. It's also interesting to note that Simmons is now marketing his products through televised retailer QVC as well as through conventional retail outlets. Even the most traditional shopper can buy them without changing shopping habits. And the infomercials do double duty as both "call-in now" and "pick-up-at-the-store" vehicles.

Another factor that would seem to bode well for a marketing channel in pharmaceuticals and health care is the complexity of the pharmaceutical side. Besides the confusion generated by the debate over brand-name versus generic prescription drugs—grist for the marketing channel's mill—there is also vast confusion concerning over-the-counter products. What, if any, are the differences between brands of pain killers? Or sinus medicines? Or cough medicines? Brand confusion is even becoming evident in the category of hemorrhoid relief products. As the collective moans and groans of aging boomers grow louder, we can be sure of a healthy health care business determined to keep us all looking and feeling young. With nearly $2 billion in advertising revenues, the marketing channel will get its share. The prognosis looks good.

❖ 12. SPORTING GOODS/RECREATION

Amount spent on advertising: $503,000,000

Major Category Advertisers

SPORTING GOODS
Media Expenditures: $100–149.9 Million

Brand	Corporation
Nike athletic footwear	Nike, Inc.
Reebok athletic footwear	Reebok International, Inc.

Media Expenditures: $25–49.9 Million

L A Gear athletic wear	L A Gear, Inc.

Media Expenditures: $15–24.9 Million

Converse athletic footwear	Converse, Inc.
Easy Spirit™ sporting footwear	U.S. Shoe Corp.
NordicTrack exerciser	NordicTrack, Inc.

Media Expenditures: $10–14.9 Million

British Knights sneakers	British Knights, Inc.
Keds footwear	The Keds Corp.
Spalding sporting goods	Spalding Sports Worldwide
Titleist golf equipment	Titleist Foot-Joy Worldwide

Media Expenditures: $5–9.9 Million

Adidas athletic footwear	Adidas USA, Inc.
Avia athletic footwear	Avia Group International
Puma™ sportswear and footwear	Etonic, Inc.
Soloflex exercise equipment	Soloflex, Inc.
Spalding golf balls	Spalding Sports Worldwide
Yamaha marine motors	Yamaha Motor Corp. USA
Zebco fishing equipment	Zebco Corp.

RECREATION
Media Expenditures: $25–49.9 Million

Brand	Corporation
Walt Disney World	Walt Disney World Co.

Media Expenditures: $15–24.9 Million

Disneyland™	The Walt Disney Co.

Media Expenditures: $10–14.9 Million

Adventureland/Tampa, FL	Busch Entertainment Corp.
Sea World parks	Sea World, Inc.
Tropworld casino and resort	Aztar Corp.

Media Expenditures: $5–9.9 Million

Busch Gardens/Tampa, FL	Busch Entertainment Corp.
Busch Gardens/Williamsburg, VA	Busch Entertainment Corp.
Caesars Palace hotel and casino	Caesars Palace
Cedar Point amusement park	Cedar Fair LP
The Mirage hotel and casino	Mirage Resorts, Inc.
Showboat casino	Showboat, Inc.
Trump Plaza hotel and casino	Trump Organization

Industry Health and Direction

Entire industries have been created out of the boomers' love of sports and recreation. Imagine trying to buy a soccer ball or a hockey stick in middle America 25 years ago. Today, you'll find a selection of both, in designer colors, in any sporting goods store in the country. The sneaker industry alone is a study in marketing success. Few categories fit today's life-styles better. And it is difficult to imagine a category better suited to a marketing channel. From the oldest boomers in America to their children and grandchildren, recreation is a very serious business.

It's likely that the real strength of a marketing channel in this category is its ability to attract cross-channel, cross-category advertisers. Sports and recreation are at the very heart of baby boomerism. Boomers play golf, tennis, and handball on a weekly basis. They hunt, fish, golf, camp out, and join company softball teams and neighborhood soccer clubs. They buy skis and ski equipment, boats, bicycles, jet skis, snowmobiles, and rollerblades. The potential for long-form commercials, enough to finance a marketing channel, is obvious. The products lend themselves to long-form commercials: witness the many successful golf-related and fishing-related commercials today. This is the kind of programming that has the ability to attract advertisers from other categories. A long-form commercial on fishing tackle, for instance, would be an impressive draw for the insertion of short-form commercials featuring campers and motor homes from the automotive category. A long-form commercial on golf or horseback riding would be an enticing lure for short-term commercials featuring resorts and dude ranches from the vacation/travel category. Products from exercise equipment to whirlpool baths to basement saunas would find a welcome home on this compatible marketing channel.

❖ 13. TOYS AND GAMES

Amount spent on advertising: $397,000,000

Major Category Advertisers

Media Expenditures: $50–99.9 Million

Brand	Corporation
Super Nintendo entertainment systems	Nintendo of America
Tyco toys	Tyco Toys, Inc.

Media Expenditures: $25–49.9 Million

Barbie™ dolls and accessories	Mattel, Inc.
Fisher-Price toys	Fisher-Price, Inc.
Milton Bradley games/toys/ puzzles	Milton Bradley Co.
Sega video games	Sega of America

Media Expenditures: $15–24.9 Million

Lego building toys   Lego Systems, Inc.
Tonka™ toys   Hasbro, Inc.

Industry Health and Direction

Virtually every segment of this market is growing. The boom in video games continues, with both Nintendo and Sega introducing CD-based systems. The preschool market, too, is active, promising to be the industry's most competitive. And the perennial cash cows like Lego and Mattel's Barbie dolls continue to regenerate themselves domestically and have turned their attention to affluent European and Asian markets. All in all, a healthy vital industry.

Remember how we said marketing channels aren't designed to compete with entertainment-based programming? Remember how we said marketing channels only attract customers as they come into the marketplace every year or two or three? And remember how we said the proper criteria for judging audiences of marketing channels was not quantity, but quality? Well, this channel is probably the exception that proves the rule. With one audience—kids—*The Toys and Games Channel* will compete with cartoons, particularly around Christmas or birthdays. So, you say, that's great for advertisers, but what about parents? Who wants the little darlings nagging them all day for the newest Nintendo game or the latest incarnation of Barbie? The fact is, marketing channels can prove a real boon to parents.

The way toy retailing works now, manufacturers select their most promising items and then put millions behind them, mostly on Saturday morning television. Kids see the ads, apply the appropriate pressure, and parents, in a knee-jerk reaction, make sure the proper toys are under the tree. But are they the proper toys? Are they safe? Are they educationally correct? What's the full spectrum available, not just the heavily advertised toys? Answers to these and other pertinent questions will be available on *The Toys and Games Channel.*

❖ 14. PET SUPPLIES

Amount spent on advertising: $292,000,000

Major Category Advertisers

Media Expenditures: $10–14.9 Million

Brand	Corporation
Alpo cat food	Alpo Pet Foods, Inc.
Alpo dog food	Alpo Pet Foods, Inc.
Fancy Feast™ cat food	Nestlé Brands Foodservice Co.
Hartz Mountain pet products	Hartz Mountain Corp.
Iams pet foods	The Iams Co.
Mighty Dog™ canned food	Nestlé Brands Foodservice Co.
Nature's Course™ dog food	Ralston Purina Co.
Pedigree™ dog food	Kal Kan Foods, Inc.
Whiskas™ cat food	Kal Kan Foods, Inc.

Industry Health and Direction

Another life-style–driven category, pet supplies continue to sell at record figures. By proliferating products and brands of products (at a rate of 271 percent in 1992 and another 125 percent for the first six months of 1993), a successful niche marketing effort has resulted in pet food sales of $7.52 billion. Niches include food for puppies/kittens, food for adolescent dogs/cats, food for adult dogs/cats, food for older dogs/cats. Meanwhile, thanks to the prevalence of the all-day empty house (Mom and Dad working, kids at day care or school), cats have overtaken dogs as America's leading pet. Cat toys and litter sales are booming.

Americans love their pets. Americans pamper their pets. Americans spend millions of dollars on their pets each year. And Americans are hungry for information about their pets. All of which makes the category of pet supplies a natural for a dedicated marketing channel. When the subject matter for long-form commercials is as varied as pets and pet supplies, the possibilities are endless . . . and engaging. Which breed of dog is right for your family? Are you providing the proper nutrition for your cat? All this plus tips from the vet and the whole story on pet cemeteries. And imagine the visual impact of infomercials on products for birds or tropical fish. From pet food marketers to franchised pet shops to aquarium manufacturers, marketing channels, like a slipper to a puppy, give advertisers something to chew on.

❖ 15. OFFICE EQUIPMENT/SUPPLIES

Amount spent on advertising: $169,000,000

Major Category Advertisers

Media Expenditures: $15–24.9 Million

Brand	Corporation
Canon copiers	Canon USA, Inc.
Lanier office equipment/ supplies	Lanier Worldwide, Inc.
Xerox business products and systems	Xerox Corp.

Media Expenditures: $10–14.9 Million

Mita copiers	Mita Copystar America, Inc.

Media Expenditures: $5–9.9 Million

Minolta copiers	Minolta Corp.
Mita facscimile machines	Mita Copystar America, Inc.
Parker pens	Parker Pens USA Ltd.
Pitney Bowes mailing systems	Pitney Bowes, Inc.
Radio Shack™ business products	Tandy Corp.
Ricoh office products	Ricoh Corp.
3M™ office products	Minnesota Mining & Mfg. Co.
Toshiba copiers	Toshiba America Info Systems

Industry Health and Direction

In many ways, this category resembles the computer industry. Constant, rapid technological changes make "just keeping up" the buyer's problem. And keeping up is important in today's business climate. Copying machines come and go with celerity. Office furniture continues to hold its price, and its value. Among the most interesting growth areas facing this category is the home market. The proliferation of home computers has spawned a new market for home office furniture. Also, fax machines continue to move from the office to the home. While a small segment of the total market, home office furniture will continue to grow as we move toward the interactive future.

While at first glance this may seem like an industrial category as opposed to a consumer category, it is felt that a viable marketing channel is possible. Products in this category are often complex, constantly changing. They lend themselves to long-form commercials extremely well. And among those in the market, prospects ranging from corporate purchasing people to architects and contractors, the interest level is very high. Two other factors weigh in as important: in the case of corporate purchasers or architects, a single sale can easily account for sales in the six-figure range, and the recent interest in home computers has led to a spate of equipment buying for home offices. In other words, while the audience for a marketing channel dedicated strictly to office equipment may be small at any given time, it only takes a few sales to rack up big profits for the advertiser.

❖ 16. PHOTO SUPPLIES/EQUIPMENT

Amount spent on advertising: $165,000,000

Major Category Advertisers

Media Expenditures: $25–49.9 Million

Brand	Corporation
Kodak film	Eastman Kodak Co.

Media Expenditures: $15–24.9 Million

Canon cameras   Canon USA, Inc.
Minolta cameras and accessories   Minolta Corp.
Polaroid One™ film   Polaroid Corp.

Media Expenditures: $10–14.9 Million

Kodak cameras   Eastman Kodak Co.
Nikon cameras and accessories   Nikon, Inc.
Olympus cameras and accessories Olympus Corp.
Polaroid instant cameras   Polaroid Corp.

Media Expenditures: $5–9.9 Million

Fuji film   Fuji Photo Film USA, Inc.
Kodalux™ processing services   Qualex, Inc.

Industry Health and Direction

This is another of those mature markets that enjoy slow, but constant growth. While the technology is complex, it changes at a much slower rate than computers and office copiers. With quality manufacturers worldwide, this is a truly global industry. It is life-style affected in that it tends to boom during times of affluence when travel and recreation increase.

One of the best reasons for a marketing channel in this category is that it is technologically complex. Sometimes, too complex. For example, in October 1991, Kodak launched a massive advertising campaign featuring its new photo CD. The product was a new concept, more complex than anything Kodak had introduced before. It allowed the user to transfer 35mm slides to a compact disk to be reproduced on a photo CD player or computers equipped with CD-ROM drives. The CD players include a remote control device capable of reducing and manipulating photos. Three months and $35 million later, the product was languishing. Due to the complexity of the photo CD and the vagueness of the benefit, Kodak had elected to run with a schedule of magazine advertisements along with 60- and 120-second direct response television commercials. Nothing seemed to work. It lowered the price. Still nothing. Early in 1992, Kodak and its advertising agency, J. Walter Thompson, finally developed a 30-minute infomercial in a last-ditch effort to jump start the product introduction. Unfortunately, by that time Phillips Consumer Electronics had come out with an improved model at a lower cost. The Phillips model also had audio capabilities.

It's too early to tell whether the product concept will ever catch on—it may be one of those ideas whose time will never come. Still, it's clear that a marketing channel would have provided Kodak with a powerful, logical place to introduce, explain, and clarify the benefits of such a complex product.

On a more positive note, in the late 1980s, Kodak along with Olympus cameras, sponsored "World of Photography," a series of 165 half-hour programs designed to inform shutterbugs, in an entertaining format, of the latest techniques, tips, and equipment. This series was produced by long-form commercial pioneer Richard Brockway and aired on *A&E, Discovery,* and *ABC* from 1984 to 1991. With a little imagination, this show's innovative blending of marketing savvy with just a hint of direct response immediacy positions it as a precursor to marketing programming designed to answer the question, "Is this the right camera for me?" High costs, product complexity, and constant popularity ensure the success of a marketing channel dedicated to this category. The picture is clear.

❖ MARKETING CHANNELS AS BRAND BUILDERS

Clearly, for certain low-involvement, low-priced products, the shopping channels are a great idea. But the fact remains that for all their potential, only 3 percent of cable viewers presently shop from shopping channels. The other 97 percent buy elsewhere, from either catalogs or retail stores. This is not to say exposure on shopping channels isn't effective. As mentioned earlier, studies have shown that the appearance of an item on a shopping channel or unscheduled infomercial causes local retail sales of that same item at a ratio of 1 to 5. As illustrated in Chapter 7, a televised presentation of a juicer, over time, is capable of causing a five to eightfold increase in juicer sales at stores. One conclusion we can draw from this is that television has enormous power to create desire/demand, to the point where people don't want to wait. A viewer can call in and order a juicer, but there's all the hassle of waiting around for the package to arrive, as well as the possibility that it might be faulty, in which case there's even more hassle involved in sending it back. In addition, the viewer may not wish to buy all the add-on items usually offered as part of the TV exclusive. How much more convenient simply to pick it up next time one shops.

While all this may sound like a windfall to marketers of branded products sold through traditional retail channels, the trouble is, these sales are uncontrolled. These shoppers are in search of a juicer, but not necessarily your juicer. They fall back on familiar brand preferences. If that preference happens to be your brand, you win. If not, well, it's time to start building brand equity.

Marketing channels provide advertisers with both the power of television's push to buy, along with a direction for retail buyers to pursue . . . straight to your brand.

Marketing channels provide buyers with better ways to buy and sellers with better ways to sell. For "sweet sixteen" marketers, they help solve heretofore unsolvable problems. Furthermore, as we greet the dawn in a five-hundred-channel world, marketing channels are not only possible, but probable. Someone is going to make them a reality. It has been speculated that the most likely candidates to introduce single-channel marketing are current catalog marketers. Perhaps. But such channels would not specifically be marketing channels. In the first place, many direct response marketers have no national retail presence. As such, the channel would be more of a shopping channel, dealing primarily in call in sales.

One of the major advantages of marketing channels is the fact that they work *with* current retailing structures. No longer created merely to promote call-in sales, they are now designed to promote store traffic and brand enhancement. Those benefiting the most from marketing channels are brands with highly visible retail presence. Remember, today only 3 percent of shoppers buy from shopping channels. And while that percentage will doubtless increase in the future, still the vast majority of Americans buy at Saks, Sears, or Service Merchandise. It is the accepted method of shopping. And it is a habit. The benefit to advertisers on marketing channels is that consumers aren't required to change long-held buying habits. The marketing channel may *sell* them, but the *sale is made* at the local retail outlet. As for marketers like L. L. Bean and Land's End, they are themselves brands. Strong brands. The kinds of brand marketers who should themselves take advantage of the brand-friendly ambiance of the marketing channel.

Marketing channels represent a new and better retailing idea. And new and better ideas always supersede the old order. Within the next few years, marketing channels will become a profitable reality for someone.

But whom?

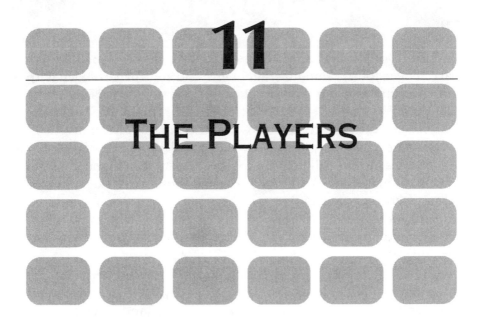

11

THE PLAYERS

"May you live in interesting times."

CHINESE CURSE

Obviously, marketing channels are not going to spring, Phoenix-like, fully formed and flying from the fires of today's television *milieu*. Or should I say *mélange*? Or even *mêlée*, which the French-English dictionary colorfully describes as a scrum (where the forwards of opposing rugby teams link arms and kick at the ball, opponents, or each other . . . whichever is closest). It's an apt definition. Facing off in the television scrum of today are a dozen different technologies in various stages of development, along with hundreds of financially intertwined companies, including broadcasters, cable operators, "entertainment" producers, and "marketing" producers. To make matters more interesting, the industry is populated by a number of incredibly gifted and effective movers and shakers—people like Barry Diller, John Malone, Gerald Levin, and Ted Turner—each with a totally different but equally plausible view of television's next decade.

Not since the early 1920s, when the possibilities inherent in broadcasting had the potential to lead the fledgling technology in any one of a hundred directions, has the industry been in such a state of flux. Many of today's visionaries, like those early executives at AT&T who regarded radio as a phonelike public service, will be proven wrong either in the short run or the long run. Others will mold it and shape it and carry it into the twenty-first century and beyond.

There is general agreement on where we will likely end up: interactivity. Barry Diller describes it vividly. He sees technology developed by a massive cooperative research and development effort between entrepreneurial television, telephone, and computer companies, probably aided and abetted by enabling government legislation. The result will be in-home technology that allows the user to shop, bank, vote, conduct business, earn a degree, trade on the market, play chess with Dad back in Saginaw, talk to Uncle Mario in the old country, and listen to music, plus watch movies and television programming—old and new—all on demand.

The world this technology promises, of course, may never come about. At best, it is decades away. Just like David Sarnoff's 1927 prediction that television would be popularly affordable by the mid-1930s, Diller's prediction is subject to such sidetracking events as worldwide depression and war. Also, just because technology makes a thing possible doesn't mean that people will like it. Even today, with a computer and a phone modem, it's possible for many people to work at home. With few exceptions, however, such people still prefer face-to-face interactivity in the office to more efficient but less personal over-the-phone interactivity from home. Human nature is remarkably resistant to technological change. Most people, for example, have no qualms about withdrawing cash from remote bank machines, yet there are still those who prefer to go to the actual bank with large deposits. They like to see the money go in and to get a receipt from a living, breathing bank teller.

While there may be general agreement on Diller's vision of the far future, theories as to the shape the technology will take are legion.

❖ CABLE COMPETITION: ALTERNATIVE DELIVERY SYSTEMS

> *"It's a long shot with a limb in the way, but it beats suckin' pond water."*
>
> JED CLAMPETT, *The Beverly Hillbillies*

Direct Broadcast Satellite

One such technology, direct broadcast satellite (DBS), would make current cable technology obsolete. Under this system, programming would be made available on a satellite with a continent-size footprint covering every home in North America. Viewers would access programming via a 15-inch dish. Obviously, this highly efficient technology has the advantage of eliminating all the paraphernalia of today's cable systems. It eliminates the need for local stations, local staff, and miles of cable. Actually, DBS technology has been around for years, since the first communications satellite was launched in the 1970s. Rupert Murdoch led a failed attempt to challenge cable with this technology at that time. In all likelihood, if the cable industry had not had such a long head start, DBS would be the primary technology in use today. And it may still be, sometime in the future. In the long run, the most efficient systems usually win out. Currently, a satellite is under construction, a venture between United States Satellite Broadcasting and Hughes Communications and is scheduled for a 1994 launch.

Most observers today, however, feel that DBS is a long shot, at least for the near future. Cable is too well entrenched (pun intended). As a system, it is up and running, and until it breaks, nobody is likely to feel the need to fix it. Barring unforeseen developments, DBS will likely remain an alternate delivery system whose primary market is probably those few homes that lie beyond the cable lines.

The Telcos and Fiber Optics

Fiber optics is another of those "definitely/someday/surely" technologies: a good idea, an improvement, but not widely practical at this time. Fiber optic cable, made up of microthin stands of glass, is the finest transmitter of information ever developed, capable of carrying 250,000 times as much information as copper phone wire. As it relates to television delivery, fiber optics has two primary advantages over current cable technologies: improved picture quality and interactivity. Also, since they follow already authorized phone rights-of-way into homes, the FCC has ruled the telcos can operate without separate franchise approval. While most telephone switches between cities are currently using fiber optics and digital technologies capable of carrying hundreds of channels, the costs to complete home wiring, the last leg, are staggering. As mentioned in Chapter 3, even with the extraordinarly deep pockets of the telcos, long-term high investment for a second place standing in the long run is a questionable goal. Apple chief John Scully commented at a recent conference "It would be silly to think that the telephone companies aren't going to play a role in this in some form." Undoubtedly there are other, better ways for the telcos to profit from the cable venture. At the time of this writing, TCI and MCI are reportedly in joint-venture discussions. In May of 1993, U.S. West announced a $25-billion investment for a 25 percent stake in Time Warner's cable and entertainment unit.

Microwave Technology

This new technology utilizes microwaves at electromagnetic frequencies much higher than conventional UHF or VHF television frequencies. Microwave reception, therefore, is far superior in both sound and picture. It has, however, one big disadvantage: it can only transmit for a short distance along a line of sight. Cellular telephone technology solves the same problem by the simple expedient of dividing large areas into several small areas, each with its own transmitter.

At this writing, Cellular Vision of New York, Inc., is testing microwave technology in Brighton Beach, Brooklyn, that delivers

© John Grimes. Courtesy New Media magazine.

several dozen channels at a cost to subscribers of just $29.95 per month. The company is working to provide specialized programming to individual neighborhoods with high immigrant populations—Russian channels, Korean channels, and so on. Also, with modifications, the 4-inch antenna can transmit signals back to the base antenna, allowing phone calls, video conferencing, data transmission, and other services.

Like DBS, microwave technology has a number of advantages over conventional cable. Its disadvantage is that it is probably too little, too late.

"Telephone and cable companies will lay the information super-highway and it will be one of the greatest technological developments of the 20th century. But someone will still have to fill up the highway."

GEORGE LUCAS, filmmaker

The Interactive Superhighway

Based on a year of experimentation in Queens, New York, Time Warner is rolling out the first few miles of the much-talked-about interactive superhighway to 4,000 subscribers in the Orlando area. Among its offerings, in addition to full cable programming, are full-motion video education from local schools and universities; Video-On-Demand, featuring movies, sporting and cultural events, and documentaries; interactive home shopping; intrasubscriber video games; and long-distance telephone service.

As we'll see in Chapter 12, interactivity is the future, and giant multimedia conglomerates like Time Warner, with holdings, interests, and alliances in the television, telephone, and computer industries, will lead the way. Time Warner calls its Orlando venture the *Full Service Network*. It is, for now. But the future range of services will be far, far fuller. Enthusiastic prognosticators, spurred by the arrival of the Full Service Network and encouraged by the Clinton administration's apparent mood of cooperation, expect the nationwide interactive superhighway to be built and busy by the end of the decade. Don't bet on it.

New technologies are being discovered every day. There are no signs of anything that could remotely be called industry standards. The giant industries are extending tentative tentacles toward one another, but only a few solid agreements have been reached.

"There will be road kill on this superhighway."

LELA COCOROS, TCI

The superhighway is a long way off. All these ideas and others represent technology, and nothing more. Most will disappear, sucking millions of dollars into the vortex with them. Some will succeed, becoming the state of the art and earning millions for their fortunate investors. New technologies—some we haven't even dreamed of yet—will replace old ones. But whatever happens technologically is largely irrelevant to the main issue.

As Rupert Murdoch has said: "Ultimately, the viewer cares not one whit whether a program comes from an analog broadcast signal, a digital broadcast signal, a coaxial cable, a glass fiber owned by TCI, a glass fiber owned by Bell-South, a satellite, a microwave system, or a microwave oven. What the viewer cares about is the program."

❖ HOW TO GET INTO THE MARKETING CHANNEL BUSINESS: A THREE-CHANNEL PHASE-IN

Regardless of tomorrow's technological developments, the fact remains that the future of television has already taken root. The seeds have been planted, the crop is already coming up. As mentioned earlier, marketing channels will probably appear piecemeal, accompanied by a great deal of pretesting that will be conducted by a company or companies in existence today. Furthermore, these companies will probably operate in the realm of broadcast/production rather than in either the computer or telephone industries.

Let's take a look at a three-channel phase-in scenario—using an automotive channel, a life-style and electronics channel, and a home and health channel—which provides a relatively low-risk basis for the establishment of future channels.

Channel 1:	Car and Automotive Products		$ 4.370B
Channel 2:	Life-style and Electronics		$ 1.632B
	Computers		$ .595B
	TV/VCR		
	Stereo equipment	$ .342B	
	Home appliances	$ .302B	
	Office equipment	$ .169B	
	Photo equipment/supplies	$ .165B	
	Jewelry and watches	$ .059B	
Channel 3:	Home and Health		$ 17.011B
	Food, beverages, and restaurants	$ 8.514B	
	Cosmetics and apparel	$ 3.424B	
	Pharmaceuticals and health care	$ 1.825B	
	Vacations and travel	$ 1.797B	
	Sporting goods/recreation	$ .503B	
	Toys and games	$ .397B	
	Pet supplies	$ .292B	
	Home furnishings	$ .259B	
	Total, Channels 1–3		<u>$23.013B</u>

Notice that the products in these three categories presently account for a total of more than $23 billion. To highlight the enormity of that figure, keep in mind that total U.S. cable ad revenues for 1992 amounted to just $3.4 billion. If marketing channels attract just 20 percent of the advertising budgets listed in these three channels, it would represent an increase of more than $1 billion over the total revenues of the entire cable industry in 1992.

Is 20 percent a likely percentage? Keep in mind, significant advertising funds in all these industries are already committed to television. As we've seen, more and more advertisers—even big blue chippers like GM, Lincoln Mercury, and Apple—are increasingly inclined to experiment with nontraditional media, especially those with a direct response slant. It would not be unreasonable to target from 20–25 percent of these total media dollars for use in the placement of long-form commercials on the appropriate category-specific marketing channel.

This three-channel phase-in allows for the development of new channels based on proven performance. Individual marketing channels will be spun off only after a given industry category has proved its ability to generate support revenue; in terms of advertising dollars, somewhere between $50 million and $100 million.

In the long run, all sixteen industries may never be represented. On the other hand, dark horse industries—gardening, perhaps—may find the audiences and advertisers they need to support independent marketing channels. Whatever happens, and however it happens, the development of marketing channels will come about not because of future technological possibilities, but because of the drive and vision of companies and individuals in the business today. Who are these companies? There are a number of possibilities.

❖ THE FIELD

As mentioned earlier, given the nature of the expertise required to establish and operate a marketing channel, players will likely come from the broadcasting/cable/programming world. Let's take a look at the leading companies in these industries.

Top Companies in Entertainment

Ranked by Market Value[1]

1. Walt Disney Co., $16,562 million
2. Paramount Communications, $5,017 million
3. Blockbuster Entertainment, $2,079 million
4. United Artists Entertainment, $1,896 million
5. King World Productions, $1,212 million

Ranked by Media Sales[2]

1. Time Warner, $7,642 million
2. News Corp., $5,427 million
3. Capital Cities/ABC, $4,957 million
4. Hachette Magazines, $4,546 million

5. Dun & Bradstreet, $4,332 million
6. Sony Corp., $3,963 million
7. Paramount Communications, $3,869 million
8. Gannett, $3,518 million
9. Times Mirror, $3,461 million
10. General Electric Co., $3,392 million

Top Companies in Motion Picture Production

Ranked by Five-Year Average Return on Equity[3]

1. General Cinema, 46.6 percent
2. Paramount Communications, 32.2 percent
3. Walt Disney Co., 26.4 percent
4. Handleman, 24.7 percent
5. Live Entertainment, Inc., 20.8 percent
6. Commtron, 18.0 percent
7. MCA, Inc., 10.6 percent
8. Time Warner, 9.4 percent
9. Orion Pictures, 4.5 percent

Ranked by Total Sales[4]

1. Warner Bros., $685 million
2. Universal, $679 million
3. Columbia/Tri Star, $673 million
4. Buena Vista, $577 million
5. Paramount, $570 million
6. MGM/UA, $304 million
7. 20th Century Fox, $286 million
8. Orion, $165 million

Top Companies in Broadcasting

Ranked by Market Value as of 1991[5]

1. Capital Cities/ABC, $8,092 million
2. Tele-Communications, Inc., $5,607 million
3. American TV & Communications, $4,635 million
4. Lin Broadcasting, $3,340 million
5. Viacom, $2,602 million
6. CBS, $2,406 million
7. Turner Broadcasting, $2,116 million
8. Comcast, $1,694 million
9. BHC Communications, $1,539 million
10. Multimedia, $851 million

Listing of 12 Global Television Interests (biggest "names" outside of U.S.)

Author's subjective ranking[6]

Patrick Le Lay, President-Director—TFI, France

Andre Rousselet, President—Canal Plus, France

Leo Kirch, President—KirchGruppe, Germany

Marc Woessner, President and CEO—Bertelsmann, Germany

Kerry Packer—Nine Network, Australia

Gaston Thorn, President/Director General—CLT Multi Media, Luxembourg

Silvio Berlusconi—Fininvest Communicazioni, Italy

Akio Morita, President—Sony, Japan

Hisashi Hieda, President—Fuji Television Network, Japan

Roberto Marinho, President and General Director—TV Globo, Brazil

Emilio Azcarraga, President—Televisa, Mexico

Top Networks

Ranked by Network Revenues[7]

1. NBC, $2,800 million
2. ABC, $2,400 million
3. CBS, $2,300 million
4. Fox, $375 million

Top Cable Companies

Ranked by Basic Subscriber Revenues[8]

1. Tele-Communications, Inc.
2. Time Warner Cable
3. Continental Cablevision
4. Comcast
5. Cox Cable
6. Cablevision Systems Corp.
7. Jones Spacelink
8. Newhouse
9. Cablevision Industries
10. Times Mirror Cable

Where one might be led to believe these lists are composed of independent, autonomous, competing companies, such is not the case. The fact is, they are all part of an incredibly complex series of investment alliances and joint ventures as difficult to unravel as the Gordian knot. Interestingly, some of the control in these companies is held by major advertisers.

Still, the most aggressive activity has come from the cable community. The Turner Broadcasting System provides a typical example of the wheeling and dealing common to the industry. Starting out with just the Atlanta-based independent station *WTBS*, Turner soon established *Cable News Network (CNN)*. Slow to take off and starved for cash, *CNN* drew the attention of John Malone, chief executive officer of giant Tele-Communications, Inc. (TCI), who kept the channel on the air in return for 12 percent of *Turner Broadcasting* (today TCI owns 22.5 percent). Once rejuvenated, *CNN* began to gain an audience, and its performance during Operation Desert Storm won the plaudits of the public and the envy of its competitors. Meanwhile, Turner followed up with *CNN Headline News, CNN Radio,* and *TNT,* another cable network. To accomplish this, Turner forged a long chain of alliances in addition to TCI, including Time, Inc., Viacom International, Warner Communications, Inc., Cablevision Systems Corp., United Artist Communication Corp., Jones Intercable, and Continental Cable. And then, in the spring of 1993, Turner announced he intended to divest himself of his holdings altogether.

In addition to its investment in Turner Communications, TCI owns 49.9 percent of Teleport, a telephone service, and stakes in both *QVC* and *The Discovery Channel* (which includes *The Learning Channel*). At the time of this writing, Liberty Media, a TCI subsidiary functioning as a holding company for programming investments, owns stakes in *Home Shopping Network* (*QVC's* major competitor), *American Movie Classics, Black Entertainment Television, Courtroom Television Network, Encore, The Family Channel, Prime Sports Channel Network,* and interest in 13 regional sports networks.

Complicating matters even further is the fact that the industry is populated with the most brilliant, flamboyant, colorful cast of individual characters this side of the medieval tales of Mallory and Scott.

In the role of Arthur: Ted Turner, who began with one station and built it into an empire on guts and foresight; who built and outfitted a yacht in quest of, not the Holy Grail, but the America's Cup; one of the few men in America who could marry Jane Fonda and *not* be called "Mr. Fonda." Now stepping down, perhaps in favor of his lovely Guinevere?

Or the always mysterious Barry Diller, as Merlin, who built Fox on his programming genius, took a hiatus, and fell in love with technology—and, to the surprise of almost everyone, cast his lot with *QVC.*

From out of the West came young Lochinvar, Michael Ovitz, who grew bored with running a successful Los Angeles talent agency and went off in search of a new vision, known only to him, and who has positioned his Creative Artists Agency (CAA) to do battle on fields of his choosing.

And as Gawaine: TCI's steady, reliable, and reclusive John Malone, who clings to his vision, who forges alliances with possible competitors, and who, thanks to his faith in technology, has forged the strongest cable of all.

Disney's Michael Eisner (the Sorcerer's Apprentice? why not?) heads an empire perhaps best positioned of all to establish marketing channels. Hi ho, hi ho, it's off to work we go.

And then, there is Ivanhoe: Time Warner's Gerald Levin, the Prince of Copyrights, the first knight on the superhighway, single-mindedly seeking technologies and channels capable of showcasing his company's businesses—publishing, programming, film, and music.

And what of the remaining knights, the global players of television? Indeed, enough intrigue to fuel a TV series all on its own.

These and perhaps a few more such brilliant individuals are all perfectly capable of putting together the funding, the people, and the organization needed to make marketing channels a reality.

❖ THE FINALISTS

The field is vast, complex, and fluid, subject to change on any given day. There is capital available and no shortage of opportunistic companies and individuals with the guts to use it. It must be admitted, however, that certain of these companies are better positioned than others to deliver on the promise of marketing channels. The chart in Figure 11-1 shows how the leading contenders (author's opinion) compare according to important criteria like integrated marketing potential, studios and facilities, distribution capability, and financial resources and stability.

Figure 11-1

Sponsor Scorecard

	Ownership of		Experience in		Integrated	Own	Distribution	Financial
	Cable Network	Broadcast Network	Entertainment Production	Marketing Production	Marketing Potential	Studios/ Facilities	Experience (rep media time)	Resources/ Stability
Liberty Media: TCI, *QVC, HSN* (Diller, Malone)	Y	N	Y	L	L	Y	Y	Y
Time Warner (Levin)	Y	Y	Y	Y	Y	Y	Y	Y
Turner Broadcast (Turner)	Y	Y	Y	L	L	Y	Y	Y
CAA (Ovitz)	N	N	Y	Y	Y	?	L	Y
Disney (Eisner)	Y	N	Y	Y	Y	Y	Y	Y
ABC	Y	Y	Y	L	Y	Y	Y	L
NBC	Y	Y	Y	L	Y	Y	Y	N
CBS	Y	Y	Y	L	Y	Y	Y	L
Film Industry (Columbia, Paramount, etc.)	L	N	Y	L	L	Y	L	?
Global Players	?	Y	Y	?	Y	Y	Y	Y

Legend: Y=Yes, N=No, L=Limited, ?=Unknown

Strengths and weaknesses of potential marketing channel owners/operators. In terms of ability to pick up the concept of marketing channels and run with it immediately, Time Warner, Disney, and TCI seem best poised. However, the concept could conceivably work to strengthen current weaknesses exhibited by some of the others, particularly in the areas of marketing potential and financial resources/stability.

❖ ENDNOTES

1. Business Week, *Business Week Top 1,000* (annual), April 1991, p. 167.

2. *Financial World*, April 16, 1991, p. 42.

3. *AdWeek*'s *Marketing Week*, "Superbrands: American Top 2,000 Brands" (Suppl.), 1990, p. 130.

4. Ibid.

5. Business Week, *Business Week Top 1,000*, p. 176.

6. Television Business International, editorial staff

7. *Fortune*, November 19, 1990, p. 98.

8. *Channels*, December 2, 1990, p. 57.

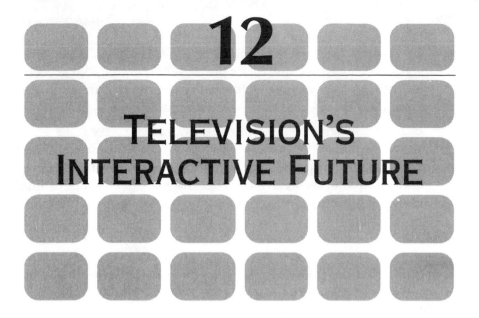

12

TELEVISION'S INTERACTIVE FUTURE

Interactivity is here today. Workable technologies are in place, public enthusiasm is growing rapidly. From Reston, Virginia, to Cerritos, California, Americans are interacting fully with television. For example,

- Subscribers to *The Nostalgia Channel* are registering to play *The Memory Game,* a half-hour, four-part game that quizzes callers through a 900 number. At the end of each part, winners are given the choice of taking their winnings and exiting the game or going on to the next part.

- In Sacramento, subscribers to *Interactive Network, Inc. (IN),* play *Jeopardy* along with the contestants while competing privately with each other. They can also join other subscribers in guessing whodunit on *Murder She Wrote* or calling the next play during live NFL football games. Among *IN*'s interested investors are General Electric's NBC and the A. C. Nielsen Company.

- In scattered markets, subscribers to *TV Answer* can bank, subscribe to magazines, and order pizza, flowers, liquor, or groceries for pickup or delivery. Interested investors include Domino's Pizza and J. C. Penney among others.

- Bars, restaurants, college lounges, and military rec halls subscribing to *NTN Communications* of Carlsbad, California, allow participants the opportunity to enjoy interactive football games and trivia contests. In an early experiment, Chevrolet ran commercials during a trivia game. At the end of each commercial, players were prompted to enter their names and addresses if they'd like more information about the car being advertised. In the fourteen-week test period, Chevrolet received 13,000 inquiries, which were then turned over to local dealers. Another interested sponsor (for obvious reasons, given *NTN*'s venue) is the Miller Brewing Company.

- Also in the works, *NTN's Cable Wagering System* will allow subscribers to open an account with a race track (thoroughbred, harness, and/or quarter horse) and bet until they're rich or until the account runs out . . . whichever comes first.

- Patrons who stay in hotels and motels served by *NTN/Lodgenet* can while away the lonely hours playing interactive games over their in-room TV sets.

- Sony, which owns more than 10,000 episodes of *Jeopardy, Wheel of Fortune, The Dating Game,* and *The Gong Show* is planning the launch of the interactive (by telephone) *Game Show Channel* in 1993.

The problem with interactive television today is not technology. While surely in its infancy, interactive television technology, mostly telephone based at this point, does work. *TV Answer,* mentioned earlier, requires a unit simply called an "appliance" rather than a telephone. The appliance, while superior to the telephone, costs about $700. Even Hewlett-Packard, the appliance developer, admits that $700 is "a little pricey." But in electronics, costs always come down. Thus, while cost may be a minor problem at present, it won't be for long.

❖ Interactivity: A Faltering Start

The fact is, interactive television has been with us for decades. Experiment after experiment, each showing great promise and introduced with great fanfare, has been conducted in the field. One by one, each failed to spark the public's imagination, despite the millions spent in development and promotion. Perhaps the nearest miss was QUBE, mentioned briefly in Chapter 3.

It was 1977 when Warner-Amex signed up subscribers in Columbus, Ohio, to this exciting new interactive cable system. The essential feature of QUBE was a second wire that allowed the subscriber to interact with the QUBE computer via a hand-held responding device. QUBE offered everything conventional cable offered, plus extras. Merchandise could be bought and paid for (this was perhaps the genesis of the home shopping channel), and polling was conducted on issues of the day and analyzed according to the database of subscriber information in the central computer. Several colleges in the Columbus area began offering courses over QUBE; exams were conducted via the hand-held interactive devices, with individual grades posted immediately to students. Initial subscriptions were in the encouraging 30,000 range, but renewals soon fell off drastically.

Why did QUBE falter? Analysis indicates that *The Polling Game* was perhaps not as much fun as its developers had anticipated. It was a little like the call in newspaper polls of today: a controversial subject such as abortion or gun control will draw thousands of responses, but a question relating to the activities of the county board of supervisors is virtually ignored.

Erik Barnouw suggests, quite rightly one suspects, that the major problem with QUBE was the question of privacy.[1] The QUBE computer came to know too much about its subscribers. It knew their politics, their buying habits, maybe even details of family income. At a time when the government seemed to be populated by an assortment of crooks and nuts (the Attorney General was under criminal indictment and the Secretary of the Interior announced that conservation was unnecessary as Armageddon would be taking place in just two hundred years, anyway), well, did one really want people like these accessing one's opinions and finances?

❖ INTERACTIVITY: A FEW SUCCESSES

It would seem that perhaps QUBE was the right idea at the wrong time. Still, there were other technologies that, while small and slow, have survived and seem actually to be growing steadily and surely. Enter the home computer. Right on time.

Interactive Computer Services: The 1990s

In 1980, the vast majority of people in the business world were checked out on electric typewriters and copying machines. By 1990, most were checked out on computers and fax machines. Even more interesting, computers and fax machines were beginning to spill over from the office into the home. With a phone modem, the efficient junior executive could work at home and transfer the fruits of his or her labors not just to a disk but directly to an office computer.

Thanks to the modem, the marriage between the computer industry and the telephone company has been consummated. This was the fusion of two of the three requisite technologies (minus television) necessary to bring about the completely interactive world.

Into the breach leapt two on-line subscription services, Compu-Serve and Prodigy, followed by others which have yet to dislodge the two leaders from the top of the heap. These companies provide their subscribers with a variety of services that boggle the mind: news, weather, instantaneous market reports, access to airline tickets (including a choice of schedules and prices), banking, shopping, games versus the computer, games versus other subscribers, tax help, sports information, bulletin boards, complete reference librar-ies including encyclopedias, plus two-way interaction with anyone and everyone on the system.

Naturally, these systems eventually attracted the attention of advertisers. As an example of how advertisers use these interactive systems, let's take a look at Ford's "advertising tree" on Prodigy. The "trunk" of an advertiser's "tree" appears on virtually every system. On various and appropriate screens throughout the Prodigy system, viewers are invited to [jump] into the World of Ford. Viewers who do are offered various branches for exploration: brands, products, financing, and more. A trip up the "financing" branch, viewers learn about Ford Credit, including financing and leasing options, as well as monthly payment calculations. Another branch takes you to a showroom displaying all Ford and Lincoln-Mercury models in all available colors. Throughout, viewers are invited to order literature and brochures. There's even a driving simulation game aimed at keeping viewers involved.

Prodigy, CompuServe, and their ilk seem to be pointing toward the future. They offer the viewer complete control of his or her selections. They offer a wide variety of subjects of interest, updated constantly. Trees, like that used by Ford, go marketing channels one better by offering information on demand. The only thing they lack is television. The narrow bandwidth of today's telephone lines prevents on-line services from offering nearly the amount of information or speed as a TV signal. And let's face it, computer graphics, no matter how sophisticated, are still no match for even a 280-line television screen.

The New Milieu: Jockeyers for Position

The interactive systems mentioned at the beginning of this chapter have one thing in common: they are interactive exclusively with existing programming. In other words, viewers are restricted to playing along with the game being shown at the time; the subscriber has no way to control programming.

The 1990s have seen the introduction of dozens of these new one-way interaction companies: small, aggressive, clever competitors aiming for the top. Leaders in this field include *TV Answer* of Reston, Virginia and two California companies, *IN* of Mountain View and *NTN* of Carlsbad. Of the three, only *NTN* has a nationwide subscriber base. In addition, there are half a dozen smaller companies up and running today and a dozen or so currently in test. They are, or will be, available to subscribers in various combinations of cable, phone, and satellite. Ultimately, both two-way computer technology and one-way television technology are less than completely satisfying. Computer technology, while satisfying to the interactive user, is less so to the advertiser. A computer tree, no matter how ingeniously designed, simply lacks the visual involvement possible with a 30-minute long-form commercial. One-way interactive TV solves the advertiser's problem, but poses a problem of its own: is it involving enough to command subscriber renewals once the novelty has worn off? Clearly, a new form of interaction is called for. And it's on the way.

Two-Way Interaction

What are the criteria for a successful two-way interactive system?

1. It must satisfy the involvement requirements of advertisers (e.g., TV rather than computer graphics).
2. It must have broad subscriber appeal; games and/or banking alone will not generate renewals.
3. It must be reasonably priced.
4. It must put at least some of the programming control in the hands of the viewer.

At this writing, it appears that the only operational two-way system is *GTE Main Street*, available in several large California cities. It currently meets all the criteria mentioned. If it has a current weakness, it is the absence of Video-On-Demand; viewers cannot call up movies and associated programming. And while this feature appears to have failed as a paid extra service and predictions would discourage much enthusiasm for its future, the feature, once included in the overall cost of the system, will make the offer somewhat more flexible. Due to the interest in this subject, a second book by this author is currently in preparation investigating methods and techniques major advertisers of national brands can use to fully utilize the interactive variable.

The next five to ten years are obviously going to be, in the words of the ancient Chinese curse, "interesting times" in the world of two-way interactive television. In deference to Ted Turner, it's going to be a real cup race. The sleek yachts are already lined up, flying proud flags: GTE, AT&T, First Cities, TCI, Time Warner, and Viacom Cable. It's going to be a long race, because there's a maelstrom ahead, waiting to tear off the masts and rip out the bottoms of the sleek ships, waiting to swallow revenues and reputations alike. It's a maelstrom resulting from two existing conditions: first, uncertainty about the kinds of interactive services the public will be willing to support and, second, lack of universally accepted standards in operating systems, hardware, and programming. Those who control the standards, or who happen by chance to develop technologies which match the standards that eventually emerge, will lead this industry into the future. They'll cross the line a-booming, with all flags flying, and claim the cup.

And the early results are coming in: AT&T and Viacom International, Inc. recently announced a joint test of interactive services by the end of 1993. Time Warner, U.S. West, Toshiba, ITOCHU Corp., and Silicon Graphics, Inc. are forming a partnership to develop full-service, interactive digital technology for the Orlando, Florida electronic superhighway. Microsoft, Intel, and General Instrument and Motorola, Scientific-Atlanta, and Apple/IBM are separate groups reportedly discussing development of digital cable TV converter boxes. And, most notably, a new company called Cablesoft is being formed by Time Warner, TCI and Microsoft. The company's mission is to create products for interactive TV programming including set-top operating software and hardware that promote a single (operating) standard across different cable networks.

❖ CHARTING THE STANDARDS

Industry standards: they're a blessing and a curse. In place, they can eventually save us all from a world of confusion. And with something as inherently confusing as interactivity, they are critical. But the wait for standards, usually prolonged, has the effect of stifling technological development. Investing in something that may or may not meet yet-to-be-established standards is not a game for the faint of heart. Yet often the race belongs to the swift, and standards are set de facto by the first company to get the upper hand in the marketplace. Cable became the standard delivery system before arguably superior DBS and microwave technologies managed to get their acts together. Thus playing it safe and waiting for the standards to become established can leave a company in the lurch, too far back to catch up. Most companies watch and wait, eventually operating on a best-guess scenario, making the investment at the last possible minute. Sometimes it pays off, sometimes it doesn't.

Remember the videotape wars fought by Beta (Sony) and VHS (Matsushita/JVC/Hitachi/et al.)? Both technologies were developed by Sony, which chose to market the superior picture quality of Betamax. VHS was discarded by Sony as inferior. Shut off from Beta, competitors like Matsushita/JVC/Hitachi et al. were forced to adapt VHS technology. Unable to compete with Beta on its strength—picture quality—they devised a twofold marketing strategy: (1) flood the U.S. home market with VHS standard VCR units, which would (2) convince the entertainment community to commit to the VHS format rather than Beta as the standard when producing prerecorded movies. Technically minded buyers, noting the superior picture quality, invested in Sony's Betamax technology. But most people, preferring quantity (a large selection of movies) to quality (a nice picture), went with VHS.

In recent years, Sony, still stinging from the Betamax defeat, has renewed the battle with its quality 8mm technology. Matsushita et al. are retaliating with VHS-C. At this writing, VHS-C, a latecomer to the race, seems to be gaining on 8mm, but it's really too close to call.

The establishment of computer standards has been even more confusing. In the early days, each computer manufacturer had its own operating system. Confused buyers, not to mention software writers, were reluctant to invest time and money in a company which may or may not be in business the next year. Finally, IBM, because of its size and reputation, ended the deadlock by actually publishing the design of its machines, thereby establishing its operating system, DOS, as the standard. It worked, but there was an unfortunate consequence—low-priced clones came on the market in direct competition with IBM.

While most computers were soon "IBM compatible," one wasn't. Apple, the largest producer of microcomputers, continued to promote its Macintosh operating system because of its "user-friendly" graphics. With the popularization of personal computers, user-friendliness became an important selling point. So important, in fact, that Microsoft developed "Windows," a DOS-based "shell" that makes DOS computers more Mac-like. The graphic user interface invented by Xerox and popularized by Mac is becoming the "standard" method of interfacing with the user.

As it turned out, the market was large and diverse enough to support two systems. Then, just as it seemed the smoke had cleared, along came UNIX. The UNIX system, as written by AT&T, was originally meant to operate on larger, science-oriented computers. As desktop models have increased in power and sophistication, however, UNIX has begun to compete with Windows and the Mac, largely due to the fact that it is not computer specific; that is, it will run on a variety of different computers.

Not everyone, however, is convinced the battle is over, even now. In addition to UNIX, there are a number of other promising science-based systems available from companies like SUN, Apollo, Hewlett-Packard, and NeXT. Also, IBM is convinced its OS-2 system has a chance to carve out a market. Who knows?

Throughout the last half of this book, ostensibly about the television industry, the computer industry has dodged in and out. The television/telephone/computer triumvirate that, most people agree, defines the future is only now taking shape. The stars of the cable and communications universe converge and align into new, megakinetic constellations. Telephones and computers continue to link up in the form of interactive services like Prodigy and Compu-Serve. QVC and Prodigy are exploring online versions of cable TV home shopping channels—theoretically, a first step toward conversion of today's interactive computer format to tomorrow's interactive television format (once established). Television and telephones continue to link up to legitimize shopping channels, infomercials, and direct response advertising and to form the basis of one-way interactive television. And now, with corporate alliances the magnitude of Time Warner/U.S. West and Time Warner, TCI and Microsoft (Cablesoft) beginning to emerge, we witness entities formidable enough to lead the way.

Fiber optic telephone lines bring us access to homes, two-way communications, and the potential for such technologies as high-definition television (HDTV).

Television brings us impact, involvement, immediacy. But computer technology would seem to be the logical minister to perform the ceremony between television and telephones. Computers can organize, react instantly, make magic happen. Which would lead one to believe that perhaps the most logical scenario . . . the Yellow Brick Road to follow . . . begins not in Hollywood (Munchkin Land), but in the Silicon Valley. We're off to see the wizard.

Bill Gates and Microsoft: Standard Setters?

Is this Oz? No, it's Microsoft. Brilliant, trendy, young people who love what they do and who are encouraged to follow their dreams cluster around fashionably and elegantly cluttered workstations, conversing in compubabble. With 140 million PCs worldwide using Microsoft's DOS operating system as of 1994, Microsoft's market value has climbed to $25 billion. And it just keeps growing all the time. It has become the symbol of corporate wealth and power. And in the courtyard lives a boa constrictor named ZsaZsa.

At the head of Microsoft is Bill Gates, not yet 40, but already a legend. Not surprisingly, Bill Gates has been thinking about two-way interactive television. And he has set his brilliant staff in search of what's been called the TV-PC. It's shaping up like this: high-definition TV will display digitized information, just like a PC, and fiber optic lines will make it possible to link TV-PCs so that vast amounts of information can be transported both to and from the home. Once these two innovations are in place (Gates believes that the cable companies will push them and figures they should be in place in the late 1990s), all that's needed is a type of cordless "air mouse" control similar to those in use on some of today's videogame machines. Finally, the entire home unit must cost less than $500 and be simple enough for even the most computer-illiterate subscriber to operate.

Armed with this air mouse, viewers won't have to waste time flipping through the five hundred available channels; instead, they can ask an on-screen "navigator" to help locate programs of choice. In the mood for a horror film? Just ask. The navigator will list the choices currently available. Can't decide which one? The navigator will allow you to check out what Siskel and Ebert had to say. If it turns out *The Texas Chain Saw Massacre* isn't everything you'd hoped, you might want to see how the Cubs are doing (another massacre?). At any time during the game you'll be able to call up a "baseball card" with stats on any player, check the line-up, or get scores on other games in progress. You could check out the availability of seats and order tickets to the game. Or you can "miter" the picture from the Cubs game into the upper left-hand corner of the screen and watch the Braves get massacred on the rest of the screen. You'll be able to order CDs from *MTV* or call up subtitles if you have difficulty understanding the lyrics. You'll be able to design a video birthday card full of sophisticated special effects and "send" it to your crazy cousin Arnie in Schenectady. You'll be able to buy everything from the sports coat Arsenio is wearing tonight to stocks and bonds.

Such is the promise of interactive television. And if computer technology is necessary to make it work, then Microsoft has the wealth, power, and bandwidth (brains) needed to bring it about. Logically, Bill Gates will be the catalyst who unites HDTV with fiber optics and brings two-way interactive television to the living rooms of America.

❖ THE RISE OF "LIFE-STYLE RETAILING"

Television's interactive future represents more—far more—than simply a revolution in communications. Perhaps its most important side effect will be a revolution in retailing. Since the very first marketplace appeared, probably around ten thousand years ago, human beings have thought in terms of "going to the store." At first, it might have been once a week or once a month, but as we advanced beyond subsistence living and moved into cities, the frequency of shopping increased. Today, few people actually produce any of the goods and services they need. We go to the store for everything. And if we don't go to the store, we order it out of a catalog or off the television screen. Interactivity will change all that.

❖ MARKETING CHANNELS IN THE TWO-WAY WORLD

If anything, marketing channels make more sense than ever on a two-way interactive system. With the air mouse replacing the telephone as the ordering device, that process is simplified. The simplicity of the system also serves to remove the VCR from the picture, with desired information simply stored for later use. This ease of storage will doubtless have the effect of widening the "window of interest" for the prospective buyer. You may not be planning to buy a new bedroom suite until next year, but if the navigator tells you Ethan Allen has a documercial running on *The Home Furnishings Channel* tonight, it's a simple matter to store it until you're ready to buy.

And how about our busy car buyer from Chapter 9? In an interactive world she'll have more options than ever before. She won't have to visit a dealership at all, if she doesn't want to. With an interactive unit in her living room she'll be able to arrange to have the dealer bring the car to her for a test drive the next day. If she decides to buy, she can arrange all the financing right there on the screen.

As we enter the new five-hundred-channel world, it behooves those of us in the communications industry to look at television not just from the perspective of traditional programmers, but from that of marketers, and to view it not just as an entertainment medium, but a new and exciting retail system. When we do, the broadcaster wins, the advertiser wins, and, best of all, the consumer wins.

Marketing channels promise much today. They promise even more in the interactive future.

In *The Popcorn Report*, futurist Faith Popcorn's latest book, she has titled Chapter 12 "The End of Shopping."[2] In it she describes today's shopping experience as "cumbersome, inefficient, a violation of trends." She foresees a world where consumers shop from the television screen, making their choices and buying directly from the producer, bypassing the retailer altogether. Homes will be equipped with holding tanks, some refrigerated, into which trucks will deliver everything from groceries to pharmacy items. Big-ticket items will be handled by sales reps who visit the home on call. Manufacturers will maintain an ongoing dialog with consumers, getting feedback on products from the development stage forward.

This provides a perfect example of the theme of this book: that technology precedes programming. Just as "entertainment" eventually became the programming of choice for radio, and later for television, so "marketing" is becoming a major alternative to entertainment as cable technology advances. As interactive technology continues to proliferate, entertainment-based programming will likely remain what it has been, while marketing-based programming will change our lives in ways we cannot yet fathom. Will we train for new jobs at home? Will we get advanced degrees from home? Will we conduct business at home? What will happen to packaging; will we need it? Will we need the post office? One thing we know for sure: for the first time in ten thousand years, it will not be necessary to go to the store.

No, we aren't there yet. We're several years away, in fact. But we're a long way ahead of where we were when the television set was just a box full of amusement-on-demand. The anomalies are there for everyone to see: from Dr. John Romulus Brinkley and his goat-gland transplants, to Ron Popeil, to Richard Simmons, to *Spring in Spring Hill*, to Saks Fifth Avenue and Calvin Klein on *QVC*, it is clear that television can sell as well as entertain. And it can move merchandise from the retail outlet as well as from the television screen. The time for marketing channels is now.

❖ ENDNOTES

1. Eric Barnouw, *Tube of Plenty: The Evolution of American Television* (New York: Oxford University Press, 1990).

2. Faith Popcorn, *The Popcorn Report* (New York: HarperCollins, 1991).

APPENDIX

Following is a company-by-company list of current advertisers in the sixteen categories designated as candidates likely to support a marketing channel. Figures shown here are taken from *AdWeek*'s 1992 supplement, "Superbrands: America's Top 2,000 Brands." The number of potential marketing channels is by no means limited to just this high-profile group. Got an idea for a channel? Look around and see if the category could generate between $50 million and $100 million in annual television advertising. Does your category meet the marketing channel criteria outlined in Chapter 10? If so, a marketing channel may be in your advertising future.

Automotive

Media Expenditures: $300–349.9 Million

Brand	Corporation
Chevrolet cars and trucks	General Motors Corp.
Ford cars and trucks	Ford Motor Co.
Toyota cars and trucks	Toyota Motor Sales USA, Inc.

Media Expenditures: $150–199.99 Million

Buick cars	General Motors Corp.
Dodge cars and trucks	Chrysler Corp.
Nissan cars and trucks	Nissan Motor Corp. USA

Media Expenditures: $100–149.9 Million

Acura cars	American Honda Motor Co., Inc.
Chrysler cars	Chrysler Corp.
Honda cars	American Honda Motor Co., Inc.
Mazda cars and trucks	Mazda Motor Corp.
Mitsubishi cars and trucks	Mitsubishi Corp.
Pontiac cars	General Motors Corp.

Media Expenditures: $50–99.9 Million

BMW cars	BMW of North America, Inc.
Cadillac cars	General Motors Corp.
General Motors corporate	General Motors Corp.
Geo™ cars	General Motors Corp.
Hyundai cars	Hyundai Motor America
Isuzu cars and trucks	American Isuzu Motors, Inc.
Jeep™ vehicles	Chrysler Corp.
Mercedes-Benz cars	Mercedes-Benz of NA, Inc.
Mercury cars	Ford Motor Co.
Midas muffler and brake shops	Midas International Corp.
Saturn™ cars	General Motors Corp.
Subaru cars	Subaru of America, Inc.
Volkswagen cars	Volkswagen of America, Inc.

Media Expenditures: $25–49.9 Million

Amoco gasoline	Amoco Oil Co.
Audi cars	Audi of America, Inc.
Chevron gasoline	Chevron USA, Inc.
Eagle™ cars	Chrysler Corp.
GMC™ trucks	General Motors Corp.
Goodyear car and truck tires	Goodyear Tire & Rubber Co.

Goodyear automotive service	Goodyear Tire & Rubber Co.
Lexus™ cars	Toyota Motor Sales USA, Inc.
Meineke discount muffler shops	Meineke Discount Mufflers, Inc.
Mobil gasoline	Mobil Corp.
Plymouth cars and vans	Chrysler Corp.
Volvo cars and wagons	Volvo North America Corp.

Media Expenditures: $15–24.9 Million

ARCO gasoline	ARCO Products Co.
Castrol GTX™ motor oil	Castrol, Inc.
Exxon gasoline	Exxon Corp.
Ford Motor corporate	Ford Motor Co.
Jaguar cars	Jaguar Cars, Inc.
Michelin tires	Michelin Tire Corp.
NAPA™ auto parts	National Automotive Parts Assn.
Pennzoil motor oil	Pennzoil Co.
STP™ oil and gas treatments	First Brands Corp.
Saab cars	Saab Cars USA, Inc.
Sears automotive centers	Sears, Roebuck & Co.
Shell petroleum products	Shell Oil Co.
Texaco gasoline	Texaco, Inc.
Trak auto parts stores	Trak Auto Corp.
Valvoline motor oil	Valvoline, Inc.

Media Expenditures: $10–14.9 Million

AC Delco automotive parts	Delco Products
AAMCO transmissions	AAMCO Transmissions, Inc.
Alfa Romeo cars	Alfa Romeo Distributors of NA
Armor all car care products	Armor All Products Corp.
B F Goodrich tires	Uniroyal Goodrich Tire Co.
BP gasoline	BP America, Inc.
Chief Auto Parts stores	Chief Auto Parts, Inc.
Conoco petroleum products	Conoco, Inc.
Firestone tires	Bridgestone/Firestone, Inc.
Ford parts and service	Ford Motor Co.
K-Mart automotive service	K-Mart Corp.

Prestone™ automotive products   First Brands Corp.
Quaker State motor oils   Quaker State Corp.
Union Oil gasoline   Unocal Corp.

Media Expenditures: $5–9.9 Million

Autolite™ spark plugs	Allied Signal, Inc.
Bridgestone tires	Bridgestone/Firestone, Inc.
Chrysler Motors parts and service	Chrysler Corp.
Citgo gasoline	Citgo Petroleum Corp.
Gumout™ automotive products	Pennzoil Co.
Havoline™ motor oil	Texaco, Inc.
Honda motorcycles and scooters	American Honda Motor Co., Inc.
Jiffy Lube™	Pennzoil Co.
Kelly-Springfield tires	Kelly-Springfield Tire Co.
MAACO auto painting and body work	MAACO Enterprises, Inc.
Mobile 1™ motor oil	Mobil Corp.
Monroe shock absorbers and struts	Monroe Auto Equipment Co.
Mopar™ auto parts	Chrysler Corp.
Motorcraft™ automotive products	Ford Motor Co.
Pep Boys auto parts stores	Pep Boys—Manny, Moe & Jack
Phillips 66™ gasoline	Phillips Petroleum Co.
Porsche cars	Porsche Cars North America, Inc.
Precision Tune tune-up shops	Precision Tune, Inc.
Quaker State™ Minit-Lube	Minit-Lube, Inc.
STP Son of a Gun™ protector	First Brands, Inc.
Scania™ heavy trucks	Saab Cars USA, Inc.
Speedy Muffler King™ mufflers	Tenneco, Inc.
Sunoco™ gasoline	Sun Co., Inc.
Turtle Wax products	Turtle Wax, Inc.
Western Auto Supply stores	Western Auto Supply Co.
Yugo cars	Yugo America, Inc.
Zerex™ antifreeze coolant	BASF Corp.

Media Expenditures: $3–4.9 Million

Brand	Corporation
Cincinnati Microwave radar detector	Cincinnati Microwave, Inc.
Fram™ oil filters	Allied Signal, Inc.
Kendall motor oils	Kendall Refining Co.
Marathon petroleum products	Marathon Oil Co.
Slick 50™ engine treatment products	Petrolon, Inc.

Vacation/Travel

Brand	Corporation

Media Expenditures: $100–149.9 Million

American Airlines	American Airlines, Inc.
Delta Air Lines	Delta Air Lines, Inc.

Media Expenditures: $50–99.9 Million

Continental Airlines	Continental Airlines Corp.
United Airlines	United Airlines, Inc.

Media Expenditures: $25–49.9 Million

Alamo car rental	Alamo Rent-a-car, Inc.
Amtrak passenger rail service	National RR Passenger Corp.
Avis car rental	Avis, Inc.
Carnival cruise line	Carnival Cruise Lines, Inc.
Hertz car rental	The Hertz Corp.
Holiday Inns	Holiday Corp.
Hyatt hotels	Hyatt Hotels Corp.
Marriott hotels and resorts	Marriott Corp.
Northwest Airlines	Northwest Airlines, Inc.
Norwegian cruise line	Kloster Cruise Ltd.
Royal Caribbean cruise line	Royal Caribbean Cruises Ltd.
Southwest Airlines	Southwest Airlines Co.
TWA Airlines	Trans World Airlines, Inc.
USAir	USAir, Inc.

Media Expenditures: $15–24.9 Million

Alaska Airlines	Alaska Airlines, Inc.
America West Airlines	America West Airlines, Inc.
Best Western hotels	Best Western International
British Airways	British Airways PLC
Budget car rental	Budget Rent-a-car Corp.
Canada tourism	Canada
Greyhound Lines	Greyhound Lines, Inc.
Hilton hotels and resorts	Hilton Hotels Corp.
Holland America Line Westours	Holland America Line Westours
Liberty travel services	Libgo Travel, Inc.
Mexico tourism	Mexico
Ryder truck rental	Ryder Systems, Inc.

Media Expenditures: $10–14.9 Million

Bahamas tourism	Bahamas
Bermuda tourism	Bermuda
Club Med travel services	Club Med Sales, Inc.
Costa cruise line	Costa Cruises
Delta shuttle	Delta Air Lines, Inc.
Embassy Suites hotels	Embassy Suites, Inc.
Enterprise car rental	Enterprise Rent-a-car
Illinois tourism	State of Illinois
Las Vegas tourism	City of Las Vegas
Lufthansa Airlines	Lufthansa German Airlines
Premier Cruises	Premier Cruise Lines Ltd.
Princess cruises and tours	Princess Tours, Inc.
Sheraton hotels	ITT Sheraton Corp.
Stouffer hotels and resorts	Stouffer Hotels & Resorts

Media Expenditures: $5–9.9 Million

Admiral™ cruises	Royal Caribbean Cruises Ltd.
Air Canada airlines	Air Canada
American Hawaii cruises	American Hawaii Cruises
Cancun tourism	Mexico
Chandris Celebrity™ cruises	Chandris, Inc.

Chandris Fantasy™ cruises	Chandris, Inc.
Choice hotels	Choice Hotels International, Inc.
Commodore cruises	Commodore Cruise Line
Cunard cruise line	Cunard Line Ltd.
Days Inns	Days Inns of America, Inc.
Dollar car rental	Dollar Rent-a-car Systems, Inc.
Florida tourism	State of Florida
Four Seasons hotels	Four Seasons Hotels
General™ car rental	Dynasty Express Corp.
Iberia Airlines	Iberia Airlines
Inter-Continental hotels	Inter-Continental Hotels Group
JAL Japan airlines	Japan Airlines Co.
Jamaica tourism	Jamaica
KLM Royal Dutch airlines	KLM Royal Dutch Airlines
Louisiana tourism	State of Louisiana
Manor Care™ hotels	Manor Healthcare Corp.
Mexicana airlines	Mexicana Airlines
Motel 6 motels	Motel 6 LP, Inc.
Nevada tourism	State of Nevada
New Orleans tourism	City of New Orleans
New York State tourism	State of New York
Outrigger Hotels Hawaii	Outrigger Hotels Hawaii
Pennsylvania tourism	State of Pennsylvania
Players Club International	Players International, Inc.
Pleasant Hawaiian Holidays	Pleasant Hawaiian Holidays
Princess hotels	Princess Hotels International
Puerto Rico tourism	Puerto Rico
Quantas airways	Quantas Airways Ltd.
Ramada inns/hotels/resorts	Ramada Franchise Systems, Inc.
Red Roof inns	Red Roof Inns, Inc.
Super 8 motels	Super 8 Motels, Inc.
Texas tourism	State of Texas
Thrifty car rental	Thrifty Rent-a-car System, Inc.
U.S. Virgin Islands tourism	U.S. Virgin Islands
Value car rental	Value Rent-a-car, Inc.
Virgin Atlantic Airways	Virgin Atlantic Airways

Virginia tourism	State of Virginia
Wyndham hotels and resorts	Wyndham Hotels & Resorts

Media Expenditures: $3–4.9 Million

Alaska tourism	State of Alaska
Alitalia airlines	Alitalia Airlines
Arizona tourism	State of Arizona
Carlson travel network	Carlson Companies, Inc.
Club America travel services	Club America Travel/Tour, Inc.
Colorado tourism	State of Colorado
Courtyard by Marriott™ hotels	Marriott Corp.
Empress travel services	Empress Travel Franchise Corp.
Georgia tourism	State of Georgia
Hawaii tourism	State of Hawaii
Helmsley hotels	Helmsley Hotels, Inc.
Howard Johnson motor lodges/restaurants	Howard Johnson Franchise System
Korean airlines	Korean Air
La Quinta inns	La Quinta Motor Inns, Inc.
Michigan tourism	State of Michigan
North Carolina tourism	State of North Carolina
Reno Air airlines	Reno Air, Inc.
Royal Viking™ cruise line	Kloster Cruise Ltd.
Sandals resorts	Sandals Resorts International
Sea Escape cruises	Sea Escape, Inc.
Superclubs resorts	Superclubs
SwissAir	SwissAir Transport Co., Inc.
Wisconsin tourism	State of Wisconsin

Furniture/Home Furnishings

Brand	Corporation

Media Expenditures: $25–49.9 Million

Ethan Allen home furnishings	Ethan Allen, Inc.
Stainmaster™ carpets	E. I. du Pont de Nemours & Co.

Media Expenditures: $15–24.9 Million

Contour™ lounge chairs	Craftmatic/Contour Industries
Craftmatic™ adjustable beds	Craftmatic/Contour Industries
Monsanto Wear-Dated™ carpets	Monsanto Co.

Media Expenditures: $10–14.9 Million

Armstrong flooring	Armstrong World Industries, Inc.
Lenox crystal and china	Lenox, Inc.
Sealy mattresses	Sealy Corp.

Media Expenditures: $5–9.9 Million

Corning cookware and dinnerware	Corning, Inc.
La-z-boy furniture	La-Z-Boy Chair Co.
Lane furniture	The Lane Company, Inc.
Lorus clocks	Seiko Time Corp.
Mannington resilient floors	Mannington Mills, Inc.
Ortho mattresses	Ortho Mattress, Inc.
Serta mattresses	Serta, Inc.
Simmons Beautyrest™ mattresses	Simmons Co.
Sleepy's mattresses	Sleepy's
Sun Valley waterbeds	Sun Valley Waterbeds
Thomasville furniture	Thomasville Furniture Inds, Inc.

Media Expenditures: $3–4.9 Million

Castro Convertible furniture	Castro Convertibles

Home Appliances

Brand	Corporation

Media Expenditures: $25–49.9 Million

Dirt Devil™ vacuum cleaners	Royal Appliance Mfg. Co.

Media Expenditures: $15–24.9 Million

Braun home appliances	Braun, Inc.
GE appliances	General Electric Co.
General Electric corporate	General Electric Co.
Maytag appliances	Maytag Co.
Whirlpool appliances	Whirlpool Corp.
Windmere™ appliances	Whirlpool Corp.

Media Expenditures: $10–14.9 Million

Carrier air conditioning/ heating products	Carrier Corp.
Eureka vacuum cleaners	The Eureka Co.
Kitchenaid appliances	Kitchenaid, Inc.
Lennox air conditioning/ heating products	Lennox International, Inc.
Regina steamer/carpet cleaner	The Regina Company, Inc.
Trane heating and cooling systems	The Trane Co.

Media Expenditures: $5–9.9 Million

Bissell carpet cleaning system	Bissell, Inc.
Black & Decker appliances	Black & Decker Corp.
Dust Buster™ power brush and vacuum	Black & Decker Corp.
First Alert™ home safety products	BRK Electronics
Frigidaire home appliances	Frigidaire Co.
Hoover vacuum cleaners	The Hoover Co.
Kenmor™ appliances	Sears, Roebuck & Co.
Magic Chef major appliances	Magic Chef Co.
Presto Saladshooter™	National Presto Industries, Inc.

Media Expenditures: $3–4.9 Million

Conair appliances	Conair Corp.
Culligan water conditioner	Culligan International Co.

Rheem air conditioning/
  heating products   Rheem Mfg. Co.
Sunbeam-Oster appliances   Sunbeam-Oster Co., Inc.

Jewelry/Watches

Brand	Corporation

Media Expenditures: $15–24.9 Million

Seiko watches and clocks	Seiko Time Corp.

Media Expenditures: $10–14.9 Million

Swatch watches and accessories	Swatch Watch USA
Timex watches	Timex Corp.

Media Expenditures: $5–9.9 Million

Citizen watches	Citizen Watch Co. of America
Franklin jewelry	Franklin Mint Corp.
Lorus watches	Seiko Time Corp.
Movado watches	Movado Watch Co.
Pulsar watches	Pulsar Time, Inc.
Rolex watches	Rolex Watch USA, Inc.

Stereo Equipment/TV/VCR/Electronics

Brand	Corporation

Media Expenditures: $50–99.9 Million

Energizer™ batteries	Eveready Battery Co.

Media Expenditures: $25–49.9 Million

Duracell batteries	Duracell USA, Inc.
Sony video equipment	Sony Corp.

Media Expenditures: $15–24.9 Million

Hitachi electronics	Hitachi Ltd.
Magnavox audio/video systems	Philips Consumer Electronics

Media Expenditures: $10–14.9 Million

Pioneer audio/video systems	Pioneer Electronics USA Corp.
RCA™ televisions	Thompson Consumer Electronics
Texas Instruments electronics	Texas Instruments, Inc.

Media Expenditures: $5–9.9 Million

BASF audio/videotapes	BASF Corp.
Canon camcorders	Canon USA, Inc.
Delco car stereo systems	Delco Products
Emerson electronics	Emerson Radio Corp.
Fuji videotape	Fuji Photo Film USA, Inc.
Goldstar electronics	Goldstar Electronics International
JVC electronics	JVC Company of America
Motorola electronics	Motorola, Inc.
Panasonic camcorders	Panasonic Co.
Philips compact disc players	Philips Consumer Electronics
Rayovac batteries	Rayovac Corp.
Sharp consumer electronics	Sharp Electronics Corp.
Sony color televisions	Sony Corp.
Sony compact disc players	Sony Corp.
TDK audio/videotapes	TDK Electronics Corp.

Media Expenditures: $3–4.9 Million

Mitsubishi audio/video systems	Mitsubishi Electronics America
Panasonic televisions	Panasonic Co.
RCA™ camcorders	Thompson Consumer Electronics
Samsung electronics	Samsung Electronics America
Sony audio/video tapes	Sony Corp.
Zenith televisions	Zenith Electronics Corp.

Computers/Computer Products

Brand	**Corporation**

Media Expenditures: $25–49.9 Million

Apple computers	Apple Computer, Inc.
Compaq computers	Compaq Computer Corp.
Digital computer systems	Digital Equipment Corp.

Hewlett-Packard computers/
  office equipment   Hewlett-Packard Co.
IBM computer systems   IBM Corp.
IBM corporate   IBM Corp.
NEC computer products   NEC Technologies, Inc.

Media Expenditures: $15–24.9 Million

Dell computers   Dell Computer Corp.
Epson computer products   Epson America, Inc.
Macintosh computers   Apple Computer, Inc.
Microsoft computer software   Microsoft Corp.
Prodigy™ on-line service   IBM Corp./Sears, Roebuck
Sharp information systems   Sharp Electronics Corp.

Media Expenditures: $10–14.9 Million

Intel computer components   Intel Corp.
Lotus computer software   Lotus Development Corp.
Tandy computer systems   Tandy Corp.
Toshiba Computer systems/
  products   Toshiba America Info Systems
Video Technology learning aids   Video Technology Industries

Media Expenditures: $5–9.9 Million

AST Computers   AST Research, Inc.
Amiga™ personal computers   Commodore International, Inc.
Ashton-Tate computer software   Ashton-Tate Co.
Compuadd computers   Compuadd Corp.
CompuServe information
  services   CompuServe, Inc.
Computer Associates software   Computer Associates Int'l, Inc.
Data General computer systems   Data General Corp.
Egghead Discount software   Egghead Discount Software, Inc.
Electronic Data Systems   Electronic Data Systems Corp.
Epson printers   Epson America, Inc.
Everex Computer Systems   Everex Systems, Inc.
IBM laser printers   IBM Corp.

Informix computer software	Informix Software, Inc.
Librex notebook computers	Librex Computer Systems
New Image computer systems	New Image Industries
Novell computer networks	Novell, Inc.
Oracle computer software	Oracle Corp.
Sun microsystems	Sun Microsystems, Inc.
Tandon computers and software	Tandon Corp.
Zenith data systems	Zenith Electronics Corp.

Media Expenditures: $3–4.9 Million

Apollo™ computers	Hewlett-Packard Co.
Aviion™ family of computer systems	Data General Corp.
NCR computer systems	NCR Corp.
Okidata computer products	Okidata Corp.
Wyse Technology computers	Wyse Technology, Inc.
Xerox desktop publishing systems	Xerox Corp.

Food

Brand	**Corporation**

Media Expenditures: $50–99.9 Million

Cheerios™ cereal	General Mills, Inc.

Media Expenditures: $25–49.9 Million

Campbell's condensed soups	Campbell Soup Co.
Eggo™ waffles	Mrs. Smith's Frozen Foods Co.
Kellogg's Corn Flakes™	Kellogg Co.
Kellogg's Frosted Flakes™	Kellogg Co.
Kellogg's Pop-Tarts™	Kellogg Co.
Kellogg's Raisin Bran™	Kellogg Co.
Nutrasweet™ sweetener	The Nutrasweet Co.
Post Grape-Nuts™ cereal	Kraft General Foods, Inc.
Total™ cereal	General Mills, Inc.
Total Raisin Bran™ cereal	General Mills, Inc.

Wrigley's Extra™ sugar-free
  gum   Wm. Wrigley Jr. Co.

Media Expenditures: $15–24.9 Million

Apple Cinnamon Cheerios™
  cereal   General Mills, Inc.
Basic 4™ cereal   General Mills, Inc.
Betty Crocker Hamburger/
  Chicken Helper™   General Mills, Inc.
Campbell's Soup-For-One™   Campbell Soup Co.
Certs™ breath mints   American Chicle Co.
Cool Whip™ frozen whipped
  toppings   Kraft General Foods, Inc.
Duncan Hines™ mixes   The Procter & Gamble Co.
Fruit Corners™ snacks   General Mills, Inc.
Gerber baby foods   Gerber Products Co.
Healthy Choice™ foods   ConAgra, Inc.
Heinz tomato ketchups   Heinz USA
Honey Nut Cheerios™ cereal   General Mills, Inc.
I Can't Believe It's Not Butter™   Van Den Bergh Foods Co.
Jell-O™ gelatin dessert   Kraft General Foods, Inc.
Jif™ peanut butter   The Procter & Gamble Co.
Kellogg's Frosted Mini-Wheats™   Kellogg Co.
Kellogg's Just Right™ cereal   Kellogg Co.
Kellogg's Nut & Honey™ cereal   Kellogg Co.
Kellogg's Product 19™ cereal   Kellogg Co.
Kellogg's Rice Krispies™ cereal   Kellogg Co.
Kellogg's Special K™ cereal   Kellogg Co.
Kraft Miracle Whip™ and
  Whip Light™   Kellogg Co.
Kraft salad dressings   Kraft General Foods, Inc.
Louis Rich turkey products   Louis Rich Co.
Lucky Charms™ cereal   General Mills, Inc.
M & M chocolate candies   M & M/Mars
Oscar Mayer luncheon meats   Oscar Mayer Foods Corp.
Perdue poultry   Perdue Farms
Philadelphia™ cream cheese   Kraft General Foods, Inc.

Post Fruity/Cocoa Pebbles™
  cereals   Kraft General Foods, Inc.
Post Honey Bunches of Oats™
  cereal   Kraft General Foods, Inc.
Post Natural Raisin Bran™
  cereal   Kraft General Foods, Inc.
Quaker Oats   The Quaker Oats Co.
Ouaker Oats instant oatmeal   The Quaker Oats Co.
Ragu pasta sauces   Ragu Foods Co.
Stove-Top Stuffing™   Kraft General Foods, Inc.
Trident™ sugarless gum   American Chicle Co.
Triples™ cereal   General Mills, Inc.
Uncle Ben's rice   Uncle Ben's, Inc.
Velveeta™ cheese   Kraft General Foods, Inc.
Wrigley's Doublemint™ gum   Wm. Wrigley Jr. Co.
Wrigley's Spearmint™ gum   Wm. Wrigley Jr. Co.

Media Expenditures: $10–14.9 Million

A-1™ steak sauce   Nabisco Foods Group
Baskin-Robbins ice cream   Baskin-Robbins, Inc.
Campbell's Chunky™ soups   Campbell Soup Co.
Campbell's Healthy Request™
  soups   Campbell Soup Co.
Cap'N Crunch™ cereal   The Quaker Oats Co.
Care Free™ sugarless gum   Planters Lifesaver Co.
Cheez Whiz™ cheese products   Kraft General Foods, Inc.
Chef Boyardee™ canned pasta   American Home Foods
Chiquita™ fruits and juices   Chiquita Brands Int'l., Inc.
Cinnamon Toast Crunch™
  cereal   General Mills, Inc.
Cocoa Puffs™ cereal   General Mills, Inc.
Contadina™ fresh pasta and
  sauces   Nestlé Brands Foodservice Co.
Crisco™ oil and shortening   The Procter & Gamble Co.
Dannon yogurt   Dannon Co., Inc.
Dentyne™ gum   American Chicle Co.
Doritos™ tortilla chips   Frito-Lay, Inc.

Eagle™ tortilla chips	Eagle Snacks, Inc.
Equal™ sweetener	Monsanto Co.
Frito's corn chips	Frito-Lay, Inc.
Golden Grahams™ cereal	General Mills, Inc.
Good Seasons™ salad dressing mix	Kraft General Foods, Inc.
Great Starts™ breakfast foods	Campbell Soup Co.
Green Giant™ vegetables	Pillsbury Co.
Häagen-Dazs ice cream	The Häagen-Dazs Co.
Hellmann's™ mayonnaise	CPC International, Inc.
Hidden Valley Ranch™ salad dressing	Kingsford Products Co.
Hillshire Farms processed meats	Hillshire Farms
Holly Farms™ poultry	Tyson Foods, Inc.
Jell-O™ pudding and pie mixes	Kraft General Foods, Inc.
Keebler Pizzerias™ crackers	Keebler Co.
Kellogg's Fruit Loops™ cereal	Kellogg Co.
Kellogg's All Bran™ cereal	Kellogg Co.
Kellogg's Corn Pops™ cereal	Kellogg Co.
Kellogg's Cracklin' Oat Bran™	Kellogg Co.
Kellogg's Crispix™ cereal	Kellogg Co.
Kellogg's 40 Percent Bran Flakes™ cereal	Kellogg Co.
Kellogg's Nutri-Grain™ bars	Kellogg Co.
Kellogg's Nutri-Grain™ cereal	Kellogg Co.
Kix™ cereal	General Mills, Inc.
Knudsen dairy products	Knudsen Dairies
Kraft dinners	Kraft General Foods, Inc.
Kraft mayonnaise	Kraft General Foods, Inc.
Kraft Touch of Butter™ spread	Kraft General Foods, Inc.
Lean Cuisine™ frozen entrees	Stouffer Foods Corp.
Life Savers™ candy	Planters Lifesaver Co.
Light 'n Lively™ dairy products	Kraft General Foods, Inc.
Minute Rice™	Kraft General Foods, Inc.
Nabisco Shredded Wheat™ cereal	Nabisco Foods Group
Nestlé Crunch™ chocolate bar	Nestlé Brands Foodservice Co.

Oreo™ cookies	Nabisco Foods Group
Orville Redenbacher™ microwave popcorn	Hunt-Wesson, Inc.
Oscar Mayer hot dogs	Oscar Mayer Foods Corp.
P B Max Real Peanut™ candy bar	M & M/Mars
Pam™ cooking spray	American Home Foods
Planters nuts and snacks	Planters Lifesavers Co.
Post Fruit & Fibre™ cereal	Kraft General Foods, Inc.
Prego™ spaghetti sauces	Campbell Soup Co.
Progresso™ soups	Pet, Inc.
Promise™ margarine	Van Den Bergh Foods Co.
Puritan™ cooking oil	The Procter & Gamble Co.
Quaker Life™ cereal	The Quaker Oats Co.
Quaker Oat Bran™ cereal	The Quaker Oats Co.
Quaker Oat Squares™ cereal	The Quaker Oats Co.
Ruffles™ potato chips	Frito-Lay, Inc.
Shake 'N Bake™ coating mix	Kraft General Foods, Inc.
Shedd's Country Crock™ margarine/spread	Van Den Bergh Foods Co.
Skippy™ peanut butter	CPC International, Inc.
Snickers™ candy bar	M & M/Mars
Starburst Fruit Chews™	M & M/Mars
Stouffer's frozen foods	Stouffer Foods Corp.
Sunchips Multigrain™ chips	Frito-Lay, Inc.
Teddy Grahams™	Nabisco Foods Group
Trix™ cereal	General Mills, Inc.
Twix™ cookie bars	M & M/Mars
Velveeta Shells & Cheese™ dinner	Kraft General Foods, Inc.
Weight Watchers frozen foods	Weight Watchers Food Co., Inc.
Wesson cooking and salad oils	Hunt-Wesson, Inc.
Wheat Thins™ snack crackers	Nabisco Foods Group
Wheaties™ cereal	General Mills, Inc.
Wrigley's Big Red™ gum	Wm. Wrigley Jr. Co.
Wrigley's Freedent™ gum	Wm. Wrigley Jr. Co.
Wrigley's Juicy Fruit™ gum	Wm. Wrigley Jr. Co.

Media Expenditures: $5–9.9 Million

Akzo salt	Akzo America, Inc.
Ball Park™ franks	Hygrade Food Products Corp.
Banquet Kid Cuisine™ frozen foods	ConAgra, Inc.
Bar None™ candy bar	Hershey Chocolate USA
Bisquick™ flour	General Mills, Inc.
Boboli™ Italian bread shells	Kraft General Foods, Inc.
Bounty™ candy bars	M & M/Mars
Breath Savers™ sugar-free mints	Planters Lifesavers Co.
Breyer's™ dairy products	Kraft General Foods, Inc.
Bryan™ foods	Sara Lee Corp.
Bubble Yum™ bubble gum	Planters Lifesavers Co.
The Budget Gourmet™ frozen entrees	Kraft General Foods, Inc.
Butterfinger™ candy bar	Nestlé Brands Foodservice Co.
California Slim low-calorie meals	California Slim, Inc.
Campbell's Home Cookin'™ soups	Campbell Soup Co.
Carnation Good Start™ baby food	Nestlé Beverage Co.
Carnation Instant Breakfast™ drink	Nestlé Beverage Co.
Chee-tos™ cheese puffs	Frito-Lay, Inc.
Clorets™ breath freshner mints	American Chicle Co.
Clusters™ cereal	General Mills, Inc.
Coffee-Mate™ coffee creamer	Nestlé Beverage Co.
Combos™ snacks	M & M/Mars
Country Pride™ chicken	ConAgra, Inc.
Craisins™ cranberry snack	Ocean Spray Cranberries, Inc.
Del Monte canned vegetables	Del Monte USA
Digiornio™ pastas and sauces	Kraft General Foods, Inc.
Domino sugar	Domino Sugar Corp.
Double Chex™ cereal	Ralston Purina Co.
Dovebar™ ice cream bar	Dove International, Inc.

Eckrich franks/sausages/ cold cuts	Armour Swift-Eckrich, Inc.
5th Avenue™ candy bar	Hershey Chocolate USA
Fig Newtons™	Nabisco Foods Group
Flowers Industries food products	Flowers Industries, Inc.
Fruitola™ dairy products	Dreyer's Grand Ice Cream, Inc.
Grey Poupon™ mustards	Nabisco Foods Group
Healthy Sensation™ salad dressings	Thomas J. Lipton Co.
Hebrew National™ foods	National Foods, Inc.
Heinz 57 sauce	Heinz USA
Hershey's Kisses™	Hershey Chocolate USA
Hershey's Symphony Bar™	Hershey Chocolate USA
Hershey's syrup	Hershey Chocolate USA
Hostess Twinkies™ and Cupcakes	Continental Baking Co.
Hunt's Manwich™ sauce	Hunt-Wesson, Inc.
Jeno's™ frozen pizza and pizza rolls	Pillsbury Co.
Keebler Elfkins™ sandwich cookies	Keebler Co.
Keebler Wheatables™ crackers	Keebler Co.
Kellogg's Apple Jacks™ cereal	Kellogg Co.
Kellogg's Honey Smacks™ cereal	Kellogg Co.
Kellogg's Kenmei Rice Bran™ cereal	Kellogg Co.
Kellogg's Mueslix™ cereal	Kellogg Co.
Kikkoman sauces	Kikkoman International, Inc.
Kraft American cheese singles	Kraft General Foods, Inc.
Kraft Spreadery™ cheese spread	Kraft General Foods, Inc.
Lea & Perrins sauces	Lea & Perrins, Inc.
Lender's bagels	Lender's Bagel Bakery
Lipton Golden Sautee™ rice dish	Thomas J. Lipton Co.
Lipton soup and dip mixers	Thomas J. Lipton Co.
Little Debbie™ snack cakes	McKee Baking Co.

Louis Kemp Crab/Lobster Delights™	Louis Kemp Seafood Co.
Mazola™ corn oil	CPC International, Inc.
Micro Magic™ convenience foods	J. R. Simplot Co.
Milky Way™ candy bar	M & M/Mars
Minute™ microwave dishes	Kraft General Foods, Inc.
Mr. Phipps™ pretzels	Nabisco Foods Group
Mrs. Dash™ seasoning	Alberto Culver Co.
Nabisco Cream of Wheat™ cereal	Nabisco Foods Group
Nestlé Alpine™ white chocolate bar	Nestlé Brands Foodservice Co.
Nestlé milk chocolate bar	Nestlé Brands Foodservice Co.
Oatmeal Raisin Crisp™ cereal	General Mills, Inc.
Old El Paso™ Mexican foods	Pet, Inc.
Ortega™ Mexican foods	Nabisco Foods Group
Orville Redenbacher™ popping corn	Hunt-Wesson, Inc.
Oscar Mayer Lunchables™	Oscar Mayer Foods Corp.
Pace Mexican sauces	Pace Foods Co.
Peter Pan™ peanut butter	Hunt-Wesson, Inc.
Peter Paul Almond Joy™ candy bar	Hershey Chocolate USA
Pillsbury baking mixes	Pillsbury Co.
Pillsbury Oven Lovin'™ cookie dough	Pillsbury Co.
Pillsbury Refrig™ bread dough	Pillsbury Co.
Pillsbury Toaster Strudel™	Pillsbury Co.
Post Alpha-bits™ cereal	Kraft General Foods, Inc.
Post Honeycomb™ cereal	Kraft General Foods, Inc.
Post Super Golden Crisp™ cereal	Kraft General Foods, Inc.
Pringle's™ potato chips	The Procter & Gamble Co.
Reese's Peanut Butter Cups™	Hershey Chocolate USA
Ritz Bits™ crackers	Nabisco Foods Group
Ritz™ crackers	Nabisco Foods Group

Roman Meal breads	Roman Meal Co.
Sara Lee frozen baked goods	Sara Lee Corp.
Sargento cheese	Sargento Cheese Co., Inc.
Seven Seas™ salad dressings	Kraft General Foods, Inc.
Skittles™ bite-size candies	M & M/Mars
Smucker's jams/jellies/ preserves	J. M. Smucker Co.
Sunbeam™ bakery products	Quality Bakers of America, Inc.
Sunkist Fun Fruit™ snacks	Thomas J. Lipton Co.
Sunsweet prunes	Sunsweet Growers, Inc.
Swanson Kids Fun Fest™ dinners	Campbell Soup Co.
Sweet 'N Low™ sugar substitute	Cumberland Packing Corp.
Swift Butterball™ turkey/ cold cuts	Armour Swift-Eckrich, Inc.
Thomas' English Muffins™	Best Foods Baking Group
3 Musketeers™ candy bar	M & M/Mars
Tic Tac™ mints	Ferrero USA, Inc.
Toblerone™ chocolate	Jacobs Suchard, Inc.
Top Shelf™ main dish entrees	Geo. A. Hormel & Co.
Totino's™ frozen pizza/pan pizza	Pillsbury Co.
La Victoria salsas and sauces	La Victoria Foods, Inc.
Wise™ snacks	Borden, Inc.
Yoplait yogurt	Yoplait USA

Media Expenditures: $3–4.9 Million

Aunt Jemima™ syrups	The Quaker Oats Co.
Beech-Nut baby foods	Beech-Nut Nutrition Corp.
Birds Eye™ frozen vegetables	Kraft General Foods, Inc.
Bob Evans Farms sausage products	Bob Evans Farms, Inc.
Bull's Eye™ barbecue sauce	Kraft General Foods, Inc.
Chips Ahoy!™ cookies	Nabisco Foods Group
La Choy™ oriental food products	Hunt-Wesson, Inc.
Creamettes™ pastas	Borden, Inc.

Del Monte Lite™ canned fruits	Del Monte USA
Entenmann's baked goods	Entenmann's, Inc.
Ferrero chocolates	Ferrero USA, Inc.
Fisher dry roasted nuts	Fisher Nut Co.
Gorton's frozen entrees	The Gorton Group
Harvest Crisps™ crackers	Nabisco Foods Group
Heinz home-style gravies	Heinz USA
Hershey baking products	Hershey Chocolate USA
Honey Maid™ graham crackers	Nabisco Foods Group
Hunt's tomato products	Hunt-Wesson, Inc.
Jimmy Dean breakfast sausage	Jimmy Dean Meat Co., Inc.
Kit Kat™ candy bar	Hershey Chocolate USA
Lawry's seasonings and spices	Lawry's Foods, Inc.
Le Menu Light™ frozen entrees	Campbell Soup Co.
Leaf candies	Leaf, Inc.
Life Savers Holes™ candy	Planters Lifesaver Co.
Lipton's Noodles and Sauce™	Thomas J. Lipton Co.
Log Cabin™ syrups	Kraft General Foods, Inc.
Mars Bar™ candy bar	M & M/Mars
Micro Cup™ single-serve soups/entrees	Geo. A. Hormel & Co.
Mini Oreo™ cookies	Nabisco Foods Group
On-Cor frozen entrees	On-Cor Frozen Foods, Inc.
Ore-Ida frozen french fries	Ore-Ida Foods Co., Inc.
Ore-Ida twice baked potatoes	Ore-Ida Foods Co., Inc.
Parkay™ margarine	Kraft General Foods, Inc.
Pepperidge Farm frozen foods	Pepperidge Farm, Inc.
Peter Paul Mounds™ candy bar	Hershey Chocolate USA
Pillsbury pizzas	Pillsbury Co.
Pillsbury refrigerated pastry	Pillsbury Co.
Post Natural Bran Flakes™ cereal	Kraft General Foods, Inc.
Quaker 100 Percent Natural™ cereal	The Quaker Oats Co.
Raisin Nut Bran™ cereal	General Mills, Inc.
Tyson frozen chicken	Tyson Foods, Inc.
Vlasic pickles	Vlasic Foods, Inc.

Wheaties Honey Gold™ cereal   General Mills, Inc.
York Peppermint Patties™   Hershey Chocolate USA

Beverages

Brand   **Corporation**

Media Expenditures: $50–99.9 Million

Coca-Cola Classic™   The Coca-Cola Co.
Diet Coke™   The Coca-Cola Co.
Diet Pepsi™   Pepsi-Cola Co.
Dr. Pepper and Diet Dr. Pepper™ Dr. Pepper Co.
Folger's coffee   Folger Coffee Co.
Maxwell House™ coffees   Kraft General Foods, Inc.
Pepsi-Cola   Pepsi-Cola Co.

Media Expenditures: $25–49.9 Million

Gatorade Thirst Quencher™   The Quaker Oats Co.
General Foods International™
   coffees   Kraft General Foods, Inc.
7-Up™   The Seven-Up Company
Sprite™   The Coca-Cola Co.
Tropicana fruit juices   Tropicana Products, Inc.

Media Expenditures: $15–24.9 Million

Diet 7-Up™   The Seven-Up Co.
Folger's decaffeinated coffee   Folger Coffee Co.
Minute Maid™ fruit juices   Coca-Cola Foods
Mountain Dew™   Pepsi-Cola Co.
Taster's Choice™ coffee   Nestlé Beverage Co.

Media Expenditures: $10–14.9 Million

A & W cream soda   A & W Brands, Inc.
Canada Dry™ beverages   Cadbury Beverages, Inc.
Crystal Light™ sugar-free
   drink mix   Kraft General Foods, Inc.

Dole juices — Dole Food Co.
Evian spring water — Evian Waters of France
Kool-Aid™ drink mixes — Kraft General Foods, Inc.
Lipton regular teas — Thomas J. Lipton Co.
Minute Maid™ orange soda — The Coca-Cola Co.
Nescafé™ instant coffees — Nestlé Beverage Co.
Ocean Spray fruit juices — Ocean Spray Cranberries, Inc.
Tropicana Twister™ juices — Tropicana Products, Inc.
V-8™ juice — Campbell Soup Co.
Veryfine juices — Veryfine Products Co.

Media Expenditures: $5–9.9 Million

A & W root beer — A & W Brands, Inc.
Celestial Seasonings teas — Celestial Seasonings, Inc.
Citrus Hill™ juices — The Procter & Gamble Co.
Country Time™ lemonade drink mix — Kraft General Foods Co.
Diet Sprite™ — The Coca-Cola Co.
Folger's Gourmet Supreme™ coffee — Folger Coffee Co.
Hi-C™ fruit drinks — Coca-Cola Foods
Hills Brothers™ coffee — Nestlé Beverage Co.
Juice and More™ beverage — Gerber Products Co.
Lipton iced tea products — Thomas J. Lipton Co.
MJB™ coffee — Nestlé Beverage Co.
Nestea™ instant teas and tea bags — Nestlé Beverage Co.
Nestlé Quik™ chocolate milk — Nestlé Beverage Co.
Ocean Spray fruit drinks — Ocean Spray Cranberries, Inc.
Perrier mineral water — Perrier Group
RC™ Cola — Royal Crown Cola Co.
Sanka™ coffee — Kraft General Foods, Inc.
Schweppes™ ginger ale — Cadbury Beverages, Inc.
Snapple natural beverages — Snapple Natural Beverage Co.
Sunny Delight™ fruit drink — The Procter & Gamble Co.

Tetley teas	Tetley, Inc.
Welch's fruit juices	Welch Foods, Inc.

Media Expenditures: $3–4.9 Million

Community coffee	Community Coffee Co., Inc.
Slice™	Pepsi-Cola Co.
Sparkletts™ bottled water	McKesson Water Products Co.
Squeezit™ fruit drinks	General Mills, Inc.
Yuban™ coffee	Kraft General Foods, Inc.

Restaurants

Brand	Corporation

Media Expenditures: $850–899.9 Million

McDonald's restaurants	McDonald's Corp.

Media Expenditures: $100–149 Million

Burger King restaurants	Burger King Corp.
Kentucky Fried Chicken™ restaurants	KFC Corp.
Pizza Hut restaurants	Pizza Hut, Inc.
Taco Bell restaurants	Taco Bell Corp.

Media Expenditures: $50–99.9 Million

Domino's Pizza delivery	Domino's Pizza, Inc.
Hardee's restaurants	Hardee's Food Systems, Inc.
Little Caesars restaurants	Little Caesars Enterprises, Inc.
Red Lobster restaurants	Red Lobster USA
Wendy's restaurants	Wendy's International, Inc.

Media Expenditures: $25–49.9 Million

Arby's restaurants	Arby's, Inc.
Dairy Queen restaurants	American Dairy Queen Corp.
Dunkin' Donuts	Dunkin' Donuts, Inc.
Jack-in-the-Box™ restaurants	Foodmaker, Inc.

Long John Silver's restaurants — Long John Silver's, Inc.
Sizzler restaurants — Sizzler International, Inc.

Media Expenditures: $15–24.9 Million

Bennigan's™ restaurants — S & A Restaurant Corp.
Carl's Jr.™ restaurants — Carl Karcher Enterprises, Inc.
Church's Fried Chicken™
 restaurants — Al Copeland Enterprises, Inc.
Denny's restaurants — Denny's, Inc.
Ponderosa™ steakhouses — Metromedia Steakhouses, Inc.
Roy Rogers™ restaurants — Hardee's Food Systems, Inc.

Media Expenditures: $10–14.9 Million

Bob Evans Farm restaurants — Bob Evans Farms, Inc.
Chi-Chi's Mexican restaurants — Chi-Chi's, Inc.
Chili's Grill & Bar — Chili's, Inc.
Popeye's Famous™ fried chicken — Al Copeland Enterprises, Inc.
Rally's Hamburger™ restaurants — Rally's, Inc.
TCBY frozen yogurt shops — TCBY Enterprises, Inc.
White Castle restaurants — White Castle System, Inc.

Media Expenditures: $5–9.9 Million

Bakers Square restaurants — Bakers Square Restaurants, Inc.
Big Boy™ drive-in restaurants — Marriott Corp.
Black Angus™ restaurants — Stuart Anderson Restaurants
Bob's Big Boy™ restaurants — Marriott Corp.
Captain D's™ restaurants — Shoney's, Inc.
Carrows Hickory Chip™
 restaurants — Grace Restaurant Co.
Carvel ice cream shops — Carvel Corp.
Chuck E. Cheese™ restaurants — Showbiz Pizza Time, Inc.
Del Taco restaurants — Del Taco Restaurants, Inc.
El Pollo Loco restaurants — El Pollo Loco
Friendly Ice Cream restaurants — Friendly Ice Cream Corp.
International House of Pancakes — IHOP Corp.

Krystal restaurants   Krystal Co.
Perkins Family restaurants   Perkins Family Restaurants
Pizza Inn restaurants   Pizza Inn, Inc.
Rax restaurants   Rax Restaurants, Inc.
Round Table Pizza restaurants   The Round Table Franchise Corp.
Shakey's pizza restaurants   Shakey's, Inc.
Skipper's seafood restaurants   Skipper's, Inc.
Village Inn™ restaurants   Vicorp Restaurants, Inc.
Whataburger restaurants   Whataburger, Inc.

Media Expenditures: $3–4.9 Million

Cocos™ coffee shops   Family Restaurant Enterprises Grp.
Outback Steak restaurants   Outback Steak Restaurants
Sonic Drive-in™ restaurants   Sonic Industries, Inc.
Steak & Ale™ restaurants   S & A Restaurant Corp.

Alcohol (Beer/Wine/Liquor)

Brand   **Corporation**

Media Expenditures: $100–149.9 Million

Budwiser™ beer   Anheuser-Busch, Inc.
Miller Genuine™ draft beer   Miller Brewing Co.

Media Expenditures: $50–99.9 Million

Bud Dry™ beer   Anheuser-Busch, Inc.
Bud Light™ beer   Anheuser-Busch, Inc.
Coors Light™ beer   Coors Brewing Co.
Miller Light™ beer   Miller Brewing Co.

Media Expenditures: $25–49.9 Million

Coors beer   Coors Brewing Co.
Gallo wines   E. & J. Gallo Winery
Heineken™ beer   Van Munching & Co., Inc.
Miller High Life™ beer   Miller Brewing Co.

Media Expenditures: $15–24.9 Million

Absolut™ vodka	Carillon Importers Ltd.
Bartles & Jaymes™ wine coolers	E. & J. Gallo Winery
Busch beer	Anheuser-Busch, Inc.
Coors Extra Gold™ beer	Coors Brewing Co.
Keystone™ beer	Coors Brewing Co.
Old Milwaukee™ beer/light beer	The Stroh Brewery Co.
Sharp's™ nonalcoholic beer	Miller Brewing Co.

Media Expenditures: $10–14.9 Million

Anheuser-Busch corporate	Anheuser-Busch, Inc.
Bacardi Breezers™	Bacardi Imports, Inc.
Bailey's Original Irish Cream™	The Paddington Corp.
Beck's™ beer	Dribeck Importers, Inc.
Colt 45™ malt liquor beer	G. Heileman Brewing Co., Inc.
Cutty Sark™ Scotch whiskey	W. A. Taylor & Co.
Dewars™ blended Scotch whiskey	Schenley Distillers, Inc.
Hennessy™ cognac	Schieffelin & Somerset Co.
Michelob™ beer	Anheuser-Busch, Inc.
Molson beer and ale	Molson Breweries USA
Seagram's wine coolers	Joseph E. Seagram Co.
Smirnoff™ vodka	Heublein, Inc.
Stolichnaya™ vodka	Monsieur Henri Wines Ltd.
Tott's™ champagne	E. & J. Gallo Winery

Media Expenditures: $5–9.9 Million

Bacardi rums	Bacardi Imports, Inc.
Ballantine's™ Scotch whiskey	Hiram Walker & Sons, Inc.
Ballatore™ champagne	E. & J. Gallo Winery
Beefeater™ gin	Hiram Walker & Sons, Inc.
Bombay™ gin	Carillon Importers Ltd.
Canadian Club™ blended whiskey	Hiram Walker & Sons Ltd.
Canadian Mist™ whiskey	Brown-Forman Beverage Co.

Carlsberg™ beer	Anheuser-Busch, Inc.
Chivas Regal™ Scotch whiskey	Joseph E. Seagram Co.
Corona Extra™ beer	Barton Beers Ltd.
E & J brandy	E. & J. Gallo Winery
Grand Marnier™ liqueur	Carillon Importers Ltd.
J & B Rare™ Scotch whiskey	The Paddington Corp.
Jack Daniel's™ whiskey	Brown-Forman Beverage Co.
Jim Beam liquors	Jim Beam Brands Co.
Johnnie Walker™ Scotches	Schieffelin & Somerset Co.
Kahlua™ liqueur	Hiram Walker & Sons, Inc.
Martini & Rossi™ wine	Bacardi Imports, Inc.
Michelob Dry™ beer	Anheuser-Busch, Inc.
Pabst beers	Pabst Brewing Co.
Remy Martin cognac	Remy Martin Amerique, Inc.
Rums of Puerto Rico™	Puerto Rico
Schlitz™ malt liquor beer	The Stroh Brewery Co.
Seagram's V O™ Canadian whiskey	Joseph E. Seagram Co.
Seagram's Crown Royal™ whiskey	Joseph E. Seagram Co.
Seagram's Extra Dry™ gin	Joseph E. Seagram Co.
Stock™ vermouth	Distillerie Stock USA, Inc.
Tanqueray™ London gin	The Guinness Import Co.

Media Expenditures: $3–4.9 Million

Amstel Light™ beer	Van Munching & Co., Inc.
Boone's™ wine	E. & J. Gallo Winery
Courvoisier™ cognac	W. A. Taylor & Co.
Gilbey's™ London gin and vodka	Jim Beam Brands Co.
Korbel™ champagnes and brandies	Brown-Forman Beverage Co.
Martell's™ cognac	Joseph E. Seagram Co.
Moussy™ nonalcoholic beer	Coors Brewing Co.
Old Style™ beer	G. Heileman Brewing Co., Inc.
Rolling Rock™ beer	Latrobe Brewing Co.

Seagram's 7 Crown™ blended whiskey	Joseph E. Seagram Co.
Southern Comfort™ whiskey	Brown-Forman Beverage Co.
Wild Turkey™ bourbon whiskey	Heublein, Inc.
Windsor Supreme™ Canadian whiskey	Jim Beam Brands Co.

Cosmetics

Brand	**Corporation**

Media Expenditures: $50–99.9 Million

Cover Girl™ cosmetics	The Procter & Gamble Co.
Sensor™ shaving system	The Gillette Co.

Media Expenditures: $25–49.9 Million

Crest™ toothpaste	The Procter & Gamble Co.
Degree™ antiperspirant	Helene Curtis, Inc.
Head & Shoulders™ shampoo	The Procter & Gamble Co.
Helene Curtis Salon Selectives™	Helene Curtis, Inc.
Huggies™ disposable diapers	Kimberly-Clark Corp.
L'Oréal cosmetics	L'Oréal Cosmetics
Maybelline cosmetics	Maybelline, Inc.
Norelco shavers	Norelco Consumer Products Co.
Oil of Olay™ lotion	Richardson-Vicks, Inc.
Pampers™ disposable diapers	The Procter & Gamble Co.
Rogaine™ men's hair growth products	The Upjohn Co.

Media Expenditures: $15–24.9 Million

Always Feminine™ hygiene products	The Procter & Gamble Co.
Aqua-fresh™ toothpaste	Smithkline Beecham Consumer Products
Arrid Extra Dry™ antiperspirant	Carter-Wallace, Inc.

Ban™ deodorant and antiperspirant	Bristol-Myers Squibb Co.
Clairol Nice 'N Easy™ hair color	Clairol, Inc.
Clairol Ultress™ hair color	Clairol, Inc.
Colgate toothpaste	Colgate-Palmolive Co.
Dove Beauty Bar™ soap	Lever Brothers Co.
Elizabeth Taylor's White Diamonds™ fragrances	Parfums International Ltd.
Escape™ fragrance	Calvin Klein Cosmetics Co.
Huggies Pull-ups™ diapers	Kimberly-Clark Corp.
Ivory™ bar soap	The Procter & Gamble Co.
Kotex™ feminine hygiene products	Kimberly-Clark Corp.
Lady Power Stick™ antiperspirant	Mennen Co.
Listerine™ antiseptic mouthwash	Warner-Lambert Co.
L'Oréal Plentitude™ cosmetics	Cosmair, Inc.
L'Oréal Studio Line™ hair products	Cosmair, Inc.
Luvs™ diapers	The Procter & Gamble Co.
Max Factor™ cosmetics	The Procter & Gamble Co.
Neutrogena™ skin care products	Neutrogena Corp.
Nexxus hair care products	Nexxus Products Co.
Old Spice™ antiperspirant/ deodorant	The Procter & Gamble Co.
Old Spice™ cologne and after-shave	The Procter & Gamble Co.
Pert Plus™ shampoo and conditioner	The Procter & Gamble Co.
Plax™ mouthwash	Pfizer, Inc.
Revlon Classic™ cosmetics	Revlon, Inc.
Schick Tracer™ razor	Warner-Lambert Co.
Scope™ mouthwash	The Procter & Gamble Co.
Secret™ antiperspirants	The Procter & Gamble Co.
Speed Stick™ antiperspirant	Mennen Co.
Spellbound™ fragrance	Estée Lauder, Inc.

Sure™ antiperspirant and deodorant	The Procter & Gamble Co.
Vaseline Intensive Care™ products	Chesebrough-Pond's USA
Vidal Sassoon hair products	Vidal Sassoon Co.

Media Expenditures: $10–14.9 Million

Arm & Hammer™ toothpaste	Church & Dwight Co., Inc.
Bain De Soleil™ suntan products	Richardson-Vicks, Inc.
Braun electric shavers	Braun, Inc.
Camay™ bar soap	The Procter & Gamble Co.
Carefree™ panty shields	Johnson & Johnson
Clarion™ cosmetics	The Procter & Gamble Co.
Close-up™ toothpaste	Chesebrough-Pond's, Inc.
Coast™ deodorant soap	The Procter & Gamble Co.
Colgate Tartar Control™ toothpaste	Colgate-Palmolive Co.
Colgate toothbrushes	Colgate-Palmolive Co.
Denorex™ medicated shampoo	Whitehall Laboratories
Finesse™ shampoo and conditioner	Helene Curtis, Inc.
Irish Spring™ deodorant soap	Colgate-Palmolive Co.
Jergens Actibath Bath Therapy™	The Andrew Jergens Co.
Jhirmack™ hair care products	Playtex, Inc.
Johnson's baby oil	Johnson & Johnson
Lancome™ cosmetics	Cosmair, Inc.
Lee press-on nails	Lee Pharmaceuticals
Lever 2000™ deodorant soap	Chesebrough-Pond's, Inc.
L'Oréal Preference™ hair color	Cosmair, Inc.
Lubriderm™ hand and body lotion	Warner-Lambert Co.
Massengill™ feminine hygiene products	Smithkline Beecham Consumer Products
Navy™ perfume	The Procter & Gamble Co.
Neutrogena™ hair care products	Neutrogena Corp.

Noxzema™ medicated skin cream	The Procter & Gamble Co.
Oral-B oral hygiene products	Oral-B Laboratories
Pantene hair care products	Pantene Co.
Power Stick™ antiperspirant	Chesebrough-Pond's USA
Reach™ toothbrushes	Johnson & Johnson
Right Guard™ antiperspirant/ deodorants	The Gillette Co.
Sanofi fragrances	Sanofi Beauty Products, Inc.
Skin Bracer™ aftershave lotion	Mennen Co.
Soft & Dri™ antiperspirants	The Gillette Co.
Suave™ hair care products	Helene Curtis, Inc.
Summer's Eve™ feminine hygiene products	C. B. Fleet Co., Inc.
Tampax™ tampons	Tambrands, Inc.
Unforgettable™ fragrance	Revlon, Inc.
Volupte™ fragrance	Sanofi Beauty Products, Inc.
Zest™ bar soap	The Procter & Gamble Co.

Media Expenditures: $5–9.9 Million

ACT™ fluoride dental rinse	Johnson & Johnson
Afta™ aftershave conditioner	Mennen Co.
Alberto VO5™ hot oil treatment	Alberto Culver Co.
Alberto VO5™ shampoo/ conditioner	Alberto Culver Co.
Almay Hypo-Allergenic™ cosmetics	Revlon, Inc.
Aramis fragrances	Aramis, Inc.
Aspen™ fragrance	Quintessence, Inc.
Baby Magic™ baby products	Mennen Co.
Bic disposable razors	Bic Corp.
Brut™ cologne and aftershave	Fabergé USA, Inc.
Caress Body™ bar soap	Lever Brothers Co.
Chanel No. 5™ perfume	Chanel, Inc.
Clairol Loving Care™ hair color	Clairol, Inc.
Clairol Option™ hair color for men	Clairol, Inc.

Clinique cosmetics for women	Clinique Laboratories, Inc.
Coppertone™ suntan products	Schering-Plough Corp.
Dial bar soaps	The Dial Corp.
Efferdent™ denture cleaner	Warner-Lambert Co.
Egoiste™ fragrance	Chanel, Inc.
Elizabeth Arden cosmetics	Elizabeth Arden, Inc.
Estée Lauder eye makeup	Estée Lauder, Inc.
Estée Lauder facial creams	Estée Lauder, Inc.
Exclamation™ fragrance	Pfizer, Inc.
Fashion Fair cosmetics	Fashion Fair Cosmetics
Freeman cosmetics	Freeman Cosmetics Corp.
Johnson's baby shampoo/ conditioner	Johnson & Johnson
Jose Eber haircare products	Jose Eber, Inc.
Just for Men™ hair color	Combe, Inc.
Keri™ body lotions	Bristol-Myers Squibb Co.
Knowing™ perfume	Estée Lauder, Inc.
Lady Speed Stick™ antiperspirant	Mennen Co.
Lady Stetson™ perfume	Pfizer, Inc.
Liquid Dial™ soap	The Dial Corp.
Merle Norman cosmetics	Merle Norman Cosmetics, Inc.
Miss Clairol™ hair color	Clairol, Inc.
Nivea™ cremes and lotions	Beiersdorf, Inc.
O B™ tampons	Johnson & Johnson
Ogilvie™ hair products	L & F Products
Panasonic Wet/Dry™ shaver	Panasonic Co.
Paul Mitchell hair care products	Paul Mitchell Systems
Perma Soft™ shampoo and conditioner	Dowbrands, Inc.
Playtex tampons	Playtex, Inc.
Pond's cold creams and lotions	Chesebrough-Pond's USA
Preferred Stock™ men's cologne	Pfizer, Inc.
Prell™ shampoo and conditioner	The Procter & Gamble Co.
Q-Tips™ cotton swabs	Chesebrough-Pond's USA
Rave™ shampoo and conditioner	Chesebrough-Pond's USA
Redken hair care products	Redken Laboratories, Inc.
Redmond hair care products	Redmond Products, Inc.

Remington men's shavers	Remington Products, Inc.
Revlon Flex™ hair care products	Revlon, Inc.
Revlon lipsticks	Revlon, Inc.
Revlon nail products	Revlon, Inc.
Safari By Ralph Lauren™ fragrance	Cosmair, Inc.
Safeguard™ deodorant soap	The Procter & Gamble Co.
Sally Hansen™ nail treatment	Del Laboratories, Inc.
Schick™ razors	Warner-Lambert Co.
Selsun Blue™ dandruff shampoo	Ross Laboratories
Sensodyne™ toothpaste	Dentco, Inc.
Serenity Guards™ shields	Johnson & Johnson
Shower-to-Shower™ body powder	Johnson & Johnson
Soft Sheen hair care products	Soft Sheen Products, Inc.
Speed Stick™ deodorant	Mennen Co.
Stayfree Maxi Pads™	Johnson & Johnson
Stetson™ cologne for men	Pfizer
Suave™ antiperspirant	Helene Curtis, Inc.
Sundown™ sunscreen	Johnson & Johnson
Tone™ bar soap	The Dial Corp.
Tribe™ cologne	Pfizer, Inc.

Media Expenditures: $3–4.9 Million

Agree™ shampoo	S. C. Johnson & Sons, Inc.
Alberto Mousse™ styling foam	Alberto Culver Co.
Aqua-fresh Flex™ toothbrush	Smithkline Beecham Consumer Prd.
Aveeno™ bath products	Rydelle Laboratories
Beautiful™ perfume	Estée Lauder, Inc.
Buf-puf™ facial cleanser	Minnesota Mining & Mfg. Co.
Calvin Klein cosmetics	Calvin Klein Cosmetics Co.
Chap Stick™ lip care products	A. H. Robins Co., Inc.
Clean & Clear™ cosmetics	Johnson & Johnson
Clinique toiletries for men	Clinique Laboratories, Inc.
Colgate Winter Fresh Gel™	Colgate-Palmolive Co.
Curel™ skin care lotion	S. C. Johnson & Sons, Inc.
Dentu-foam™ denture cleaner	Dentco, Inc.

Edge™ shaving gel	S. C. Johnson & Sons, Inc.
Eternity™ perfume	Calvin Klein Cosmetics Co.
FA™ Shower Gel	Cosmetics Imports International
FDS™ feminine deodorant spray	Alberto Culver Co.
Finesse™ hair spray	Helene Curtis, Inc.
Jergens aloe and lanolin soap	The Andrew Jergens Co.
Jergens lotion	The Andrew Jergens Co.
Jovan Musk™ fragrance	Quintessence, Inc.
Lacome™ facial cream and lotion	Cosmair, Inc.
Obsession for Women™	Calvin Klein Cosmetics Co.
Phisoderm™ cleansing bar and lotion	Eastman Kodak Co.
Polo By Ralph Lauren™ fragrance	Cosmair, Inc.
Rembrandt™ toothpaste	Den-Mat Corp.
Sea Breeze™ skin cleanser	Clairol, Inc.
Soft Soap personal care products	Softsoap Enterprises, Inc.
Sure & Natural Maxi Pads™	Johnson & Johnson
Teen Spirit™ antiperspirant	Mennen Co.
Tom's of Maine™ natural toiletries	Tom's of Maine Toiletries
Toni Home Permanent™	The Gillette Co.
Tresor™ fragrance	Cosmair, Inc.

Apparel/Accessories

Brand	Corporation

Media Expenditures: $50–99.9 Million

Levi's jeans and sportswear	Levi Strauss & Co.

Media Expenditures: $25–49.9 Million

Dockers™ sportswear	Levi Strauss & Co.

Media Expenditures: $15–24.9 Million

Bugle Boy clothing	Bugle Boy Industries, Inc.
Cotton, Inc.	Cotton, Inc.
Fruit of the Loom men's/boys' underwear	Fruit of the Loom, Inc.

Fruit of the Loom women's underwear	Fruit of the Loom, Inc.
Haggar apparel	Haggar Apparel Co.
Lee jeans and sportswear	The Lee Apparel Co., Inc.
Polo/Ralph Lauren™ apparel	Polo/Ralph Lauren Corp.

Media Expenditures: $10–14.9 Million

Fruit of the Loom casualwear	Fruit of the Loom, Inc.
Gitano sportswear and accessories	The Gitano Group
Guess? sportswear	Guess? Inc.
Hanes men's underwear	Hanes Underwear Co.
Hanes Silk Reflections™ hosiery	Hanes Hoisery, Inc.
Jordache apparel	Jordache Enterprises, Inc.
Sheer Energy™ pantyhose	L'Eggs Products, Inc.
Totes accessories	Totes, Inc.

Media Expenditures: $5–9.9 Million

Bali women's underwear	Bali Co.
Bass shoes	G. H. Bass Co.
Calvin Klein sport sportswear	Calvin Klein Sport, Inc.
Esprit apparel	Esprit De Corps
Eve of Milady gowns	Eve of Milady, Inc.
Feminine-Style™ underwear	Union Underwear Co., Inc.
Florsheim shoes	The Florsheim Shoe Co.
Haband apparel	The Haband Co., Inc.
Hanes Her Way™ underwear	Hanes Underwear Co.
Hanes sportswear	Hanes Printables, Inc.
Isotoner gloves	Aris Isotoner, Inc.
Isotoner slippers	Aris Isotoner, Inc.
Jantzen sportswear and swimwear	Jantzen, Inc.
Maidenform bras and lingerie	Maidenform, Inc.
No Nonsense™ pantyhose	Kayser-Roth Corp.
Playtex bras	Playtex, Inc.
Samsonite luggage	Samsonite Corp.
Sheer Elegance™ pantyhose	L'Eggs Products, Inc.

Totes Toasties™ socks	Totes, Inc.
Wrangler jeans and sportswear	Wrangler Co.

Media Expenditures: $3–4.9 Million

Champion sportswear	Champion Products, Inc.
Chanel Boutique™ apparel	Chanel, Inc.
Jockey underwear	Jockey International
Perry Ellis apparel and accessories	Manhattan Industries, Inc.
Rockport footwear	The Rockport Co.
Tulavision™ activewear	Tultex Corp.

Pharmaceuticals/Health Care

Brand	Corporation

Media Expenditures: $100–149.9 Million

Nutri/System weight loss centers	Nutri/System, Inc.

Media Expenditures: $50–99.9 Million

Advil™ pain reliever	Whitehall Laboratories
Ultra Slim-fast weight loss program	Slim Fast Foods Co.
Tylenol™ and Extra Strength Tylenol™	McNeil Consumer Products Co.

Media Expenditures: $25–49.9 Million

Alka-Seltzer Plus™ cold/allergy	Miles, Inc.
Anacin™ tablets and caplets	Whitehall Laboratories
Dynatrim™ diet drink	Lederle Consumer Health Products
Excedrin™ tablets and caplets	Bristol-Myer Squibb Co.
Gyne-Lotrimin™ cream	Schering-Plough Corp.
Jenny Craig weight loss centers	Jenny Craig International
Monistat-7™ cream	Johnson & Johnson
Nyquil™ cold medication	Richardson-Vicks, Inc.

Robitussin™ cough medicines   A. H. Robins Co., Inc.
Tylenol™ cold medication   McNeil Consumer Products Co.
Weight Watchers weight-loss
  program   Weight Watchers Intl., Inc.

Media Expenditures: $15–24.9 Million

Bayer Aspirin™/Extra Strength
  Aspirin™   Glenbrook Laboratories
Bufferin™ tablets and caplets   Bristol-Myers Squibb Co.
Centrum™ multivitamins   Lederle Consumer Health Products
Charter Medical Corp.   Charter Medical Corp.
Dexatrim™ appetite suppressant   Thompson Medical Corp.
Dimetapp™ cold and allergy
  products   A. H. Robins Co., Inc.
Imodium A-D™ diarrhea
  medicine   McNeil Consumer Products Co.
Maalox™ antacid   Rhone-Poulenc Rorer, Inc.
Medi-flu™ cold and flu
  medicine   Warner-Lambert Co.
Metamucil™ laxative   The Procter & Gamble Co.
Motrin IB™ analgesic   The Upjohn Co.
Mylanta™ antacid   Johnson & Johnson
Nuprin™ tablets   Bristol-Myers Squibb Co.
Preparation H™ products   Whitehall Laboratories
Rolaids™ antacid tablets   American Chicle Co.
Thera-flu™ cold remedy   Sandoz Pharmaceuticals Corp.
Tums™ antacid tablets   SmithKline Beecham
                                    Consumer Products
Tylenol PM™   McNeil Consumer Products Co.
The Upjohn Co.   The Upjohn Co.

Media Expenditures: $10–14.9 Million

Actifed™ cold medicine   Burroughs Wellcome Co.
Alka-Seltzer™ antacid   Miles, Inc.
Anacin 3™ analgesic   Whitehall Laboratories
Band-Aid™ adhesive bandages   Johnson & Johnson

Benadryl™ allergy capsules/elixir	Warner-Lambert Co.
Benadryl Plus™ cold medicine	Warner-Lambert Co.
Comtrex™ cold products	Bristol-Myers Squibb Co.
Contac™ cold medicine	Smithkline Beecham Consumer Products
Correctol™ laxative	Schering-Plough Corp.
Depend™ incontinence products	Kimberly-Clark Corp.
Dimetapp Extend™ tablets	A. H. Robins Co., Inc.
Dr. Scholl's™ foot products	Schering-Plough Corp.
Dristan™ tablets and capsules	Whitehall Laboratories
Drixoral 12-Hour™ cold tablets	Schering-Plough Corp.
EPT™ pregnancy test	Warner-Lambert Co.
Fibercon Fiber™ laxative	Lederle Consumer Health Products
Flintstones™ vitamins	Miles, Inc.
Marion Merrell Dow pharmaceuticals	Marion Merrell Dow, Inc.
Miracle Ear™ hearing aids/ centers	Dahlberg, Inc.
Pepto-Bismol™ stomach remedy	The Procter & Gamble Co.
Robitussin™ cough medication	A. H. Robins Co., Inc.
Seldane™ decongestant	Marion Merrell Dow, Inc.
Sinutab™ analgesic/decongestant	Warner-Lambert Co.
Sudafed™ cold medicine	Burroughs Wellcome Co.
Triaminic™ cold syrup and tablets	Sandoz Phamaceuticals Corp.
Tylenol™ sinus pain reliever	McNeil Consumer Products Co.
Vicks Formula 44™ cough medication	Richardson-Vicks, Inc.

Media Expenditures: $5–9.9 Million

Acutrim™ appetite suppressant	Ciba-Geigy Pharmaceuticals
Afrin 12-Hour™ decongestant	Schering-Plough Corp.
Attends™ briefs and undergarments	The Procter & Gamble Co.
BC™ headache powders and tablets	Block Drug Co., Inc.
Bally's health and tennis clubs	Bally's Health & Tennis Corp.

Beltone™ hearing aids/ audiometers	Beltone Electronic Corp.
Ben-gay™ analgesic rub	Pfizer, Inc.
Caladryl™ lotion	Warner-Lambert Co.
Chlor-trimeton™ allergy medication	Schering-Plough Corp.
Chloraseptic™ throat medication	The Procter & Gamble Co.
Clearasil™ acne medication	Richardson-Vicks, Inc.
Coadvil™ cold remedy	American Home Products Corp.
Coricidin™ decongestant	Schering-Plough Corp.
Cortaid™ cream ointment and lotion	The Upjohn Co.
Dimetapp Elixir™ cold medicine	A. H. Robins Co., Inc.
Doan's™ backache pills	Ciba-Geigy Pharmaceuticals
Ex-Lax™ laxatives	Sandoz Pharmaceuticals Corp.
Excedrin PM™ tablets and caplets	Bristol-Myers Squibb Co.
Fact Plus™ pregnancy test	Ortho Pharmaceutical Corp.
Fixodent™ denture adhesive cream	Richardson-Vicks, Inc.
Gas-x™ tablets	Sandoz Pharmaceuticals Corp.
Glaxo™ ethical drugs	Glaxo, Inc.
Hall's™ cough tablets	American Chicle Co.
Interplak™ plaque removal instruments	Bausch & Lomb, Inc.
Jack La Lanne™ health clubs	Bally's Health & Tennis Corp.
Kaopectate™ diarrhea medicine	The Upjohn Co.
Kick the Habit™ antismoking device	Vipont Pharmaceutical, Inc.
Micatin™ athlete's foot remedy	Ortho Pharmaceutical Corp.
N'ice™ lozenges and spray	Smithkline Beecham Consumer Products
Neosporin™ nasal spray	Burroughs Wellcome Co.
Nicorette™ nicotine gum	Marion Merrell Dow, Inc.
Nutrition Headquarters products	Nutrition Headquarters, Inc.
Oxy™ acne remedies	Smithkline Beecham Consumer Products

Pediacare™ children's cold products	McNeil Consumer Products Co.
Phillips Milk of Magnesia™	Glenbrook Laboratories
Polident™ denture products	Dentco, Inc.
Primatene™ mist and tablets	Whitehall Laboratories
Ramipril™ high blood pressure medicine	Hoechst-Roussel Pharmaceutical
Riopan/Riopan Plus™ antacid	Whitehall Laboratories
Sinex™ nasal spray	Richardson-Vicks, Inc.
Sucrets™ lozenges and spray	Smithkline Beecham Consumer Products
Therapeutic™ mineral ice	Bristol-Myers Squibb Co.
Tinactin™ antifungal powder/cream	Schering-Plough Corp.
Today™ contraceptive sponge	Whitehall Laboratories
Trental Vasotherapeutic™	Hoechst-Roussel Pharmaceutical
Tucks™ premoistened pads	Warner-Lambert Co.
Tylenol™ children's pain reliever	McNeil Consumer Products Co.
Unisom Sleep Aid™ tablets	Pfizer, Inc.
Vicks Pediatric Formula 44™ medicine	Richardson-Vicks, Inc.
Vicks Vaporub™	Richardson-Vicks, Inc.

Media Expenditures: $3–4.9 Million

Anbesol™ analgesic	Whitehall Laboratories
Anusol™ hemorrhoid medication	Warner-Lambert Co.
Aspercreme™ pain reliever rub	Thompson Medical Co., Inc.
Ben-gay Sports Balm™	Pfizer, Inc.
Bufferin AF Nite Time™ caplets	Bristol-Myers
Dristan™ nasal spray	Whitehall Laboratories
Dulcolax™ suppositories and tablets	Boehringer-Ingelheim Ltd.
Fiberall™ laxative	Ciba-Geigy Pharmaceuticals
First Response™ pregnancy test	Carter-Wallace, Inc.
Holiday Spa™ health clubs	Bally's Health & Tennis Corp.
Lanacane Cream™ lotion and spray	Combe, Inc.

Midol PMS Maximum Strength™ tablets	Glenbrook Laboratories
Minitran Transdermal Nitro™ patch	Minnesota Mining & Mfg. Co.
Nytol™ sleep-aid tablets	Block Drug Co., Inc.
Pamprin™ pain relief medication	Chattem, Inc.
Prokine™ pharmaceutical	Hoechst-Roussel Pharmaceutical
Sine-aid™ sinus remedy	McNeil Consumer Products Co.
Sominex™ sleep aid	Smithkline Beecham Consumer Products
Sudafed™ sinus tablets	Burroughs Wellcome Co.
Super Poli-Grip™ denture adhesive	Block Drug Co., Inc.
Theragran™ vitamin tablets	Bristol-Myers Squibb Co.
Vivarin™ stimulant	Smithkline Beecham Consumer Products

Sporting Goods

Brand	Corporation

Media Expenditures: $100–149.9 Million

Nike athletic footwear	Nike, Inc.
Reebok athletic footwear	Reebok International, Inc.

Media Expenditures: $25–49.9 Million

L A Gear athletic wear	L A Gear, Inc.

Media Expenditures: $15–24.9 Million

Converse athletic footwear	Converse, Inc.
Easy Spirit™ sporting footwear	U.S. Shoe Corp.
NordicTrack exerciser	NordicTrack, Inc.

Media Expenditures: $10–14.9 Million

British Knights sneakers	British Knights, Inc.
Keds footwear	The Keds Corp.

Spalding sporting goods	Spalding Sports Worldwide
Titleist golf equipment	Titleist Foot-Joy Worldwide

Media Expenditures: $5–9.9 Million

Adidas athletic footwear	Adidas USA, Inc.
Avia athletic footwear	Avia Group International
Puma™ sportswear and footwear	Etonic, Inc.
Soloflex exercise equipment	Soloflex, Inc.
Spalding golf balls	Spalding Sports Worldwide
Yamaha marine motors	Yamaha Motor Corp. USA
Zebco fishing equipment	Zebco Corp.

Media Expenditures: $3–4.9 Million

Boston Whaler fishing boats	Boston Whaler, Inc.
Etonic athletic footwear	Etonic, Inc.
Huffy bicycles	Huffy Corp.
K-swiss athletic footwear	K-swiss, Inc.
Kawasaki jet skis and watercraft	Kawasaki Motors Corp. USA
Taylor Made golf clubs	Taylor Made Golf Clubs
Wilson golf products	Wilson Sporting Goods Co.

Recreation

Brand	Corporation

Media Expenditures: $25–49.9 Million

Walt Disney World	Walt Disney World Co.

Media Expenditures: $15–24.9 Million

Disneyland™	The Walt Disney Co.

Media Expenditures: $10–14.9 Million

Adventureland/Tampa, FL	Busch Entertainment Corp.
Sea World parks	Sea World, Inc.
Tropworld™ casino and resort	Aztar Corp.

Media Expenditures: $5–9.9 Million

Busch Gardens/Tampa, FL   Busch Entertainment Corp.
Busch Gardens/Williamsburg, VA Busch Entertainment Corp.
Caesars Palace hotel and casino Caesars Palace
Cedar Point amusement park   Cedar Fair LP
The Mirage hotel and casino   Mirage Resorts, Inc.
Showboat casino   Showboat, Inc.
Trump Plaza hotel and casino   Trump Organization

Media Expenditures: $3–4.9 Million

Bally's casino resort   Bally's Casino Resort
Harrah's casino and hotel   Harrah's
Knott's Berry Farm   Knott's Berry Farm
Marine World Africa USA   Marine World Foundation
Walt Disney World hotels/resorts Walt Disney World Co.

Toys and Games

Brand   **Corporation**

Media Expenditures: $50–99.9 Million

Super Nintendo Entertainment
  Systems   Nintendo of America
Tyco toys   Tyco Toys, Inc.

Media Expenditures: $25–49.9 Million

Barbie™ dolls and accessories   Mattel, Inc.
Fisher-Price toys   Fisher-Price, Inc.
Milton Bradley games/toys/
  puzzles   Milton Bradley Co.
Sega video games   Sega Of America

Media Expenditures: $15–24.9 Million

Lego building toys   Lego Systems, Inc.
Tonka toys   Hasbro, Inc.

Media Expenditures: $10–14.9 Million

GI Joe™ toys and accessories	Hasbro, Inc.
NEC Turbografx-16 video games	NEC Technologies, Inc.
Teenage Mutant Ninja Turtles™ toys	Playmates Toys, Inc.

Media Expenditures: $5–9.9 Million

Bandai video games	Bandai America
Cabbage Patch Kids™ dolls	Hasbro, Inc.
Electronic Arts Sports Network™ video game	Electronic Arts
Hot Wheels™ vehicles/ accessories	Mattel, Inc.
Matchbox toys	Matchbox Toys USA Ltd.
Micro Machines™ toys	Lewis Galoob Toys, Inc.
Nintendo Game Boy™ video game	Nintendo of America
WWF™ wrestling figures	Hasbro, Inc.

Media Expenditures: $3–4.9 Million

Duplo™ building toys	Lego Systems, Inc.
L'il Miss™ dolls	Mattel, Inc.
Little Tikes toys	The Little Tikes Co.
Nerf Sport™ toys	Parker Brothers
Play Doh™ products	Kenner Products, Inc.
Pressman games	Pressman Toy Corp.
See'N Say™ toys	Mattel, Inc.
Trivial Pursuit™ game	Hasbro, Inc.

Pet Foods/Supplies

Brand	Corporation

Media Expenditures: $10–14.9 Million

Alpo cat food	Alpo Pet Foods, Inc.
Alpo dog food	Alpo Pet Foods, Inc.
Fancy Feast™ cat food	Nestlé Brands Foodservice Co.

Hartz Mountain pet products   Hartz Mountain Corp.
Iams pet foods   The Iams Co.
Mighty Dog™ dog food   Nestlé Brands Foodservice Co.
Nature's Course™ dog food   Ralston Purina Co.
Pedigree™ dog food   Kal Kan Foods, Inc.
Whiskas™ cat food   Kal Kan Foods, Inc.

Media Expenditures: $5–9.9 Million

Control™ cat litter   The Clorox Co.
Cycle™ dog food   The Quaker Oats Co.
Friskies™ cat food   Nestlé Brands Foodservice Co.
Heartgard-30™ pet medication   Merck & Co., Inc.
Hill's pet foods   Hill's Pet Products, Inc.
Ken-L Ration Kibbles & Bits™   The Quaker Oats Co.
Milk-Bone™ dog biscuits   Nabisco Foods Group
Purina™ dog chow   Ralston Purina Co.
Purina Kit'N Kaboodle™ cat food Ralston Purina Co.
Purina™ puppy chow   Ralston Purina Co.
Reward™ dog food   Heinz Pet Products
Science Diet™ pet food   Hill's Pet Products, Inc.
Sheba™ cat food   Kal Kan Foods, Inc.
Tidy Cat™ cat litter   Golden Cat Corp.
Fresh Step™ cat litter   The Clorox Co.
Friskies Kitten Formula™   Nestlé Brands Foodservice Co.
Purina One™ dog food   Ralston Purina Co.

Office Equipment/Supplies

Brand   **Corporation**

Media Expenditures: $15–24.9 Million

Canon copiers   Canon USA, Inc.
Lanier office equipment/
   supplies   Lanier Worldwide, Inc.
Xerox business products and
   systems   Xerox Corp.

Media Expenditures: $10–14.9 Million

Mita copiers   Mita Copystar America, Inc.

Media Expenditures: $5–9.9 Million

Minolta copiers	Minolta Corp.
Mita facsimile machines	Mita Copystar America, Inc.
Parker pens	Parker Pens USA Ltd.
Pitney Bowes mailing systems	Pitney Bowes, Inc.
Radio Shack™ business products	Tandy Corp.
Ricoh office products	Ricoh Corp.
3M™ office products	Minnesota Mining & Mfg. Co.
Toshiba copiers	Toshiba America Info. Systems

Media Expenditures: $3–4.9 Million

Canon facsimile machines	Canon USA, Inc.
Cross writing instruments	A. T. Cross Co.
Kodak Coloredge™ copier	Eastman Kodak Co.
Mead business papers	Mead Corp.
Montblanc™ writing instruments	Koh-I-Noor, Inc.
Sharp copiers	Sharp Electronics Corp.
Sharp facsimile machines	Sharp Electronics Corp.

Photo Supplies/Equipment

Brand   Corporation

Media Expenditures: $25–49.9 Million

Kodak film   Eastman Kodak Co.

Media Expenditures: $15–24.9 Million

Canon cameras	Canon USA, Inc.
Minolta cameras and accessories	Minolta Corp.
Polaroid One™ film	Polaroid Corp.

Media Expenditures: $10–14.9 Million

Kodak cameras	Eastman Kodak Co.
Nikon cameras and accessories	Nikon, Inc.
Olympus cameras and accessories	Olympus Corp.
Polaroid Instant™ cameras	Polaroid Corp.

Media Expenditures: $5–9.9 Million

Fuji film	Fuji Photo Film USA, Inc.
Kodalux processing services	Qualex, Inc.

Media Expenditures: $3–4.9 Million

Fuji cameras	Fuji Photo Film USA, Inc.

BIBLIOGRAPHY

ASSAEL, HENRY, *Consumer Behavior and Marketing Action.* Belmont, CA: Kent, 1981.

BARNOUW, ERIK, *The Sponsor: Notes on a Modern Potentate.* New York: Oxford University Press, 1978.

BARNOUW, ERIK, *Tube of Plenty: The Evolution of American Television.* New York: Oxford University Press, 1990.

BARR, DAVID S., *Advertising of Cable: A Practical Guide for Advertisers.* Englewood Cliffs, NJ: Prentice-Hall, 1985.

BARWISE, T. P., and A. C. S. EHRENBERG, *Television and Its Audience.* London: Sage Publications, 1988.

BATRA, RAJEEV, and RASHI GLAZER, eds., *Cable TV Advertising: In Search of the Right Formula.* New York: Quorum Books, 1989.

BROWN, LESTER L., *Les Brown's Encyclopedia of Television,* 3rd ed. Detroit: Visible Ink Press, 1992.

EICOFF, AL, *Eicoff on Broadcast Direct Marketing.* Lincolnwood, IL: NTC Business Books, 1988.

FOOTE, JOE S., *Television Access and Political Power.* New York: Praeger, 1990.

HEETER, CARRIE, and BRADLEY S. GREENBURG, "Cableviewing." In *Communications and Information Science,* ed. Brenda Dervin. Norwood, NJ: Ablex, 1988.

HEIGHTON, ELIZABETH, and DON R. CUNNINGHAM, *Advertising in the Broadcast and Cable Media.* Belmont, CA: Wadsworth, 1984.

HOLLIN, TIMOTHY, *Beyond Broadcasting: Into the Cable Age.* London: BFI, 1984.

MEDVED, MICHAEL, *Hollywood vs. America: Popular Culture and the War on Traditional Values.* New York: HarperCollins, 1992.

POPCORN, FAITH, *The Popcorn Report.* New York: HarperCollins, 1991.

RIES, AL, and JACK TROUT, *Positioning: The Battle for Your Mind.* New York: Warner Books, McGraw-Hill, 1986.

RIES, AL, and JACK TROUT, *The 22 Immutable Laws of Marketing: Violate Them at Your Own Risk.* New York: HarperCollins, 1993.

SMITH, F. LESLIE, *Perspectives on Radio and Television: Telecommunications in the United States,* 2nd ed. New York: Harper & Row, 1985.

STEINBERY, CORBETT S., *TV Facts.* New York: Facts on File, 1980.

STEWART, DAVID W., and DAVID H. FURSE, *Effective Television Advertising.* Lexington, MA: Lexington Books, 1986.

WEITZEN, H. SKIP, *Hypergrowth: Applying the Success Formula of Today's Fastest Growing Companies.* New York: John Wiley & Sons, 1991.

WITEK, JOHN, *Response Television.* Chicago: Crain Books, 1981.

MAGAZINES, PERIODICALS, AND NEWSLETTERS

The subject matter in this field is extremely topical. The following publications, which contributed significantly to content of this book, were faithfully read and reviewed.

Newspapers

> *Cedar Rapids Gazette*
> *Chicago Tribune*
> *Los Angeles Times*
> *Louisville Courier-Journal*
> *The New York Times*
> *St. Paul Pioneer Press & Dispatch*
> *St. Petersburg Times*
> *USA Today*
> *The Wall Street Journal*

Newsletters and Trade Publications

Advertising Age

AdWeek

Agrimarketing

American Demographics

Boomer Report

BrandWeek

Broadcasting

Business Marketing

CableAwards

Cablevision

Channels

Company Reports and Literature (various)

Consumer Reports

DeLay Letter

Direct Marketing

DM News

Friday Report

Homeworld

Interactive Cable News

Interactive World

Marketing

Marketing News

Mediaweek

Modern Media

Multichannel News

New Media

Presentation Products

Public Pulse

Research Alert

Response TV
Sales & Marketing Management
TV Guide
Television Business International
Videobusiness

Business and General Interest

Business Week
Entertainment Weekly
Esquire
Forbes
Fortune
Inc.
Money
Newsweek
People
Success
The New Yorker
Time
U.S. News & World Report
Working Woman

GLOSSARY

Basic Cable The basic package of channels offered by cable companies, excluding extras such as pay-cable channels and Pay-Per-View.

Documercial Long-form, 30-minute commercial, usually promoting a high-involvement, considered-purchase product or service. Production values are usually higher than those of infomercials, with a priority on brand or corporate image. Documercial objectives range from building traffic in local dealerships to positioning against other products, to simple image enhancement.

Entertainment Programming Programming designed to attract the largest possible audience as a lure to advertisers.

Grazing Using the remote control to check out programming on other channels. Also called *surfing*.

Infomercial Long-form commercial, from 2 to 30 minutes in length, whose objective is to stimulate immediate call-in sales.

Long-Form Commercial Also called program-length advertising, any commercial that exceeds 2 minutes in length; including infomercials and documercials.

Marketing Channel A channel dedicated to a single product category—for example, automobiles—which allows marketers to schedule marketing programming in the same way entertainment programming is scheduled on other channels.

Marketing Programming Programming designed to appeal to a highly interested, highly specific, ready-to-buy audience.

MSO (Multiple System Operator) A cable TV company that owns and operates more than one cable system. Examples are Tele-Communications, Inc. (TCI), Time Warner, Continental, and Cox.

Paradigm Shift Phenomenon that takes place when a new concept or idea changes traditional ways of looking at cultural archetypes. As used here it describes a new way of looking at television programming, from entertainment based to marketing based.

Pay Cable Channels such as *HBO* or *The Disney Channel* for which subscribers pay a charge over and above the charge for basic cable channels.

Pay-Per-View A service offering first-run movies and special sporting and cultural events, for which viewers pay a one-time charge over and above their basic cable charge.

Program-Length Advertising Also called long-form commercials, any commercial that exceeds 2 minutes in length; including infomercials and documercials.

Surfing Using the remote control to check out programming on other channels. Also called grazing.

Video-On-Demand At present, an experimental service wherein the viewer requests, and pays extra for, specific movies.

Zapper Remote control device for changing channels. Also, the person who uses the zapper.

Zapping Escaping undesirable programming or commercials by using the remote control device. Currently no match for its major competition—video rental—it promises to play a significant role in the interactive future, offering not just movies, but past and present television shows, documentaries, and so on.

INDEX